Hsieh Liang-tso and the *Analects* of Confucius

Recent Titles in
AMERICAN ACADEMY OF RELIGION
ACADEMY SERIES

SERIES EDITOR
Carole Myscofski, Illinois Wesleyan University
A Publication Series of
The American Academy of Religion
and
Oxford University Press

*The Grace of Difference: A Canadian
Feminist Theological Ethic*
Marilyn J. Legge

*The Intersubjectivity of the Mystic: A Study
of Teresa of Avila's Interior Castle*
Mary Frolich

*Narrating History, Developing Doctrine:
Friedrich Schleiermacher and Johann
Sebastian Drey*
Bradford E. Hinze

*Analogical Possibilities: How Words Refer
to God*
Philip A. Rolnick

Womanist Justice, Womanist Hope
Emilie M. Townes

*Women Don't Count: The Challenge of
Women's Poverty to Christian Ethics*
Pamela K. Brubaker

The Exploration of the Inner Wounds—Han
Jae Hoon Lee

*Comprehending Power in Christian
Social Ethics*
Christine Firer Hinze

*The Greening of Theology: The Ecological
Models of Rosemary Radford Ruether,
Joseph Stiller, and Jürgen Moltmann*
Steven Bouma-Prediger

*The Spirit and the Vision: The Influence of
Christian Romanticism on the Development
of 19th-Century American Art*
Diane Apostolos-Cappadona

*The Freedom of the Spirit: African Indige-
nous Churches in Kenya*
Francis Kimani Githieya

*Bridge-makers and Cross-bearers: Korean-
American Women and the Church*
Jung Ha Kim

*God Bless the Child That's Got Its Own:
The Economic Rights Debate*
Darryl M. Trimiew

*Energies of the Spirit: Trinitarian Models in
Eastern Orthodox and Western Theology*
Duncan Reid

*The Goddess Laksmi: The Divine Consort in
South Indian Vaisnava Tradition*
P. Pratap Kumar

*Creative Dwelling: Empathy and Clarity in
God and Self*
Lucinda A. Stark Huffaker

*Hospitality to Strangers: Empathy and the
Physician-Patient Relationship*
Dorothy M. Owens

*The Bonds of Freedom: Feminist Theology
and Christian Realism*
Rebekah L. Miles

*The Specter of Speciesism: Buddhist and
Christian Views of Animals*
Paul Waldau

*Incarnation and Physics: Natural Science in
the Theology of Thomas F. Torrance*
Tapio Luoma

*Of Borders and Margins: Hispanic Disciples
in Texas, 1888–1945*
Daisy L. Machado

*Hsieh Liang-tso and the Analects of
Confucius: Humane Learning as a
Religious Quest*
Thomas W. Selover

AMERICAN ACADEMY OF RELIGION

Hsieh Liang-tso and the *Analects* of Confucius

Humane Learning as a Religious Quest

Thomas W. Selover

OXFORD

UNIVERSITY PRESS

2005

OXFORD
UNIVERSITY PRESS

Oxford   New York
Auckland   Bangkok   Buenos Aires   Cape Town   Chennai
Dar es Salaam   Delhi   Hong Kong   Istanbul   Karachi   Kolkata
Kuala Lumpur   Madrid   Melbourne   Mexico City   Mumbai   Nairobi
São Paulo   Shanghai   Taipei   Tokyo   Toronto

Published by Oxford University Press, Inc.
198 Madison Avenue, New York, New York 10016

www.oup.com

Oxford is a registered trademark of Oxford University Press

Library of Congress Cataloging-in-Publication Data
Selover, Thomas Whitfield.
Hsieh liang-tso and the analects of confucius :
humane learning as a religious quest / Thomas W. Selover
p. cm. — (American Academy of Religion academy series)
Includes bibliographical references and index.
ISBN 0-19-515610-2
1. Confucius. Lun yè. 2. Religion and the humanities.
3. Xie, liangzuo, ca. 1050–ca.1120 I. Title. II. Series.
PL2471.Z7 S425 2003
181'.112—dc21   2002027432

2 4 6 8 9 7 5 3 1

Printed in the United States of America
on acid-free paper

Foreword

Tu Wei-ming

The central meaning shared by verbs such as *think, cogitate, reason, reflect,* and *speculate* is "to use the power of the mind, as in conceiving ideas and drawing inferences." Whether or not we subscribe to the exclusive dichotomy of body and mind, thinking seems inevitably intertwined with the cognitive function of the mind. We assume that mind thinks and body acts and that it is appropriate for us to think clearly before we act. We further assume that theory is intellectually superior to practice and that even if concrete practice is often necessary for validating and refining the theory, it is of secondary significance in the life of the mind. In the value scale of thinking, theoria is more fundamental than praxis.

The Chinese idea of *t'i-chih* 體知 (*tizhi*, "experiential knowing") suggests a mode of thinking ("embodied thinking") that involves the body as a constitutive part of the "mental" process. We think not only with our head but also with our heart; we feel, sense, and will as we think. We can discipline ourselves to cogitate and reason in a disinterested manner devoid of feelings, but in our ordinary daily living, there is always an affective dimension to our thinking. Understandably, aesthetic, ethical, or religious reflection takes as its primary datum the experience rooted in the bodily sensations.

Through rigorous self-cultivation, we learn to appreciate that thinking as self-reflexivity is essential for human flourishing. Either in the Socratic dictum that the unexamined life is not worth living or in the Confucian conviction that self-cultivation is the root of an educated person, the scope of thinking is more than conceiving ideas and drawing inferences. Thinking is necessarily a transformative act. The mind not only has the capacity of speculation but is also self-awakening and self-enlightening.

In *Hsieh Liang-tso and the* Analects of Confucius: *Humane Learning as a Religious Quest*, Tom Selover, through empathetic understanding and analogical imagination, presents a succinct analysis of the core value in Confucian thought, *jen* 仁 (*ren*, humanity or co-humanity). Intent on capturing the "kernel" of this commonly shared and profoundly ineffable way of being human, Selover straightforwardly defines *jen* as sensitivity. We humans, so conceived, are primarily sentient beings rather than rational animals. The way we see, hear, smell, touch, taste, and sense defines who we are. Concrete feeling, instead of abstract thinking, provides the authentic access to human wisdom. This mode of philosophizing as a way of living entails self-cultivation, an ethical and religious discipline that integrates the body and mind as a spiritual attainment.

While Selover is deeply moved by this deceptively simple vision of human flourishing, he does not present it as his own faith. Rather, he articulates the humanist insight of Ch'eng Hao (Cheng Hao, 1032–1085), arguably the most brilliant proponent of the learning of the heart-and-mind in the Sung (Song, 960–1279) dynasty. Actually, Selover's strategy of a focused investigation on Ch'eng Hao's single most significant philosophical move of conceptualizing humanity as sensitivity is roundabout. Instead of addressing Ch'eng directly, he elucidates the Master's seminal idea through an informed and critical analysis of the thought of his gifted student, Hsieh Liang-tso (Xie Liangzuo, c.1050–c.1120). Furthermore, Selover makes a deliberate choice to navigate through the fragmented landscape of Hsieh's commentary on the Confucian *Analects* as a tack of encompassing the "realms of sensitivity" as defining characteristics of humanity. In so doing, he manages to bring in all four dimensions of the religio-philosophical enterprise—scripture, tradition, reason, and experience.

Selover employs Hsieh's scriptural commentary to demonstrate that the "religious" dimensions of the Confucian tradition can be best illuminated in a comparative framework. He examines the Neo-Confucian claims to authentic transmission by a nuanced interpretation of their communal critical self-awareness. He probes the semantic field in which "humanity" is disclosed not only as thought but also as action. Especially noteworthy is his idea of humane learning "as an on-going personal endeavor [which] leads to increased awareness of and sensitivity to the full range of one's human situation, embedded not only in a network of human relations that in principle cannot exclude anyone, but also in a cosmos infinite in extent and in complexity." In Selover's thought-provoking interpretation, Master Ch'eng's dictum that humanity "forms one body with Heaven, Earth and myriad things" is a paradigmatic expression of experiential knowing and embodied thinking with important theological implications.

Preface

A Brief Autobiography of the Inquiry

This study originally grew out of research interest in relationships among what have traditionally been called the "Three Teachings" of China—Confucian, Taoist, and Buddhist —during the Sung dynasty (960–1279). Sparked in a graduate seminar with Wilfred Cantwell Smith, that interest led to a focus on the interweaving of these three religious traditions in the thought and practice of some key Sung dynasty figures, with a background predisposition to favor the more "ecumenical" among them. The matter, however, turned out to be more complex.

There is, indeed, a concrete historical sense in which the traditional Chinese aphorism "the three teachings return to one" (*san-chiao kuei-i* 三教歸一) is true for the Sung period, namely that they together shaped the heritage informing Chinese literati culture during that time. This basic fact of mutual influence is observable at every turn. Nevertheless, many of the seminal thinkers of the period were intent on distinguishing and defending the authentic line of interpretation in their own tradition from any confusion with others. Therefore, pursuit of the Confucian line in that sometimes cacophonous concerto of Sung thought led to the issue of authentic transmission, and that in turn led to a focus on Hsieh Liang-tso 謝良佐 (c.1050–c.1121).

Hsieh Liang-tso (later known as master Shang-ts'ai 上蔡先生) was one of the leading direct disciples of the brothers Ch'eng Hao 程顥 and Ch'eng I 程頤 in the early days of the Confucian revival known as "Tao-hsüeh" 道學 (The Learning of the Way) in Northern Sung China. Hsieh was thus among the first to recognize and follow the insights of the Ch'eng brothers as definitive of the authentic Confucian tradition, a recognition that became, directly or implicitly, the conviction of nearly all of the later Confucian scholarly community. The focus of this study is on Hsieh's engagement with the Confucian *Analects* 論語 as a key text, particularly important for understanding *jen* 仁 (humaneness, humanity). My translation and analysis of Hsieh's commentary on the *Analects*, drawn from the composite work *Lun-Meng ching-i* 論孟精義 (Essential Meanings of the *Analects* and *Mencius*) compiled by Chu Hsi 朱熹 (1130–1200), forms the textual basis of this study, and selections from it are included in the appendix.

For Chu Hsi and his contemporaries, it became an issue whether or not Hsieh's interpretations of the *Analects*, and particularly his controversial understanding of *jen* as *chüeh* 覺 (awareness, sensitivity), represented an authentic transmission of Confucian teaching as taught by the Ch'eng brothers. This controversy is explored in various ways throughout the book. My research thus demonstrates some of the variety and intellectual tensions within what Hoyt Tillman has felicitously called the Tao-hsüeh "fellowship," particularly in terms of the dynamic of savoring the scriptural and traditional resources (*wan-wei* 玩味) and attaining personal realization (*tzu-te* 自得). It also shows that the understanding of *jen* was a much more central issue for the Tao-hsüeh masters than is generally represented in the secondary literature.

In comparative perspective, these concerns with authentic transmission and the humane learning (*jen-hsüeh* 仁學) can be seen as bearing significant similarity to the practice of theology in the West. As will be set out in some detail, this similarity is manifested in a fourfold interpretive pattern comprising scripture, tradition, reason, and experience. Thus, Hsieh Liang-tso's thought, the Tao-hsüeh movement in general, and by implication the resources of the Confucian tradition as a whole are worthy of consideration in the wider context of comparative religion and comparative theology.

In the chapters that follow, the comparative framework, which emerged last but was implicit all along, is put first. The introduction starts from modern questions concerning the religious dimensions of the Confucian tradition and then proceeds through historical antecedents of those questions in the works of Matteo Ricci and James Legge to an initial mapping of a concept of comparative theology, based on the four warrants of scripture, tradition, reason, and experience. Chapter 1 places Hsieh in the context of the rise of Sung dynasty Tao-hsüeh, with special attention to the Ch'eng brothers' claims to the authentic transmission of Confucian learning. Chapter 2 places Hsieh's commentary on the Confucian *Analects* among other commentaries of the time and discusses its particular features. Chapter 3 treats Hsieh's most important contributions on the Confucian problematique of "knowing *jen*." Chapter 4 returns to the question of authentic transmission as raised by Chu Hsi, drawing out implications of Hsieh's insights for later Confucian learning. In the concluding chapter, further ramifications of this study for contemporary and comparative theology are suggested.

The first desideratum of comparative work in cultural and religious studies is that it be thoroughly grounded in the traditions of scholarship for its area of special inquiry. On this basis, the wider comparative frame of reference can provide an enhanced understanding. This book, therefore, can be read in at least two ways. Chapters 1–4 are intended to stand on their own merits as an account of the issues of authentic transmission and humane learning surrounding Hsieh and his commentary on the *Analects*, acceptable to the canons of Confucian scholarship in particular and sinology in general. The comparative concerns raised in the introduction do not explicitly intrude in most of this account, so that in principle one could begin with chapter 1 and leave the comparative religious context aside, at least temporarily. On the other hand, the larger comparative issues set out in the introduction are pertinent at every point of the account, and if they are borne in mind throughout, a wider range of resonances can be appreciated.

The subtitle of the book, "Humane Learning as a Religious Quest," is intended to suggest a trajectory forward to the present time, at the outset of the twenty-first century. We are engaged now, I believe, in a collective intellectual and spiritual process of culling the inherited resources of humankind's philosophical and religious traditions, seeking shareable wisdom for our common human life. The Confucian is one major strand in humankind's long pilgrimage, which deserves to be recognized as having contributed to our spiritual and temporal well-being. After more than a century of intense critique, it yet contains living ideas that can significantly enhance our emerging global culture. As this book tries to suggest, humane learning is vital to us today, as both a personal and a corporate quest.

A Note on Textual Matters

As is already clear, I have used the Wade-Giles romanization system throughout this book, with the exception of names of contemporary Chinese who use the Pinyin system for spelling their names. Abbreviations for sources are given at the beginning of the selected bibliography. Passages cited from the Confucian scriptural classics are given according to standard English translations, with modifications noted. Translations from Neo-Confucian works, particularly those of Hsieh Liang-tso, are my own unless otherwise noted. I have endeavored throughout to resist the gender bias inherent in the language of those standardized English translations, and in the earlier Confucian tradition itself, though I realize that I may not have done so completely. "Learning to be human" is a continuous process of widening horizons.

Acknowledgments

"To learn and to acknowledge from time to time those from and with whom one has learned, is it not a pleasure?" The core research for this book was presented as my doctoral dissertation in Comparative Religion at Harvard University's Divinity School. My dissertation advisor, Prof. Tu Wei-ming, guided me with unfailing patience, persistence, and sensitivity to think and feel more and more as a Confucian in approaching both historical research and comparative theological concerns. He and his wife, Roseanne Hall, have treated me with great hospitality, and I am also indebted to him for his gracious foreword. John Carman helped me at many points in feeling at home on the cusp between religious studies and theology, and in addition, he and Ineke Carman quietly provided a model of intellectual and spiritual leadership for interreligious community for those of us living at Harvard's Center for the Study of World Religions. Peter Bol, specialist in Chinese intellectual history, prodded me to think more contextually about the figures, texts, and issues treated here. Robert C. Neville, dean of the Boston University School of Theology, encouraged me with his own comparative theological reflections on Confucian thought. I also want to acknowledge and thank two earlier mentors whose guidance has proved lasting. Wilfred Cantwell Smith's influence has already been noted, and will be found herein at many points. William R. Shealy, of Virginia Wesleyan College, first inspired in me an intellectual passion for the study of religion, through lectures on " the relational mode of life" that still ring in my ears.

Among many special friends, I owe a particular debt of gratitude to Huang Po-ch'i for friendship and assistance, textual and contextual. Chiang I-pin gave unsparingly of his time in assisting my research and translation. Chen Lai and Ren Yuan offered help and encouragement in early stages of my research. Chu Ron Guey and Zhu Hanmin also gave timely assistance, as did Janine Sawada. Yen-zen Tsai shared the journey through Harvard's Th.D. program in comparative religion, and Wang Zhiqiang was also very helpful. Three other special friends, Anthony Guerra, Andrew Wilson, and Patricia Guenter-Gleason have shared deeply with me the joys and vicissitudes in the way of common vocation.

I want to sincerely thank David S. C. Kim, Edwin K. Ang, and Therese Stewart, without whose personal support this work, and much else, could never have been accomplished. I gratefully acknowledge having received financial support from UTS Continuing Education fund during my doctoral studies, and a publications grant from the University of Saskatchewan, where I now teach, to assist in manuscript preparation. To Barbara Holdredge and her anonymous reviewers for the Academy Series of the American Academy of Religion (AAR), and to Barbara DeConcini and the AAR staff for the felicitous publication arrangement with Oxford University Press, I offer my earnest appreciation. OUP editors Cynthia Read, Theo Calderara, and Bob Milks have helped to make the actual production of this book a positive (if sometimes painful) pleasure.

My father and mother, Will and Lila Selover, have "kept on keeping on" in their faith in me, demonstrating the indispensability of what Confucians call "primordial ties." There are no words adequate to thank my wife, Grace Lee Selover, who has labored with me to bring this work into being, and our sons David Willfield and Andrew Thomin, who have shared their dad with a documentary sibling. Finally, I want to thank Rev. Drs. Sun Myung Moon and Hak Ja Han Moon for their unfailing inspiration, along with their son Hyo Jin Moon, to the rhythm of whose music this book was originally written.

Contents

Hsieh Liang-tso and the *Analects* of Confucius

A COMPARATIVE FRAMEWORK

Hsieh Liang-tso 謝良佐 (c.1050–c.1120), master Shang-ts'ai 上蔡先生, was one of the leading disciples of Ch'eng Hao 程 顥 (1032–1085) and his younger brother Ch'eng I 程 頤 (1033–1107).[1] Together, they were central figures in the early Tao-hsüeh 道學 or Neo-Confucian movement.[2] Concentrating on Hsieh and his interpretation of the Confucian *Analects* 論語, the main theme of this book is "humane learning" or *jen-hsüeh* 仁學,[3] supplemented by the concept of "authentic transmission."

The wider interpretive context for this inquiry is the comparative study of religion, with emphasis on what could be called "comparative theology." This introduction will briefly set out relevant features of the comparative context, exploring the religiousness of the Confucian tradition as one of its central features. In so doing, the introduction will trace some of the historical antecedents to this line of inquiry, particularly in the work of Matteo Ricci (1553–1610) and James Legge (1815–1897). Beginning from the general interpretive question of Confucian religiousness, the discussion will proceed to two specific issues that concerned both Ricci and Legge, namely the scriptural status of the Confucian classics and the commensurability of Chinese terms with Christian ideas of God. It will be seen that the issues with which Ricci and Legge wrestled are still intriguing and fruitful from a wider comparative point of view. The argument will then move on to construct a comparative notion of religious and theological reflection centered on the concept of "authentic transmission" and a fourfold pattern of resources: scripture, tradition, reason, and experience. This comparative pattern then provides an interpretive framework for the examination of a specific moment in the development of Tao-hsüeh.

Religious Dimensions of the Confucian Tradition

It may be questioned whether "religion" is the proper rubric for the study of what in the West is commonly known as "Confucianism."[4] It has been argued both in East Asia and in the West that the Confucian tradition properly belongs under the heading of "philosophy."[5] For example, Frederick Mote writes in his foreword to a collection of essays by Tu Wei-ming that he has been "quite satisfied with a perception of a Confucianism that can be a complete system of ideas and values, at the level of a philosophy that does not require one to admit any specifically religious content."[6] Mote goes on to define that which he is disinclined to admit as a characterization of the Confucian tradition:

> "Religion," as I would define it for purposes of this discourse, no matter how rational-minded it in general may be, must nonetheless in some degree accept certain aspects of its truth on faith; it must admit a degree of non-rationality into its system of thought.[7]

Mote's definition of religion as "non-rational" clearly depends on the Western assumption of a sharp dichotomy between the domains of reason and faith, without which the definition would make little sense. However, as Irene Bloom has noted, "a distinction between the divine and the natural or between faith and reason has scarcely any analogue in the history of Chinese thought."[8] The presupposition of a faith/reason split, therefore, would hinder comparative work and tend to foreclose the possibility of being informed by alternative understandings of "good reasons."[9]

By employing a definition of religion that is less culturally specific, one can rather easily point to similarities between the Confucian tradition and other traditions generally recognized as "religious." Rodney Taylor has explored various "religious dimensions" of Confucian traditions in this way, drawing upon Frederick Streng's work for a functional definition of religion as "a means toward ultimate transformation."[10] In a description that resonates well with Confucian themes to be developed in subsequent chapters here, Streng writes of the "ultimate dimension" that it "refers to the reality that emerges or appears when a person lives within an extraordinarily deep sensitivity to life or a very profound strategy for action."[11] Tu Wei-ming's phrase "ultimate self-transformation" in his description of "the Confucian way of being religious" also seems to link up with Streng's approach.[12]

An indigenous confirmation of the religious character of the Confucian tradition may be found in the fact that Confucian teaching was for much of Chinese history considered to be one of the "Three Teachings" (*san-chiao* 三 教), with Taoist and Buddhist teachings as the other two.[13] Throughout a rich history of interaction, views on the relationship among the three teachings varied from mutual hostility to grand harmonization.[14] However, there was a common assumption that the three were addressing the same kinds of concerns, concerns that can be appropriately marked by the term "ultimate transformation."

Returning to Mote's comment more heuristically, it can be noted that in the background of his distinction between the religious and the philosophical on grounds of rationality lies the complex history of the dual-source Western tradition. Before the modern sense of conflict or antagonism between the two traditions, Hellenistic and Hebraic, there was a long period when they were synthesized in a two-tiered structure of thought. Such was the philosophical and theological frame of reference for the man whom N. J. Girardot has called both "the founding father of Sinology" and "the first great interpreter of Chinese religions," namely the Italian Jesuit missionary Matteo Ricci (1553–1610).[15] A brief look at Ricci's work will provide some historical depth for the issues under discussion.

The most influential document that Ricci authored was the *T'ien-chu shi-i* (True Meaning of the Lord of Heaven), in the form of a Socratic dialogue between a Western man of letters and a Chinese man of letters.[16] In this text, called by its English translators a "pre-evangelical dialogue,"[17] Ricci sets out to lay the groundwork for Christian teaching, as he explained to his superiors and colleagues back in Rome:

> This [text] does not treat of all the mysteries of our holy faith . . . but only of certain principles, especially such as can be proved and understood with the light of natural reason . . . preparing the way for those other mysteries which depend upon faith and revealed wisdom.[18]

Ricci thus assumes the Thomistic distinction between natural theology (that is, philosophy) and revealed theology, or general and special revelation. As George Dunne, S.J., explains,

> [Ricci] adopted the same attitude vis-à-vis Confucian thought that the early Fathers of the Church had adopted towards Greek thought: endeavoring to preserve all those elements of natural truth which it contained, to add other truths which it lacked in the natural order, and to introduce the whole new order of supernatural truth contained in Christian revelation.[19]

However, what Ricci was proposing was not simply to install the Christian gospel on the foundation of Confucian thought but rather to introduce the full synthesis of biblical gospel and Greek thought to the Chinese. Stressing the differences between Christian and Confucian perspectives, Jacques Gernet comments that Ricci

> very well understood the necessity first to teach the Chinese to reason properly, that is, to distinguish between substance and accident, the spiritual soul and the material body, the creator and his creation, moral good and natural good. How else could the Christian truths be put across?[20]

Nevertheless, it was on the presumed-as-shared level of natural reason (philosophy) that Ricci joined the Chinese debate.

The Jesuit view, that Confucian thought operated on the level of natural reason, provided a natural entrée for the introduction of Chinese culture to Europe. David Mungello has traced the seventeenth-century Latin translation project on the Confucian Four Books[21] as an ongoing, team project among the Jesuit missionaries, beginning in Ricci's time. This translation was to serve not only as a primer for missionaries learning Chinese but also as a way to publicize and promote the China mission.[22] The project culminated in *Confucius Sinarum Philosophus* (1687). Ironically, the writings of "Confucius the Chinese philosopher" later provided ammunition for anti-Christian sentiments during the French Enlightenment, as evidence for the idea that natural reason could get along perfectly well without the imposition of revealed religion.

For the nineteenth-century Protestant missionaries, the situation was quite different. In the eyes of the Scottish Independent missionary James Legge (1815–97), it was no longer a question of a two-tiered system of natural philosophy and revealed religion. Writing in 1879, Legge states unequivocally that "Confucianism is the religion of China *par excellence.*"[23] Furthermore, he was convinced that the early rulers of China "were not without considerable knowledge of God."[24] As for Confucius himself, Legge went so far as to say that "his teachings suggest important lessons to ourselves who profess to belong to the school of Christ."[25]

Nevertheless, and somewhat paradoxically, Legge judged Confucius to have been "unreligious," by which he meant that Confucius's influence was "unfavorable to the development of ardent religious feeling among the Chinese people generally."[26] On this point, Legge's evangelical sense of the religious—and perhaps also his frustration as a foreign missionary—seems to have overtaken his positive assessment of Confucius. Alternatively, one could say that the dichotomy and conflict between evangelical religion and anti-religious "philosophy" in the modern West had already taken its toll on Legge's evaluation of Chinese religion.[27]

Confucian Scripture?

A question related to the "religious dimensions" of the Confucian tradition is the extent to which Confucian texts can be understood as belonging in the arena of "scripture," as it is being increasingly understood cross-culturally.[28] There is now an expanding literature of tradition-oriented, genre-oriented, or thematically oriented collections of scriptural texts from the religious traditions of the world.[29] There have also been sophisticated comparative studies, exploring notions of scripture in different traditions.[30]

The question of whether or not Confucian texts should be included in this category is sometimes phrased in terms of whether they should be called "scriptures" or "classics." In his *Scripture, Canon, and Commentary*, subtitled "A Comparison of Confucian and Western Exegesis," John B. Henderson discusses the phenomenon of scriptural commentary cross-culturally, taking Confucian texts as his main line of reference. But Henderson does not offer a formal definition of "scripture," mentioning an oft-given one only in passing:

> Whether or not a canon is, strictly speaking, "scripture" or held to be divinely inspired, appears not to have greatly affected the exegetical devices employed in the commentarial traditions to which it is related.[31]

In his opening chapter, Henderson seems almost indifferent to any distinction between scripture and classic, writing that "the Confucian canon (or canons) is as diverse in its origins and complicated in its development as that of almost any major classical or scriptural tradition."[32] In her introduction to *Rethinking Scripture*, Miriam Levering also treats scripture and classic together, noting that "the concepts of scripture and classic result from the hope that the tradition-valued word can be transmitted just as it has been received."[33] There are other scholars, however, who feel strongly that Confucian texts should be classified as "scriptures" rather than "classics."[34]

Although an explicitly generic use of the word "scripture" would have been foreign to both Ricci and Legge, they implicitly treated texts of the Confucian canon as scriptural. Beyond appealing to reason, Ricci also cited the Confucian canon to prove to his Chinese audience that the ancient sages had known much of what Ricci was trying to communicate. Legge's English translations from the Confucian canon were published in two formats, *The Chinese Classics* series and as several volumes in F. Max Müller's *Sacred Books of the East*. If Müller's collection represents one of the first large-scale applications of a generic notion of scripture, it is significant that the Confucian Five Classics were prominently included. Legge himself averred that both the *Analects* and the *Mencius* book belonged among the *Sacred Books of the East* as well.[35]

The positive scriptural evaluation of the Confucian classics by both Ricci and Legge was part of their sense that these texts could be interpreted as preparing for (Ricci), or bearing witness to (Legge), Chinese faith in God. This issue, in turn, was seen as hinging on the "term question" of how to correlate Western theistic terminology with Confucian textual resources.

Chinese Words for God?

One of Ricci's main theses was that for "early Confucians," particularly as evidenced in the *Book of Documents* (*Shu-ching* 書經) and the *Book of Odes* (*Shih-ching* 詩經), worship centered on a monotheistic deity called *Shang-ti* 上 帝 (Sovereign on High) or *T'ien* 天 (Heaven), which could be equated with the Christian God. The Jesuits did not themselves use the indigenous term "*Shang-ti*" but developed a new term, "*T'ien-chu*" 天主 (lit., Heaven-master, Lord of Heaven) as their translation for "God" (*Deus*).[36] However, Ricci argued that "Our Lord of Heaven is the Sovereign on High mentioned in the ancient [Chinese] canonical writings," and then proceeded to give numerous citations from the classics.[37] As John D. Young comments, "Ricci became the first missionary in China to believe (or discover) that the idea of God was evident in the Confucian classics."[38] In advocating this view of the original Confucian teaching, Ricci opposed the prevailing interpretations put forward by the Sung Confucians, especially Chu Hsi, as distorting the Sage's pious wisdom and leading people away from monotheism toward agnosticism, materialism, and atheism. Ricci attacked Chu Hsi's notions of *T'ai-chi* 太極 (Supreme Ultimate), *li* 理 (principle or pattern), and *ch'i* 氣 (vital energy) in favor of the Lord of Heaven as the source and creator of all things.[39]

Like the Jesuits before him, Legge was also interested in the connection between the early Chinese classics and the Christian gospel. This was among the reasons why he joined the Protestant version of the term controversy, arguing vigorously for "*Shang-ti*" as the proper Chinese translation for the terms for God in the Old and New Testaments.[40] Legge also reciprocated in his English translations of the Chinese classics, translating "*Shang-ti*" and "*Ti*" in the *Book of Documents* and the *Book of Odes* as "God." Noting the "offence" that some missionaries and others had taken to what they called his "private interpretation," Legge rejoined:

> [W]hen I examined the question . . . with all possible interest and all the resources at my command, I came to the conclusions that Ti, on its first employment by the Chinese fathers, was intended to express the same concept which our fathers expressed by God, and that such has been its highest and proper application ever since.[41]

Legge put the matter succinctly: "I can no more translate *Ti* or *Shang Ti* by any other word but *God* than I can translate [*jen*] by anything else but *man*."[42] Legge even criticized Confucius for "avoiding" the "personal name" for God, "*Shang-ti*," and "preferring" to speak of "Heaven":

[B]y his frequent references to Heaven, instead of following the phras-
eology of the older sages, he gave occasion to many of his professed
followers to identify God with a principle of reason and the course of
nature.[43]

Among the "professed followers" of Confucius, Legge clearly had in mind the
Tao-hsüeh Neo-Confucians, whom Ricci had also criticized. In Legge's
estimation, Confucius had "prepared the way for the speculations of the
literati of medieval and modern times, which have exposed them to the charge
of atheism."[44] Unlike the Jesuits, however, Legge the translator appreciated
Chu Hsi's classical commentaries and often took his views as a guide.[45]

Because both Ricci and Legge found classical references to "*Shang-ti*" to be
the point of contact between Confucian and Christian teaching, they were
bound to feel that Confucius had obscured the truth about God, and that the
Neo-Confucians had subverted it entirely. From the Sung Neo-Confucians'
point of view, however, the tradition was being enhanced rather than
degraded: Confucius the Sage was *the* authoritative embodiment of the
classical religious tradition, and they in turn were his true inheritors,
interpreters, and transmitters.

In retrospect, the limitation of a narrow focus on terms becomes apparent.
Apart from the question of how best to translate the personalistic language for
God in the Christian scriptures into Chinese, the more general comparative
issue is how to discern the kind of "ultimate dimension" in the Confucian
tradition that Christian words for God have traditionally marked. Such
discernment depends upon at least a provisional comparative understanding of
theology.

Toward a Comparative Concept of Theology

As is the case with "religion" and "scripture," using "theology" as a comparative category requires a stretching exercise, taking the concept beyond the
limits of what has traditionally been understood by it. The Catholic and
Protestant term controversies over "God" and "*Shang-ti*" make apparent the
difficulties of defining what counts as theology in terms of its putative object.[46]
Deciding whether or not two such terms have a common referent is in itself a
complex theological judgment.

In his prolegomenon to "world theology," Wilfred Cantwell Smith pro-
poses the following definition of theology:

By ["theology"] I mean, quite literally, talk about God; or more
generically, about the transcendent dimension of human life and of

the universe to which the history of religion (the history of man's spirit) bears witness and which it elucidates, and to which Christians have historically given the name "God."[47]

Smith's attempt is to offer a widely applicable general definition of theology. However, to posit "the transcendent dimension of human life and of the universe" in the singular is of course to make a particular theological statement about the religious content of the many religious traditions. For this reason, a generic description of theological concerns for comparative purposes cannot wait to be defined in terms of whether or not there is a common referent.

The emerging field of comparative ethics may provide suitable suggestions for comparative theology.[48] Comparative ethics does not presuppose a specific answer to the normative question of what is right and good (nor even to whether there is such a thing as right and good in a univocal sense), but it does endeavor to provide a field upon which such questions can be meaningfully explored. In the same way, comparative theology cannot depend on prior answers to such questions as whether "God" and "*Shang-ti*" or "Heaven" have a common referent. As in comparative ethics, comparative study of theological reflection may contribute to informing, but does not determine, normative decisions about which traditions a given theologian will take seriously.

Like Smith, Robert Neville argues for understanding theology as a form of inquiry not bound by the limits of the Christian tradition that originally gave rise to its significant issues.[49] But not all contemporary Christian theologians would agree on the propriety of availing oneself of insights from other religious traditions. As George Lindbeck might say, Confucian texts and the Christian theological tradition represent different cultural-linguistic systems; they belong to different symbolic universes that for the most part have not shared a common history.[50] The generic interpretations of theology proposed by Smith and Neville contrast with orientations such as Lindbeck's that see theology as properly "intra-textual" within a cultural-linguistic tradition.

One of the interesting features of Lindbeck's cultural-linguistic notion of religion, and its theological implications, is that one must learn the "grammar" of a religious tradition in order to become a part of it, to see its truth, and to have its significant experiences. An implication that could be drawn for the comparative study of religion is that it is salient to pay attention to the "grammar" of a tradition's scriptural texts. Such familiarity with or "feel for" the text would include not only key passages but also the corpus as a whole. For a discussion of "scriptural grammar" in Hsieh Liang-tso's *Analects* commentary, see chapter 2.[51]

Lindbeck is critical of what he calls the "liberal experiential-expressive" theory of religion, according to which all religions are held to express a common religious experience, though in particular forms. Yet neither Smith nor Neville argues for a common core of religious experience, but rather for the responsibility of contemporary theology to take humankind's disparate religious experience seriously. Although Lindbeck is surely right that appreciation of the cultural-linguistic uniqueness of a religious tradition is necessary to proper understanding, the present time is characterized by cultural and even linguistic cross-fertilization between traditions that seems likely to accelerate in the future.

Lindbeck's argument seems to presuppose that a person can legitimately belong to one religion at most. However, as Smith has cogently argued, this presupposition is historically inaccurate and, more controversial, theologically unnecessary.[52] If this presupposition were dropped from Lindbeck's "cultural-linguistic" approach, it would be better able to account for the phenomenon that a person can be "schooled" in more than one religious tradition, as one can learn to speak and to think with more than one language.

Although it has in fact contributed to the historical vitality of religious traditions at myriad points, including the rise of the Tao-hsüeh movement, such religious cross-fertilization does not always lead to syncretism in practice, as the history of the "three teachings" in China amply shows. Nor does recognizing it in theory necessarily imply the sort of "liberal experiential-expressive" view of religion that Lindbeck opposes. After all, the fruitfulness of learning another tongue is precisely that one may speak—and think—differently.

Authentic Transmission: Scripture, Tradition, Reason, Experience

Of course, every cultural-linguistic tradition lives in history through a process of transmission from generation to generation. However, as an intellectual discipline in the West, it is theology more than philosophy that accepts authoritative sources and recognizes its concern with the authentic transmission and reinterpretation of those sources. Theological reflection interprets what it takes to be sources of authentic wisdom not randomly available, and is thus centrally concerned that such insight be transmitted with integrity from one generation to the next.

This concern for authentic transmission often manifests in terms of a familiar set of resources—scripture, tradition, reason, and experience. Neville discusses these four as theological sources in *Behind the Masks of God*, subtitled "An Essay Toward Comparative Theology."[53] Though Neville is speaking primarily of Christian theology at this point in the text, and though he later refers to the four as the "Wesleyan quatrilateral" (p. 156), he draws some of his examples from the wider history of religion. Indeed, this fourfold set of resources and warrants for "theological" reflection can be fruitfully explored as the basis for a useful comparative understanding of theology.

Some of the nuances of "scripture" as a comparative category have been briefly suggested earlier. Levering makes the point that concern for authentic transmission of "the tradition-valued word" is one of the marks of a text being treated as scriptural, underscoring the point that "scriptures" are embedded within "traditions."[54] Within Christianity, "tradition" has meant primarily the interpretive tradition for particular scriptural texts, and the office and authority that provide the context for theological interpretation. "Tradition" can be said to include not only the interpretive traditions relevant to specific scriptural texts but also the ritual or liturgical tradition in which those texts are embedded. Whatever an interpreter may think of a particular received tradition with reference to scriptural texts, those older traditions still form part of the interpretive context that has to be dealt with, whether reiterated, reconstructed, or overthrown. By the same token, new work on scriptural texts is itself tradition-forming, in such a way that new canons of interpretation may be generated.

As for "reason" and "experience," it will be helpful for comparative work to think of these not in the limited terms of the rationalism-empiricism debate in Western philosophy, but in more the general terms of shared good reasons and the (at least partially) shareable familiarity of learning from experience.[55] Leaving aside all kinds of scholarly debates about the status, unity, or even existence of something called "reason," a working empirical definition would be those patterns of thinking actually relied upon explicitly in argument, that constitute "good reasons" in the rhetorical sense. Naturally, these thinking patterns are carried in, or generated by, language and grammar structures. An appeal to "reason" then would be an appeal to a culturally recognized or culturally plausible pattern of thinking.

"Experience" can refer to specific experiences, either cultivated or spontaneous, such as divine "contact," personal transformation, and so on. It can also mean the general seasoning process of life and its attendant development of pragmatic wisdom. Of course, as Rosemary Ruether has pointed out, all four types of warrants are "experiential," because "scripture" and "tradition" are also "codified collective human experience."[56] Speaking of experience as a distinct warrant can also refer to the "test of experience" by which past formulations in scripture and tradition are judged on their adequacy for contemporary life.[57] All of these four "warrants" are brought to bear on the question of how to discern an authentic transmission.

Tao-hsüeh and Theology

In a telling passage found in the introduction to his translation of the Confucian *Analects*, Arthur Waley offers the following critique of Chu Hsi's interpretive work:

> Chu Hsi has been called a great scholar, but no one would call him so who had any experience of the difference between scholarship and theology. For though Chu Hsi was not a theologian in the literal sense of the term, though he is concerned with a Truth rather than with a God, his methods are at every point those of the theologian, not those of the scholar. It was not his aim to discover, as a scholar would have done, what the Classics meant when they were written. He assumed that there was one Truth, embodied equally in the teachings of the brothers Ch'eng and in the sayings of Confucius . . . Chu Hsi was a great popular educator, a great evangelist; but in no sense was he a scholar.[58]

Like Mote's definition of religion as "non-rational" cited earlier, Waley's sharp contrast between "scholarship" and "theology" bespeaks the context of modern Western polemics. It is inapt and misleading to assert, as Waley does, that the Sung Confucians were unconcerned with determining and explaining the "original meaning" of the *Analects* and other Confucian scriptural classics. It was precisely the sense that they *had* done so that gave a certain evangelical zeal to their teaching.

Yet without compromising the tradition's widely held and centuries-long respect for Chu Hsi's scholarship, Waley's comment may still be seen as inadvertently on the mark in sensing that Chu Hsi's work was "theological" in a comparative sense. This "theological" sense is to be found in Chu's concern for the authentic transmission of the correct interpretation of scriptural texts, making them reasonably adequate to contemporary experience. As will be seen throughout the following chapters, Confucian Tao-hsüeh has had its own canon of scriptural classics, complex tradition of interpretation, fund of good reasons, and wealth of cultivated experience. All of these sources and warrants for constructive reflection were aimed at authentic transmission of the kernel of Sagely wisdom.

Having sketched this comparative framework, I will now proceed to a detailed examination of the issues surrounding Hsieh Liang-tso. Chapter 1 will place Hsieh in the context of Sung dynasty Tao-hsüeh, with special attention to the Ch'eng brothers' claims to the authentic transmission of Confucian learning. Chapter 2 will focus specifically on Hsieh's commentary on the Confucian

Analects. Chapter 3 treats Hsieh's significant contributions on the key problematique of "knowing *jen.*" Chapter 4 returns to the question of authentic transmission as raised by Chu Hsi, drawing out implications of Hsieh's insights for later Confucian learning. In the concluding chapter, further ramifications of this study for contemporary and comparative theology will be suggested.

CHAPTER ONE

Disciple of the Ch'eng Brothers

A Memorial to the Throne

In 1136, Chu Chen 朱 震 (1072–1138) submitted a memorial to the emperor Kao-tsung (r. 1127–62) containing the following description of the transmission of the Tao:

> Your servant humbly states that the Tao of Confucius was transmitted to Tseng Tzu, Tseng Tzu transmitted to Tzu-ssu, and Tzu-ssu transmitted to Mencius. After Mencius there was no transmission. Coming to our dynasty, Ch'eng Hao and Ch'eng I of the western [capital] Loyang transmitted his (or: their) Tao more than a thousand years afterwards. Those engaged in learning shouldered satchels and hiked up their garments [in hurrying] to personally receive their instruction, spreading it to the four directions. Some in secret and some openly—none can exhaust the record. Their major disciples were: Hsieh Liang-tso, Yang Shih, and Yu Tso . . . [Hsieh] Liang-tso, as a worthy, personally transmitted the Tao learning (*Tao-hsüeh*). None in the world could match him.[1]

Hsieh Liang-tso 謝良佐 (c.1050–c.1120), known in Confucian circles as master Shang-ts'ai 上蔡先生, was one of the principal direct disciples of the brothers Ch'eng Hao 程 顥 (1032–1085, master Ming-tao 明道先生) and Ch'eng I 程 頤(1033–1107, master I-ch'uan 伊川先生) identified in Chu Chen's memorial as the preeminent figures at the beginning of the Tao-hsüeh 道學 (Tao learning) intellectual and spiritual revival.[2] The emerging movement was characterized by an acute sense that although the *Analects* and other records of Confucius's teaching had been transmitted over many centuries, the authentic meaning and import of the texts had been lost. The Tao-hsüeh Confucians felt they had both the opportunity and the responsibility to recover and realize that meaning. Or, perhaps, the sense of the loss of transmission was retrospective, after they came to believe that they had rediscovered the authentic meaning. Those who constituted the Tao-hsüeh fellowship shared a new sense of being able to emulate the Sage himself through their study and practice.[3]

15

It is important to note that the Ch'eng brothers were not the sole central figures of this fellowship. In the later Confucian tradition, they have been considered as two among the "five Confucian masters" of the Northern Sung period (960–1127). The other three are Chou Tun-i 周敦頤 (Lien-hsi 濂溪, 1017–1073), Chang Tsai 張載 (1020–1077), and Shao Yung 邵雍(1011– 1077).[4] During the Sung period itself, the grouping was more flexible; for example, the *Chu-ju ming Tao chi* 諸儒鳴道記 (Records of various Confucians calling out the Tao) also includes the statesman-scholar Ssu-ma Kuang 司馬光 (1019–1086) and his followers.

The Ch'eng's Claim to Authentic Transmission

In 1085, Ch'eng Hao was eulogized by his younger brother Ch'eng I as having discovered and made available the "untransmitted learning" (*pu-ch'uan chih hsüeh* 不傳之學) that had been obscured for fourteen hundred years. The younger Ch'eng wrote:

> After the passing of the Duke of Chou, the Tao of the sages was not practiced; after Meng K'o [Mencius] died, the learning of the sages was not transmitted. [Since] the Tao was not practiced, there was no good government for a hundred generations; [since] the learning was not transmitted, there were no true Confucians [*chen-ju* 真儒] for a thousand years. When there was no good government, literati [*shih* 士] were still able to illuminate the Tao of good government by learning indirectly from others and transmitting it to later times. [But] without true Confucians, the realm was lost and no one knew where to go, human desires [*jen-yü* 人欲] were indulged and Heavenly principle [*T'ien-li* 天理] was obliterated. The master [Ch'eng Hao] was born 1400 years later. He apprehended the untransmitted learning in the surviving Classics and was intent upon "using this Tao to awaken [*chüeh* 覺] this people."[5]

This sense of Ch'eng Hao's singular achievement was shared by the various disciples and friends who wrote eulogistic comments in his memory.[6] As Ch'eng I put it, though they differed in content according to each person's understanding, they all agreed in the opinion that "after Mencius there was only one person [i.e., Ch'eng Hao] who transmitted the Sagely Way."[7] Even with allowances for eulogistic hyperbole, there was still a remarkable and historically long-lasting sense of a rejuvenation of authentic transmission.[8]

There is surely a family resemblance between the sense of rejuvenation of authentic transmission that was developing in the Ch'eng brothers' circle and the expansion of Ch'an 禪 (Zen) Buddhist transmission lineages during the same period.[9] Though they could be vehement in their criticism of Buddhist (and Taoist) "heterodox" traditions, the Tao-hsüeh Confucians also owed much to their collegial rivals. Indeed, the concern for authentic transmission is commonly shared among those who disagree sharply with each other.[10]

As an "event," the Sung Tao-hsüeh perception of a renewal of authentic transmission from the ancient sages and wise teachers, especially Confucius and Mencius, cannot be fully understood by looking at Ch'eng Hao or his brother Ch'eng I alone. Those who received the teaching from them, their disciples and friends, were an integral part of the matrix of the Tao-hsüeh revival in the reciprocity of teaching and learning. In this sense, the first-generation disciples of the Ch'eng brothers played a larger role in the Tao-hsüeh phenomenon than is often recognized. Among the direct disciples, Hsieh was known as one of the "Four Masters of the Ch'eng school,"[11] and sometimes praised as the most earnest.

Hsieh as Disciple

Hsieh Liang-tso is generally considered to have been born around 1050, in Shang-ts'ai 上蔡 district in present-day Honan.[12] He would thus have been approximately twenty-eight years old in the first year of the Yüan-feng reign-period (1078), when he journeyed to the district of Fu-kou (in present-day Honan) to see Ch'eng Hao, who was serving there as district magistrate (*chih-hsien* 知縣).[13]

According to one account of their first meeting, Ch'eng Hao said of him, "This *hsiu-ts'ai* 秀才 (flourishing talent) has potentiality and shows promise for the future."[14] According to another account, when Hsieh first arrived, Ch'eng Hao treated him with the ceremony due a guest, but Hsieh protested that he wanted to become his student. He was then housed in a corner without heat or light, until he came to some realization. Because after more than a month he was not deterred, Ch'eng Hao finally accepted him as a formal student.[15]

Hsieh has been known primarily through the *Shang-ts'ai yü-lu* 上蔡語錄 (Recorded Sayings of [Master Hsieh] Shang-ts'ai, hereafter STYL), a collection of Hsieh's sayings as recorded by Tseng T'ien 曾恬 (dates uncertain) and Hu An-kuo 胡安國 (1074–1138).[16] Chu Hsi 朱熹 (1130–1200), the primary systematizer of Tao-hsüeh insights, edited the STYL in 1159 as his first major work.[17] One of the most important features of the STYL is the light that it sheds on the teacher-disciple relationship between Hsieh and the Ch'eng brothers.

One of the few mentions of the spiritual discipline of "quiet-sitting" (*ching-tso* 靜坐) in the Ch'eng brothers' collected sayings is a record of Ch'eng Hao's instruction to Hsieh.[18] The elder Ch'eng at one point criticized their students for only studying his words, urging them to devote themselves to practice. When Hsieh asked what he should practice, he received the direction to practice quiet-sitting.[19] The passage continues that whenever Ch'eng I saw the students engaged in quiet-sitting, he commended their being good at learning. In a passage that likely describes Ch'eng Hao's own practice of quiet-sitting, Hsieh said, "When Ming-tao sat down, he was like an earthen figure, but when he associated with people, he was completely a sphere of peaceful disposition." [20] The later commentator Chang Po-hsing remarks on this passage, "Were it not that [Hsieh] Shang-ts'ai had silently understood in heart-and-mind and gotten something of it [himself], he would not have been able to describe [Ch'eng Hao] like this."[21]

The most famous encounter between Hsieh and Ch'eng Hao was an incident in which his teacher caught Hsieh's attention when he was showing off his knowledge and redirected his vocation in an opportune moment of teaching:

> At first, Master Hsieh took rote memorization to be learning and had a high opinion of himself as erudite.[22] In front of Master Ming-tao [i.e., Ch'eng Hao] he recited a book of history without leaving out a single character. Ming-tao said, "My worthy friend, you have indeed memorized a great deal. [This] could be called 'trifling with things and losing purpose.'"[23] When Hsieh heard these words, he [immediately reacted by] perspiring all over and reddening in the face. Ming-tao then remarked, "Exactly this is 'the heart-and-mind of natural compassion.'"[24]

Ch'eng Hao induced an intense reaction in Hsieh, and then pointed to his visceral response as a manifestation of natural compassion, the "beginning" of *jen*.[25] The account continues:

> When it [later] came to seeing Ming-tao [himself] reading histories, determining the phrasing and reading through without mistaking a single character, Hsieh felt very resentful. Afterwards, he reflected and came to a realization [*hsing-wu* 省悟]. Then he even took this incident as a topical case [*hua-t'ou* 話頭], to guide literati of extensive learning.[26]

Thus, Hsieh utilized his own direct experience of Ch'eng Hao's exemplary teaching as a guide for others. Something of the quality of the teacher-disciple relationship that characterized the Tao-hsüeh fellowship comes across in this anecdote that became well known among later Confucians.

Hsieh often incorporated Ch'eng Hao's poetry in his own teaching as a way to invoke a model of naturalness. A particularly evocative line that Hsieh quotes in STYL is "Wan-wu ching-kuan chieh tzu-te" 萬物靜觀皆自得 ("All things viewed in tranquility are at ease with themselves").[27] After another poem of Ch'eng Hao cited in the same STYL passage, Hsieh comments, "[We] can see that his affections are truly excellent, of the same kind as Tseng Tien's."[28] Hsieh continues, "I've been in the school of [Ch'eng] Ming-tao from early on and am able to free myself. For he 'transforms all whom he passes by.'"[29] Apparently, it was this free and easy approach to serious cultivation that Hsieh found inspiring and transformative. He was known as a diligent disciple who took his mistakes very seriously. On one occasion, after a year's effort, he reported to Cheng I that he had finally succeeded in getting rid of "boasting" (*chin* 矜), no doubt a difficult accomplishment to report without undoing it.

There are frequent references to both Ch'eng brothers in the *Shang-ts'ai yü-lu*. The *Erh-Ch'eng wai-shu* 二程外書, also edited by Chu Hsi, contains a large section of sayings of the Ch'eng brothers derived from the STYL, showing that Chu regarded the STYL as a reliable source for sayings of the Ch'engs. These include the sole instance of Ch'eng Hao's famous statement that "*T'ien-li*" 天理 (Heavenly principle or pattern) was what he gained on his own.[30]

Hsieh also respected Ch'eng Hao for his attitude toward government service. In the *Fu-kou hsien-chih* 扶溝縣志, it is recorded that Ch'eng Hao kept on the right side of his desk the saying "*Shih-min ju-shang*" 視民如傷 ("Regard the people as if [treating] the injured") from the *Tso-chuan*.[31] Seeing this, Hsieh is said to have remarked, "With investment of heart (*yung-hsin* 用心) such as this, naturally there will be no instances of excessive punishment."[32]

Following in Ch'eng Hao's footsteps (and differing from Ch'eng I), Hsieh studied for the imperial examinations, preparing for an official career. He received the *chin-shih* 進士 in the eighth year of Yüan-feng, 1085. As he later reported, he had had a dream in which he foresaw the mourning for the emperor at the time of his becoming a *chin-shih*. Indeed, the dream was prophetic, for Emperor Shen-tsung passed away in the third month of 1085. This was also the year in which Hsieh's beloved teacher Ch'eng Hao died.

Hsieh as Official and Teacher

According to the *I-Lo yüan-yüan lu* 伊洛淵源錄, Hsieh received an appointment at a prefectural school during the Yüan-yu period (1086–94). Hu Yin 胡寅 (1098–1156) records that Hsieh served as supervisor of education in Ch'in-t'ing during that period.[33] He later served in several local government posts, including Ying-ch'eng 應城 in modern Hupei and Mien-ch'ih 澠池 in modern Honan, and also held a post at the Imperial Library.[34]

It was while Hsieh was serving in Ying-ch'eng that Hu An-kuo came to see him. Hu was one of the main sources for Hsieh's sayings collected in the STYL and can be considered one of his most important followers (see chapter 4). It is recorded that Hu came in the capacity of intendant of education, but was so impressed with the discipline evident among those serving in Hsieh's outer courtyard that, instead of approaching him as a superior, he presented himself first as a student.[35] Later, Hu An-kuo often remarked about how Hsieh Shang-ts'ai's words were very good at opening up a person's intelligence.[36]

Hsieh's service in Mien-ch'ih, to the west of Lo-yang in present-day Honan, may have been either before or after his service at Ying-ch'eng, but in any case before the death of Ch'eng I in 1107.[37] It is recorded in the *Mien-ch'ih hsien-chih* 澠池縣志 (gazetteer) that:

> [When Hsieh] received orders for Mien-ch'ih, he came to Loyang to see [Ch'eng] I-ch'uan and stayed more than ten days. I-ch'uan said to Yin T'un that if he saw [Hsieh] Hsien-tao, he should try asking what he gained in coming this time. Yin went to ask. Hsieh said, "Every time [in the past] when I heard the master's words, I had many doubts and uncertainties. This time when I saw the master and heard his words, decidedly there was no doubt." Yin told this to I-ch'uan, who said, "I saw it in him. It is indeed like that." [38]

At this point, already well established on his own, Hsieh came to have a new level of faith and confidence in Ch'eng I and his teaching.

The height of Hsieh's political career seems to have been the imperial audience granted him by Emperor Hui-tsung, who ascended the throne in 1101. The *Sung shih* 宋史 records, "In the first year of Chien-chung ching-kuo (1101), while Hsieh was an official in the capital metropolitan area (*ching-shih*) he received a summons to an audience at court."[39] However, this audience did not lead to any high appointment. The Ying-ch'eng gazetteer gives the following account:

> At the beginning of Chien-chung ching-kuo, [Hsieh] had responsibility as an official in the Imperial Library [*shu chü kuan*]. He was

summoned to an audience [at court] and offended the [imperial] will, [so that he] was exiled to the provinces. He became magistrate of Ying-ch'eng. Transforming the people by virtue, [he] expected to have no legal cases; he was simple yet able to inspire awe, stern and yet not fierce.[40]

This brief account of his offense in standard terminology does not give any details. From other sources, there are two incidents recorded relating to his demotion. It is reported that after his audience, Hsieh commented that the emperor's intent was not sincere ("*Shang-i pu-ch'eng*" 上意不誠). Subsequently he was assigned to a minor post as superintendent of woods and bamboo (*chien chu-mu ch'ang* 監竹木場) in Loyang.[41]

According to another account, someone observed to Hsieh that the reign-period title "Chien-chung" 建中 declared in 1101 was the same as a title proclaimed under Emperor Te-tsung of T'ang during a period of unrest, and therefore was not auspicious. Hsieh rejoined that indeed general chaos might ensue. For this remark, it is said, he was thrown into jail, his official rank was taken away, and he was reduced to the status of a commoner.[42] Such an incident becomes plausible in light of the intense political controversies that were rampant at court during this period, stirred up by the vigorous reform program that was instituted under chief minister Wang An-shih 王安石 (1021–1086, Chieh-fu 介甫), and then by the "conservative" backlash.[43] James T. C. Liu's description of the political climate around 1100 provides the context of this alleged incident:

> A revengeful political persecution on a large scale sent hundreds of the conservatives to humiliating local government posts far away. One notable exception to the prevailing political climate occurred in 1100 when Emperor Che-tsung was succeeded by his brother Hui-tsung. Tseng Pu, the only one of Wang [An-shih]'s early associates to regain some measure of leadership, introduced a policy of reconciliation and unity by naming the reign "Establishment of a Middle Course" (Chien-chung) and by recommending some conservatives to high offices, in the hope of ameliorating factional antagonism. Unfortunately, this short-lived policy failed to please the other leaders of the postreform or to appease the embittered conservatives. [44]

In such a climate, Hsieh's critical remark about the reign-period title "Chien-chung" would have had more than passing significance, portraying the title as an ill omen rather than an olive branch.[45]

Apparently, as suggested by both of these incidents, Hsieh was implicated by rumor and suffered the vicissitudes of the factionalism and strife during the post-reform period, leading up to the loss of north China to the Jurchen Chin. The 1136 memorial by Chu Chen cited at the opening of this chapter contains the following description of the plight of Hsieh's family:

> Only [Hsieh] Liang-tso [among the chief disciples of the Ch'eng brothers] ended with being [merely] superintendent of woods and bamboo. His name was linked with the [Yüan-yu] faction and displayed on stone [steles]; his life ended without opportunity.
>
> One son, K'o-chi, entered officialdom, but later K'o-chi met up with notorious bandits in Te-an district and the whole family was destroyed. Another son crossed the ridges and entered Min [Fukien]; he died of malaria. Another son, K'o-nien, is still alive, wandering as an outcast in T'ai-chou, completely impoverished and destitute, with no provisions from morning to night.
>
> [Hsieh Liang-tso] died as a victim of the prohibition [against the Yüan-yu faction], and his sons weakened and declined. This is extreme misfortune.[46]

The point of this account in the memorial is a plea that Hsieh Liang-tso should be given posthumous recognition as one of the chief disciples of the Ch'engs. Whereas by that time the other two main Ch'eng disciples, Yang Shih and Yu Tso, had either received high office themselves or had it given to their sons, Hsieh's sole surviving son, Hsieh K'o-nien (謝可念), was living a refugee life of poverty and oblivion in T'ai-chou. The opening passage setting forth the line of authentic transmission (see further discussion in chapter 4) functions as an elaborate "whereas" clause to Chu's petition for a government post for Hsieh K'o-nien, as a belated official recognition of Hsieh Liang-tso's worth. Furthermore, as one of Hsieh's students who had risen to central government office, Chu Chen was performing his "filial" duty.

Hsieh's Literary Traces

By the time of the compiling of the *I-Lo yüan-yüan lu* by Chu Hsi in 1173, Hsieh's epitaph (*mu-chih ming* 墓志銘) by Yu Tso had already been lost, although his *wen-chi* (literary collection) was still available.[47] The *wen-chi*, which might have provided a fuller explication of Hsieh's relations with his fellow students and other contemporaries, is no longer extant. As for his cultural interests, the only record remaining is an intriguing colophon by Ch'ao Pu-chih 晁補之 (1053–1110), one of the four major followers of the multi-talented Su Shih 蘇軾, for a seal-character scroll in Hsieh's possession, from which it is possible to infer that he was a person who shared in the broad literati culture of his time.[48]

As mentioned earlier, the STYL was edited by Chu Hsi in 1159 as his first major work. In his postface to the STYL, Chu remarks that "among all those who followed [the two Ch'eng brothers], what was seen [by Hsieh] is most exhilarating (or: unconventional/transcendental, *ch'ao-yüeh* 超越)."[49] Chu Hsi further reports that he himself was a student of Hsieh's sayings long before he undertook to collate the different versions at the age of twenty-nine:

> Before I was twenty, I obtained [one version of] *Shang-ts'ai yü-lu* and read it. At first I used vermilion ink to mark the apt passages; on second reading they appeared different, so I used white ink. The third time, I used black ink. After several times, [the marked passages] were completely different from the first time.[50]

Such editorial judgments on aptness—and thus authenticity—also entered into Chu's eventual compilation and standardization of the STYL. In his 1168 postface, he remarks that he found fifty-odd passages that did not seem to belong and "could not have been" said by Hsieh, and so he expunged them. Later, he claims, he found those very passages word for word in another work, the *Pien-Tao lu* 辨道錄 (Distinguishing the Tao collection) by Chiang Min-piao 江民表, thus vindicating his editorial intuition.[51] There is probably no way now to get behind Chu Hsi's redaction; even the very thorough Wing-tsit Chan has had to admit that "it is impossible to know to what extent [Chu Hsi] edited the text."[52] In a sense, this problem is endemic to any "sayings source." However, the general rule pertains that passages further from the redactor's own viewpoint, when identifiable, should be given the more weight as likely to be more authentic (in the sense of closer to the original). Thus, the emphasis here is on themes in Hsieh's sayings that differ from Chu Hsi's own interpretive perspective.

The only literary work of Hsieh's that survives intact as a separate text is his "*Lun-yü chieh hsü*" 論語解序, the preface to his commentary on the *Analects*, included by Lü Tsu-ch'ien 呂祖謙 (1137–81) in the *Huang-ch'ao wen-chien (Sung wen-chien*, "Mirror of the Prose of the Imperial [Sung] Dynasty)."[53] There is also a shortened version of the preface in the *Lun-yü ching-i* 論語精義 (Essential Meanings of the *Analects*), compiled by Chu Hsi.

From this preface, it is evident that the *Analects* occupied a very important place in Hsieh's life and thought.[54] In his postface to Hsieh's *Analects* commentary, Hu Yin states:

> Mr. Hsieh Shang-ts'ai attained the Way from the Masters Ch'eng of Honan. In the Yüan-yu period, he supervised education in Ch'in-t'ing.

Thereupon he authored the *Lun-yü Chieh* to express what his heart-and-mind had attained, and break through worldly scholars' far-fetched, shallow and obstinate theories.[55]

It is fitting for an investigation of Hsieh's thought, as a disciple and teacher of the Tao-hsüeh revival, to focus on his interpretation of the *Analects* because, in the words of Hu Yin's postface, Hsieh himself expressed his personal attainment of understanding (*hsin-te* 心得) in the form of his *Analects* commentary.

CHAPTER TWO

"The *Analects* Can Be Hard to Read"

Interpreting Scriptural Classics in the Sung

Tao-hsüeh interpretations were part of a general Sung period re-evaluation of the Confucian scriptural heritage. Steven Van Zoeren describes this period as "a major turning point in the history of classics studies, analogous in many ways to the revolution in the reading and authority of scripture in the Christian Reformation."[1] On the other hand, as John Henderson has pointed out, "such classical revivals, renaissances, and reformations . . . often obscure significant continuities in these traditions."[2] While apparently conflicting, these two readings of the situation can be seen to correct for each other. From the *Tao-hsüeh* thinkers' own point of view, their insight was at once a major turning point and a profound continuity, precisely because they believed they had accomplished what previous commentators in the tradition had not been able to do, namely to recover the original meaning of the texts. Their specific sense of that accomplishment was embedded in both a long tradition of shared meanings and an array of new ways of looking at the classical texts in the Sung period.

Daniel Gardner has suggested a threefold outline of approaches to the classics during the Sung, under the headings "critical," "programmatic," and "philosophical."[3] Van Zoeren offers another threefold classification, the main difference being that he divides the texts and approaches called "philosophical" by Gardner into two categories, "metaphysical" and "personal/devotional."[4] However they are classified, it was an overlapping of the various emphases that supported the eventual emergence of *Tao-hsüeh* as the leading interpretation of the Confucian canon. As an example of this overlapping, the political reformer Wang An-shih 王安石 (1021–1086), who is identified by Gardner with the "programmatic approach" and whose faction was responsible for the early proscription of some of the *Tao-hsüeh* fellowship, nevertheless promoted policies that contributed to the rise of *Tao-hsüeh.*[5]

As a matter of emphasis, the *Tao-hsüeh* thinkers tended to favor certain portions of the classical "canon," with special attention to the texts that later came to be known as the Four Books.[6] Chu Hsi's commentaries on these four texts were first grouped as "the Four Masters" and published as such in 1190.[7] There has been an understandable tendency to attribute this change in the

25

effective canon ("from the Five Classics to the Four Books") solely to Chu Hsi as the most influential thinker of the *Tao-hsüeh* movement.[8] But it is clear from the recorded sayings of the Ch'eng brothers and their followers that much of the currency of their discussions was drawn from the texts that became the Four Books. This observation is also supported by a saying of Ch'eng I that Chu Hsi cites:

> Those engaged in learning ought to take the *Analects* and the *Mencius* as the basis [of their studies]. Once the *Analects* and *Mencius* are mastered, then the Six Classics can be clarified without being mastered.[9]

The Ch'eng brothers and the other early *Tao-hsüeh* masters were significant interpreters of the Four Books, as shown in their recorded sayings. Moreover, Hsieh Liang-tso and several other prominent Ch'eng disciples wrote full commentaries on the *Analects.*

Seen in this light, Chu Chen's 1136 memorial cited in the previous chapter was an early formal statement of what was becoming the new "canon within the canon" of the Confucian scriptural classics. The first four figures in Chu Chen's transmission list, Confucius, Tseng Tzu, Tzu-ssu, and Mencius, were the presumed authorial sources for the *Analects*, the *Great Learning*, the *Doctrine of the Mean*, and the *Mencius*, respectively. In the order of transmission, the *Analects* has priority.

Before turning to the *Analects* directly, it is important to take note of the particular *Tao-hsüeh* hermeneutic practice of "savoring the text" (*wan-wei* 玩味). In praising Ch'eng Hao's methods of teaching the *Odes,* Hsieh Liang-tso remarked that instead of getting bogged down in analyzing phrases, Ch'eng Hao just "savors them in a carefree way, intoning them high and low, and thus brings it about that people get something from it."[10] After citing Hsieh's description of Ch'eng Hao's reading of the *Odes*, Van Zoeren comments:

> The interesting thing about this passage . . . is what it can tell us about [Ch'eng Hao's] practice of "exploring the savor" of the text and about his hermeneutical practice generally. It seems that exploring the savor of a passage was not necessarily an "internal," private activity, but something that could be done out loud, for other people . . . [I]n the main he communicated and perhaps in a sense derived his understanding of the passage in question simply by reading it aloud— that is, by modulations of tone and emphasis. He thus restored to the text the animating and defining presence of the living voice, removing ambiguities and opening the way to understanding.[11]

By the time of the Sung, the language of the *Odes* was already archaic and sometimes difficult. Yet through "the animating presence of the living voice," Ch'eng Hao was able to make the text come alive with significance and beauty. The practice of savoring the text, then, was a matter of learning to be at ease with difficulty.

Van Zoeren argues that the development of "savoring" as a method of reading represented an extension of sensibilities developed for the *Odes* to the rest of the canon. He cites the following passage from Ch'eng I:

> Just take the Sage's words and savor them [*wan-wei*] for a while, then naturally there will be something gained. [You] ought to seek deeply in the *Analects*, taking the disciples' questions as your own questions and the Sage's answers as what your ears have heard today, then naturally you will get something. If Confucius and Mencius were to live again, they would not go beyond this in teaching people. If you can search deeply in the *Analects* and *Mencius* and savor them, then your cultivation will become complete to the point of extraordinary *ch'i*-endowment![12]

It is clear that the practice recommended by Ch'eng I owes something to traditions for studying the *Odes*. However, the special sense here is one of savoring the "living voice" of the Sage, thereby re-creating the original dialogical encounter between Confucius or Mencius and their immediate disciples. The benefits of this practice were expected to reach all the way to transforming one's physical endowment, surely a great impetus for the renewed study of classical texts!

The "Correct Meanings" of the *Analects*

In 999 CE, early in the Sung dynasty, the emperor Chen-tsung commissioned Hsing Ping 邢昺 (932–1010) to produce an official master commentary on the *Analects*. This commentary, known as the *Lun-yü chu-shu* 論語注疏 (Commentary and Sub-commentary on the *Analects*), was patterned after the T'ang dynasty *Wu-ching cheng-i* 五經正義 (Correct Meanings of the Five Classics) and was also referred to as the *Lun-yü cheng-i* 論語正義 (Correct Meanings of the *Analects*).[13] In his work, Hsing Ping included the established commentarial glosses as selected many centuries earlier by Ho Yen 何晏 (c. 190-249 CE) in his *Lun-yü chi-chieh* 論語集解 (Collected Explanations of the *Analects*).[14] To these, Hsing Ping added his own paraphrase of the classic text and glosses, which were called the "correct meaning(s)" (*cheng-i* 正義). As a modern bibliographer notes, after Hsing Ping's work was submitted and approved, it was "distributed to officials of studies and diffused everywhere in the country as a standard interpretation of the [*Analects*]."[15]

Hsing Ping's work superseded earlier annotations of Ho Yen's collection such as the *Lun-yü i-shu* 論語義疏 (Explication of the Meanings of the *Analects*) by Huang K'an 皇 侃 (488–545). For his part, Huang had referred to other commentators in his annotations, such as the "Neo-Taoist" Wang Pi 王 弼 (226–249), and explored the philosophical significance of the text. Hsing Ping's annotations, on the other hand, are simply a contemporary paraphrase of Ho Yen's work. Thus, at the beginning of the Sung period the *Analects* was given enhanced official status, though the interpretation of it was conventionalized. This conventionality was in marked contrast to the way the *Analects* would be read during the formative years of *Tao-hsüeh.*

Hsing Ping's work was eventually replaced as the orthodox standard for the civil service examinations, by Chu Hsi's *Lun-yü chi-chu* 論語集註 (Collected Commentaries on the *Analects*, hereafter LYCC). The LYCC was officially adopted in 1212 and promulgated as the standard by imperial decree in 1313, remaining so officially until 1905.[16] Like Hsing Ping's work, Chu Hsi's commentary is also a multi-layered text. At the most basic level are unattributed character glosses, many of which were taken over from Ho Yen's sources. At the other end of the spectrum, there are Chu's own editorial comments, sometimes introduced in polite self-deprecation. In between, there are more directly didactic statements culled primarily from sayings and writings of the Ch'eng brothers, their associates, and immediate disciples; these comments are clearly identified as such by Chu Hsi.[17] When Chu's collection became the government sanctioned "correct meaning" of the *Analects* for purposes of examination learning, it spawned many sub-commentaries over the succeeding centuries. Thus, Hsing Ping's official commentary, at one end, and the later official adoption of Chu Hsi's commentary, at the other, marked the temporal boundaries of a particularly fruitful period in the study of the *Analects*, when its meanings and significance were explored afresh in the commentaries and teachings of the early *Tao-hsüeh* movement.

"Essential Meanings" of the *Analects*

In 1172, approximately five years before the LYCC was first circulated,[18] Chu Hsi had already edited another major composite work, the much larger *Lun-yü ching-i* 論語精義 (Essential Meanings of the *Analects*, hereafter LYCI).[19] This text is an arrangement of extensive comments on the *Analects* by eleven northern Sung figures: the two Ch'eng brothers, Chang Tsai, Hsieh Liang-tso, Yang Shih, Yu Tso, and five others, compiled under Chu Hsi's auspices.[20] The LYCI is a verse-by-verse compilation, thus totally incorporating several whole commentaries as well as drawing from several *yü-lu* 語錄 collections. Unlike the later LYCC, which is built upon Chu Hsi's editorial selections from earlier commentaries, the LYCI contains a wealth of differing comments on each passage.

Chu Hsi told his disciples that the LYCI should function as a resource book for students' "investigation of things" (*ko-wu* 格物).[21] They were to weigh each comment on each passage and determine for themselves which commentator had gotten the point of the *Analects* passage. Although Chu himself had strong opinions on that subject, he told his students that he did not want them to approach the commentaries with a preconception of which one was right, but rather to develop their own perception to find it out for themselves (*tzu-te* 自得). Chu's description of the LYCI as a textbook for *ko-wu*, asking his students to discern which of the northern Sung *Tao-hsüeh* commentators got the point of the particular passage, assumes that there is one unitary, essential meaning to each of the passages of the *Analects* text, and further that only one of the commentators really hit upon it. Even so, the pedagogical procedure is for those engaged in learning to discover it on their own.

The LYCI is available in three major collections, the *Chu-tzu i-shu* 朱子遺書 (Surviving Works of Master Chu), the massive *Ssu-k'u ch'üan-shu* 四庫全書, and the *Hung-shih T'ang shih ching kuan tsung-shu* 洪氏唐石經館叢書 (Mr. Hung's Collection from the Office of T'ang Stone Classics). This third edition, found in the Chinese library of the Humanities Research Institute of Kyoto University, has been used as the textual basis for the translations presented in the course of this book.[22] The main reason for this selection is contextual rather than textual, heuristic rather than text-critical, in the following way: although there is no doubt about Chu Hsi's editing of the LYCI collection, it is important to see that the LYCI text can be appreciated in a wider context than simply as a "surviving work of Master Chu." The resources preserved in the LYCI can be read without necessarily moving directly to Chu Hsi's selective conclusions.

Gathering Hsieh's Commentary

Chu Hsi reports that he began his serious study of the *Analects* with Hsieh Liang-tso's commentary:

> In my study as a young man, I already loved the study of principle [*li-hsüeh* 理學] by age sixteen . . . Later I obtained Hsieh Hsien-tao's [commentary on the] *Analects* and was very happy; I studied it thoroughly.[23]

From the time I was twenty, I wanted to get at the innermost of moral principles. Once I read [Hsieh] Shang-ts'ai's *Lun-yü* [*chieh*] [Explanation of the *Analects*]. At first I marked passages with red ink, then green ink, and then yellow ink. After several times, I finally used black ink. That was to get at the essence.[24]

Unfortunately, Hsieh's commentary on the *Analects*, the *Shang-ts'ai Lun-yü chieh* 上蔡論語解 (hereafter STLYC), is no longer extant as an independent text.[25] However, there are comments by Hsieh preserved in the LYCI on virtually every one of the 532 passages of the *Analects*, and these comments form the primary textual basis for this investigation.[26]

There is some evidence of differing versions of Hsieh's *Analects* commentary. According to Hu Yin's 胡寅 postface to the commentary (see chapter 1), he found that there had been amendments made to the text of the STLYC by 1122. In addition, the preface by Hsieh himself included in the LYCI seems to be an abridgement of that found in the *Sung wen-chien* 宋文鑑 collection by Lü Tsu-ch'ien 呂祖謙 (1137–81).[27] Thus, there can be no guarantee that the passages of Hsieh's commentary themselves were not abridged or altered when they were collected in the LYCI. Yet the abridged preface preserves all the major points of the larger version of the text intact (see later discussion). Moreover, the LYCI has been used to reconstruct the *Lun-yü* commentary of another of the Ch'eng brothers' disciples, Yu Tso, suggesting that the LYCI is a reliable source for the different commentaries.[28] Unlike the case of the LYCC, there would have been little motivation for Chu Hsi to "correct" the LYCI comments, since the very point of the compilation was for students to make judgments of correctness on their own. Further corroborating evidence for the textual integrity of the passages collected in LYCI is found in discussions of the various *Analects* passages in the *Chu-tzu yü-lei* 朱子語類 (CTYL). These CTYL comments by Chu Hsi, and also numerous references in his *Wen-chi* 文集, all confirm that Chu Hsi had mixed opinions about Hsieh's comments, agreeing with some and adamantly disagreeing with others. When his comments are cited in those other sources, they agree with the LYCI.

In the course of the research for this book, all of Hsieh's comments preserved in the LYCI were gathered and translated. As a representative selection from this corpus, Hsieh's commentary on chapters 1 and 2 of the *Analects* is found in appendixes 1 and 2, respectively. The first two chapters were chosen because they contain the fullest examples of Hsieh's interpretations on many key themes; his comments tend to become progressively shorter in later chapters. These two chapters also provide extended examples of both intertextuality and intratextuality, as characteristic features of Hsieh's interpretive methods.

Intertextuality and Scriptural Voice

The most noteworthy feature of Hsieh's commentary as a whole, indicating the kind of engagement with the text that he manifests and recommends, is his constant use of scriptural citations and allusions. His comments evince what could be called "scriptural voice," an authentic "ring" of scriptural and classical verses resounding in his discourse. This scriptural voice combines two aspects, "intertextuality" and "intratextuality."

Intertextuality

It is a striking feature of Hsieh's commentary, especially in comparison with Chu Hsi's LYCC, that Hsieh copiously cites from the Five Classics and the Four Books in his explanations. This feature of his comments, which may be called "intertextuality," points to the larger exegetical and hermeneutical context in which Hsieh is working. Almost always, his citations and allusions are not explicitly marked; explicit marking was unnecessary in Hsieh's time and place because his immediate audience shared with him the fluent mental resources of scriptural classics learned by heart.

There are intertextual citations and allusions in Hsieh's comments on virtually every passage of the *Analects.* Table 2.1 gives an approximately complete listing of the classical citations in Hsieh's reconstructed *Analects* commentary, listed in descending order of frequency.

As can be seen in the table, the largest number of citations is drawn from the *Li-chi* 禮記 (Record of Ritual). That this ritual text is particularly prominent among Hsieh's quoted sources is not surprising, given that ritual is a major topic in the *Analects.* Throughout his commentary, Hsieh pays particular attention to the fine points of the rituals mentioned and discussed. In addition, his parallel passages often come from the *Li-chi.* This is a natural predilection, for Hsieh's special study for the *chin-shih* 進士 examination was in the field *Li-chi* studies. Hsieh cites from the whole *Li-chi* text, not only from the "Great Learning" and the "Doctrine of the Mean" that later became two of the Four Books. Nevertheless, according to this calculation, passages from three of the Four Books (besides the *Analects* itself) account for nearly half (177 out of 375) of the intertextual references and quotations.

Thus, as evidenced by Hsieh's commentary, the *Analects* is embedded in a whole family of other texts, from quite different sources with quite different form and content. For a canonical reading of the *Analects,* even a highly interpretive one, the wider context of other canonical literature must be taken into account. In Hsieh's commentary, passages cited from other classical sources are presented not as proof-texts that might close or clinch an argument in favor of a particular interpretation but rather as supporting material to

Table 2.1. Intertextual Citations in STLYC

Li-chi (total)	128	Lao Tzu	4
"Doctrine of the Mean"	36	Chou Li	3
"Great Learning"	14	Hsün Tzu	3
Mencius	127	Hsiao-ching	2
I-ching (total)	32	Lieh Tzu	2
Hsi-tz'u chuan	17	Han Fei Tzu	1
Shih-ching	27	Huai Nan Tzu	1
Shu-ching	20	Shih-chi	1
Chuang Tzu	15	Yang Hsiung	1
Tso-chuan	8	Total	375

further extend the domain of the *Analects* (for example, see appendix 1 on *Analects* 1:1).

Although such "intertextuality" supports notions of the unity and comprehensiveness of the canon, this need not be seen as a tendentious usage; the other classic texts are the most natural resources for the commentator's elaborations. A further point of interest in table 2.1 is the prominence of the *Chuang Tzu* among Hsieh's cited sources, suggesting that "canonical" should not be taken too literally here. In any case, "intertextuality" should be seen not merely as a "strategy" of interpretation but as a recognition of the larger tradition in which both the text and the interpreter stand.[29]

Intratextuality

Hsieh's comments are also "intertextual" on the level of specific passages of the *Analects* itself; this feature can be described as the "intratextuality" of his commentary. Embedded in Hsieh's comments, there are 196 direct references to other passages within the *Analects* text, collectively drawn from every chapter. These intra-textual citations for the whole commentary are listed in Table 2.2.

Table 2.2. Intratextual Citations in the STLYC

Passage cited	Cited at	Passage cited	Cited at	Passage cited	Cited at
Chapter 1		Chapter 5		Chapter 7, cont.	
01.01	07:06	05.03	15:10	07.20	04:15
01.02	01:03	05.05	06:01	07.21	02:16
01.14	11:06	05.09	01:15	07.23	06:09
	17:14	05.13	02:05	07.24	17:19
01.15	03:08	05.14	08:17	07.26	11:21
01.16	20:03	05.23	04:12	07.38	01:14
		05.26	16:05		
Chapter 2				Chapter 8	
02.02	20:01	Chapter 6		08.03	01:13
02.04	20:03	06.01	05:05		06:22
02.11	19:05	06.02	06:01		07:13
02.12	05:04	06.03	01:08	08.04	01:03
02.15	15:31		02:09		01:10
	19:25	06.07	02:10		10:01
02.23	03:14	06.11	01:01		13:02
			01:14		19:12
Chapter 3			02:01	08.07	02:21
03.01f	01:12	06.18	11:01	08.09	02:15
03.04	03:06	06.22	02:24		02:20
03.10	03:15		12:01	08.10	14:04
03.20	02:02		12:21	08.15	09:15
		06.30	01:06	08.18	08:21
Chapter 4			09:01		
04.02	02:10			Chapter 9	
04.05	01:01	Chapter 7		09.02	04:15
	03:03	07.02	03:20	09.03	03:18
	07:06		05:05	09.09	05:22
04.06	07:30		07:34		07:05
04.09	09:27	07.04	10:07	09.18	01:07
	14:02	07.05	05:22	09.23	17:26
	19:01	07.06	01:06	09.29	03:03
04.11	02:12	07.08	01:15		12:04
04.14	14:30	07.14	06:07		
04.15	15:03	07.15	04:12	Chapter 10	
	15:24	07.16	01:01	10 all	03:18
04.16	02:12		01:14	10.01	01:14
			15:38	10.02	01:10
			20:01		01:12
					01:14

continued

Passage cited	Cited at	Passage cited	Cited at	Passage cited	Cited at
Chapter 10, cont.		Chapter 13, cont.		Chapter 16	
10.03	01:13	13.14	01:10	16:01	11:24
10.04	01:03	13.21	01:14	16.03	02:05
10.08	10:27	13.17	01:14	16.05	17:24
10.16	10:08		06:14		
		13.20	09:04	Chapter 17	
Chapter 11			15:37	17.03	01:08
11.05	08:21	13.21	02:11	17.04	07:02
11.06	01:13		05:22	17.05	05:22
11.08	03:15		08:16		06:09
	05:08	13.27	05:10		07:05
11.13	06:09		09:01	17.06	01:02
11.16	03:04			17.07	02:15
11.17	06:09	Chapter 14			06:09
	16:01	14.06	02:10		14:32
11.19	19:25		02:12	17.12	01:03
11.22	01:11	14.17	03:22		05:25
	15:36		05:09		20:01
11.24	17:15	14.23	02:12	17.19	02:12
11.25	01:05	14.24	14:29	17.21	03:01
	19:13		19:05	17.24	11:23
11.26	06:02	14.28	07:33	17.25	04:12
		14.31	06:26		
Chapter 12		14.35	02:04	Chapter 18	
12.01	01:02		02:12	18.03	14:37
	01:08		02:15	18.08	01:13
	02:09		04:14		
12.02	01:02		19:12	Chapter 19	
	13:19	14.43	01:12	19.06	01:14
12.03	01:02	14.44	06:14		02:18
12.05	01:13		07:29		04:17
12.08	06:18				05:26
12.10	02:15	Chapter 15		19.21	15:30
12.11	12:07	15.03	04:15	19.25	01:05
12.20	07:15	15.06	07:02		
12.24	12:23	15.08	01:03	Chapter 20	
		15.10	01:08	20.02	01:08
Chapter 13		15.11	03:14		
13.05	06:08	15.15	04:12		
13.06	12:17	15.33	06:01		
	13:13	15.34	02:12		
			14:23		

In the table, the first column of each listing gives the *Analects* passage that is cited or alluded to, while the second gives the comment(s) wherein that passage is cited. One hundred and thirty-five different verses are cited; the most often cited are *Analects* 8:4 and 14:35 (five times each),[30] and 7:16, 13:21, and 19:6 (four times).

One of the purposes of this chart is to show how tightly interwoven Hsieh's citations from other passages in the *Analects* are, such that the entire text is being brought to bear on the interpretation of each passage. For this reason, Hsieh's commentarial approach could be called an extended exercise in "exegetical reasoning." His understanding and presentation of the particular *Analects* passage on which he is commenting is governed by a constant back-and-forth with the rest of the *Analects* text and with the other major texts in the Confucian tradition, especially the *Li-chi.*

Other Features of Hsieh's Commentary

Hsieh seems to rely on the existence of philological notations elsewhere, such as those that are found in the official commentary compiled by Hsing Ping, for he very rarely gives any textual notes or glosses. The only *Analects* commentaries that Hsieh obviously worked from are those by Wang An-shih 王安石 (1021–1086, Chieh-fu 介甫) and his son Wang Fang (Yüan-tse). In all, there are nine comments attributed to Wang An-shih and five attributed to Wang Fang, while there is only one attributed to Ch'eng I and none to other Sung dynasty figures. This prevalence of quotations from Wang An-shih and Wang Fang in Hsieh's comments is rather surprising, given the enmity that grew up between the Yüan-yu faction and some of Wang An-shih's followers.[31] Since Wang An-shih's commentary is no longer extant, it is not possible to read behind Hsieh's citations to see how he is using the borrowed text. It could be that these quotations represented political expediency during what James T. C. Liu has called the "post-reform" phase at the turn of the twelfth century; perhaps they were even revisions to an earlier version. However such "politically correct" expedients would belong in prominent places at the beginning of the commentary, whereas Hsieh's citations of the Wangs begin with *Analects* 7:15 and run to 15:10. In addition, the only explicit reference to Wang An-shih in the STYL is quite complimentary. It seems reasonable, therefore, to conclude that in these instances Hsieh found the interpretations of Wang An-shih and Wang Fang congenial enough to simply cite, rather than writing his own comment. This usage may indicate a larger overlap of interest between the two "factions" than has generally been assumed.

One of the "timely topics" in Hsieh's comments—particularly relevant for his time and also for later—has to do with the proper attitude toward wealth, rank, and status. Confucius's saying, "Wealth and rank attained unrightfully have as much to do with me as passing clouds," appears several times in Hsieh's commentary, including in his preface (discussed later).[32] In his comment on this passage, Hsieh amplifies Confucius's saying, remarking that "[the Sage] looked upon rightful wealth and rightful rank also as passing clouds, how much more the unrightful!" One of the life issues sure to be faced by members of the literati status group, particularly in uncertain times, was the possibility of sudden and even capricious demotion, based on court jockeying. How to face the fates with equanimity was one of the moral skills taught by the Sage, who himself suffered not a few humiliating rejections. The issue of when to take office and when to decline was also pressing, particularly during the rise, fall, and rise again of Wang An-shih's radical reform faction. With almost every worthy scholar-official in the late eleventh to early twelfth century exiled at one time or another, the unappreciated Confucian sage became a familiar rhetorical figure.

There are only a couple of passing references to Buddhists and Taoists in the whole set of Hsieh's comments, and these are predictably critical. Yet something of a more generous attitude toward "heterodox" ideas (*i-tuan* 異端) may be gleaned from his handling of *Analects* 2:16. The common interpretation of this passage is something like Legge's translation, "The study of strange doctrines [*i-tuan*] is injurious indeed!"[33] The same basic interpretation is followed in Chu Hsi's LYCC, wherein Chu quotes a saying of Fan Tsu-yü on Yang [Chu] 楊朱 and Mo [Ti] 墨翟 (opposed by Mencius) as classical examples of *i-tuan*. Then, lest there be any doubt about the identity of the most dangerous *i-tuan*, Chu adds a quotation from Ch'eng Hao to the effect that the Buddhists' teachings are more harmful than Yang and Mo. In contrast, Hsieh interprets Confucius's saying as, "*Attacking* heterodox views [*i-tuan*] brings nothing but harm." Though novel in the context of the received interpretation, Hsieh's more "liberal" reading seems to be an authentic possibility for the meaning of the text. Indeed, it seems to be the more obvious interpretation of the passage.

Hsieh's approach to the *Analects* was described earlier as "exegetical reasoning," interpreting the text on the basis of the text itself, from the inside out. This exegetical reasoning can be contrasted with systematic reasoning, according to which the individual passages would be fitted into a larger systematically coherent picture.[34] For Hsieh, the hermeneutic endeavor is to perceive the essential meanings of the most familiar scriptural passages and to make them come alive as texts for personal cultivation. Naturally, Hsieh's interpretations reflect his own world of thought, having the Four Books and Five Classics as his primary reference, seen through the eyes of his experience in mid-northern Sung China with the Ch'eng brothers as his teachers. His is an exegetical or even "theological" commentary in the sense that he is

interested in encouraging his readers to think more deeply about the implications of the *Analects* passages as a form of spiritual practice. This emphasis
on practice comes out clearly in his preface.

Hsieh's Preface: The *Analects* as "Hard to Read"

While paying homage to the Ch'eng brothers as his teachers, Hsieh refers in
the preface of his commentary to his arduous experience in studying the
Analects text:

> I once offered sprinkling and sweeping at the gate of the Honan
> Masters [i.e., Ch'eng Hao and Ch'eng I], and scarcely got even a
> hair's breadth from [the *Analects*] sentences in reading between the
> text and meaning, and this added to my believing that this book is
> hard to read.[35]

Hsieh's emphasis on the difficulty of reading the *Analects* is reminiscent of a
remark by Confucius's best disciple, Yen Hui 顏 回, concerning the Sage's
direct instruction: "The more I look up at it the higher it appears. The more I
bore into it the harder it becomes."[36] That is, even though Yen Hui was able to
study with the Sage directly, it was difficult to fully grasp his teaching. How
much more so when one must depend upon study of the *Analects* text, after so
many centuries of "misunderstanding"!

Hsieh's claim, in this highly understated reference to the Ch'eng brothers,
has several facets. One is the difficulty of the *Analects* text itself, for reasons
that Hsieh proceeds to explain further (see later discussion). But his own
having "difficulty" with the text is attributed to his study with the Ch'eng
brothers; that difficulty itself is the starting point for his serious, fruitful
engagement with the text. Hsieh argues that even though a kind of lip service
is typically paid to the high position of Confucius, in reality there is little effort
expended on getting at the real meaning of his teaching for daily practice. He
begins from Mencius's premise that even though Confucius never held high
office, his achievement surpassed that of the ancient sage-emperors. Hsieh's
subsequent comments on the *Analects* bring together the traces of transmission from the Sage himself with Hsieh's own attempt to make the Sagely
heart-and-mind accessible, paradoxically by heightening readers' sense of the
"difficulty" of the text. In this way, he also furthered the insights gained
through his teachers, the Ch'eng brothers.

One of the reasons that the *Analects* can be "hard to read" is that it is quite
plain when compared with other texts in the cultural tradition. It is not as
intricate, informative, exhilarating, and so forth, as other texts in the cultural

repertoire. Therefore, Hsieh notes, enterprising scholars have a hard time imagining that study of the *Analects* would repay the effort. The *Chuang-tzu,* the famous poets, the historians, and so on, seem to be much richer:

> But this book (the *Analects*) doesn't have even one [of these special features]! If you want quick, brilliant, outstanding, and talented literati [*shih*] to spend their energies in its midst, how can they not laugh, and even ridicule you?[37]

Compared with the other elements of culture (*wen* 文), the *Analects* seems to be plain, ordinary, even tasteless.

A second, more intrinsic source of difficulty in reading the *Analects* comes from habitual attitudes that inhibit or prevent the reader from taking the text seriously, or having faith in it. In a passage that represents an extended dialogue with the text, Hsieh writes:

> When one's discrimination between things and self is too profound, [and] in one's breast there is a lance and sharp spear (a deep sense of separation and defensiveness), then in reading of what is called the reciprocity [*shu* 恕] which can be practiced for one's whole life (*Analects* 15:24), can one really know the taste of it? When one shrugs and smiles fawningly [to curry favor] and tries to catch [advantage] through words, then in reading of what is spoken of as "cunning words and an ingratiating face [seldom express *jen*]" (*Analects* 1:3), one will rather disparage *jen.* When someone who is not yet able to be commonly poor and lowly and is ashamed of poor quality clothes and food (cf. *Analects* 4:9) reads it, how can they know ". . . the eating of coarse rice and the drinking of water, the using of one's elbow for a pillow" (*Analects* 7:16) has not destroyed my joy. When those who focus their heart-and-mind on profit, not having yet gotten it but already worried about being hindered in their progress (cf. *Analects* 17:15), read it, who [among them] can believe that "wealth and rank attained through immoral means" really are "as passing clouds" (*Analects* 7:16)?[38]

Thus, one's reaction to the *Analects* passages reveals the state of one's own heart-and-mind (to one's self and to others). For a person with all sorts of barriers "inside," the teaching of the *Analects* cannot make experiential sense. In other words, a deep appreciation of the *Analects* depends upon clearing away the barriers to awareness within oneself, through study and practice. But the converse also holds true—by taking the words of the Sage and early disciples seriously, personally, there is leverage for grappling with those habitual attitudes. That indeed is the benefit of studying the text.

One of the most practical challenges of trying to live by the *Analects* is that it does not contain a clear set of injunctions, unlike many scriptural texts in other traditions. Instead, there are encounter-dialogues with the Sage, and descriptions of his conduct on particular occasions.[39] Indeed, several of the most didactic passages in the *Analects* are in the words of Confucius's disciples rather than the Sage himself, as in Tseng Tzu's daily reflection on three points (*san-hsing* 三省) in 1:4 and Yu Tzu's teaching on *jen* in 1:2. This lack of specific injunctions means that the process of discerning how to live up to the standard set by Confucius and suggested for his disciples is a process of reflection and personal cultivation. The process is subtle to the point of seeming flavorless at times, like the taste of water.

If serious students do not concentrate in their study on the *Analects*, Hsieh warns, this will lead to a slackness in their thinking, which only makes it more difficult to appreciate and follow the direct teaching of the Sage:

> Therefore, if [one] indulges (lit., drowns) the heart-and-mind in what is shallow, near, and useless, then one's perceptive faculties (of hearing and seeing) will daily be withered and lost, and even though one wants to read [the *Analects*], [one] will not be able to get to the gate and enter.[40]

Hsieh's argument here is that the *Analects* is by no means shallow or near, but requires disciplined study in order to bear fruit in the student's life and thought:

> The Sage's words are near, but their meaning is distant; the words have their limit, but the meaning is inexhaustible. That which has its limits can be sought through philological commentary, but the inexhaustible must be comprehended spiritually.[41]

The text of the *Analects* itself is not difficult, and it is not that it contains a hidden, esoteric meaning.[42] Rather, only when personally reflected upon does the *Analects* reveal its potent wisdom. The *Analects* should be as familiar as the face of a friend:

> It is like observing people: in the past we recognized their face (external features), today we see their heart-and-mind. So far as I am concerned (from my point of view), then the appearance and expression have changed, but as for the people, they are still the same. For this reason it is hard to read.[43]

The Confucian student must become thoroughly familiar with the text in order for the personality behind it, the Sagely heart-and-mind, to appear. Once having seen and heard that personality, it is apparent that it was there all along. What might be called the "gestalt of recognition" means that previous perceptions are altered in a fundamental way. One must become thoroughly familiar with the text in order for the Sagely heart-and-mind to appear.

Hsieh closes his preface with a section that traces a dialectic pattern of hidden and manifest, obvious and abstruse, in the process of recognizing the Sage. The main thread of this section is taken from *Analects* 7:24, in which Confucius says, "My friends, do you think I am secretive? There is nothing which I hide from you. There is nothing I do which I do not share with you, my friends." The dialectic pattern is set up by juxtaposing parts of two additional *Analects* passages, 17:17 and 5:13, that also refer to hidden and manifest. The section concludes by pointing to recognizing the non-difference of "something hidden" and "nothing hidden" as the key to Confucian spiritual cultivation. Here is the closing section in full:

> If one says, "there is nothing hidden from you" (7:24), then [there are the passages such as] "What does Heaven ever say?" (17:17) and "one cannot get to hear the Master's views on human nature and the Way of Heaven" (5:13). If one says that there is something hidden from you, then [there are the passages like] "there are the four seasons going round and there are the hundred things coming into being" (17:17) and "One can get to hear about the Master's accomplishments" (5:13). As for these, how could one not be able to hear about them! The *Odes* says, "The hawk flies up to heaven; the fishes leap in the deep."[44] This is the most obvious thing in the world; how could the Sage make it hidden? This is what is called "[I] have nothing I do which I do not share with you, my friends" (7:24). "For Heaven's high dealings are profound / And far transcend all sense and sound."[45] This is the most abstruse in the world; how could the Sage make it manifest? It was appropriate that the disciples thought "there is something hidden from us." To know that "there is something hidden" and "there is nothing hidden" are not two—if one abandons this book, wherein can one see it?[46] Those who know that "there is something hidden" and "there is nothing hidden" are not two—how could they not be spacious, bright, and comprehensive *chün-tzu* 君子 [exemplary persons]? Could all of you not have [sincere] intent about this?[47]

The dialectic sense of the hiddenness of the manifest is developed throughout Hsieh's commentary, as he tries to elaborate on—and at times to dislodge—the obvious or traditional meaning of the text.

In his comments on the *Analects*, Hsieh has not paraphrased the text in the manner of Hsing Ping, nor glossed difficult characters, nor provided background context. In that sense, he does not explain what the text means but rather shows an example of how to savor the text, so that its meaning can be personally experienced by the reader. This developed skill of reflecting on and savoring the words of the text, so that their meaning will be disclosed, is referred to as "knowing the flavor." "Knowing the flavor" of the text is a form of skill-knowing based on practice. In turn, the learning to which such reading of the text leads is also in a sense a skill, the skill of knowing how to be a humane human being, a person of *jen*, in human community and among all things. For Hsieh, the "difficulties" of the *Analects* text are the difficulties of practice, and "attainment after doing what is difficult" 先難而後獲 (*Analects* 6:22) is one of Confucius's characterizations of *jen*.

This chapter has been primarily concerned with two of the four "theological" warrants discussed in the introduction: "scripture," especially the *Analects*, and "tradition," especially the new interpretive traditions of the Sung. The next chapter will focus on an issue that, while still embedded in scripture and tradition, can be fruitfully understood in terms of "reason" and "experience."

CHAPTER THREE

Knowing *Jen*

Opening the Issue

Neo-Confucians of the Tao-hsüeh revival shared, along with Confucius's direct disciples and with recent interpreters of the *Analects* in the West, the sense that *jen* is both key to the Tao taught by Confucius and very difficult to define exactly. The problem in any case is not really one of definition, but of developing an experiential knowing, or taste, for what it means to be *jen*. Before turning to Hsieh's approach to this problem, this section will first briefly review something of the recent discussion among modern interpreters of the *Analects* concerning *jen*.

Tu Wei-ming refers to a consensus among Chinese and Japanese exegetes that *jen* is the center of "the hierarchy of values" in the *Analects*, even though the text itself gives no synthetic definition.[1] Robert Eno has remarked of *jen* that "its elusiveness makes it the focus of the [*Analects*] text."[2] In the introduction to his well-known *Analects* translation, Arthur Waley refers to *jen* as "a mystic entity,"[3] emphasizing the difficulty of understanding the nature of *jen*. Concerning a particular instance of interpretive difficulty, the philosopher Herbert Fingarette complains, "When opposite interpretations can be given to a passage on such a central question, it becomes all too evident that the concept of *jen* is obscure."[4] Appreciating Fingarette's perplexity in the course of his response, Tu agrees that "*jen*, in the *Analects*, appears to be discouragingly complex."[5]

In the face of this complexity, Fingarette has offered a still controversial account in which he argues against any tendency to read the *Analects* as recommending particular "attitudes, feelings, wishes and will." He is adamant: "The thing we must *not* do is to psychologize Confucius' terminology in the *Analects*."[6] For Fingarette, the language of "inner states" is precisely what the *Analects* will call into question, in favor of a recognition of the performative character of attitudes and dispositions toward action.

To some extent, the discussion surrounding Fingarette's interpretation may have been conditioned by the Weberian hypothesis, which imputed to the Confucian gentleman a lack of inner self-consciousness in favor of a serendipitous combination of learned social responses, producing "adjustment to the world."[7] There has been a tendency to defend the Confucians against the charge of this imputed deficiency. But Fingarette is pointing to what he sees as the performative character of *all* human consciousness and applauding Confucius for recognizing it explicitly.[8]

Among others, Benjamin Schwartz has been sharply critical of Fingarette's analysis, charging that it "reflects Fingarette's own involvement with the modern Western psychology/sociology antithesis rather than anything found in the *Analects*."[9] For his part, Schwartz presents *jen* in the *Analects* as the inner virtue par excellence:

> Avoiding words like "psychology" and "psychic states," I shall thus allow myself here to define *jen* as referring to the inner moral life of the individual person that includes a capacity of self-awareness and reflection.[10]

He further comments that "*Jen* is marked above all by an inner serenity, equanimity, and indifference to creaturely matters of fortune and misfortune over which one has no direct control."[11]

The problem of "inner and outer" that shapes the interpretive debate between Fingarette and Schwartz is integral to understanding *jen* in the *Analects*; parsing this issue was also part of *Tao-hsüeh* reflections. As will be shown in the following sections, Hsieh Liang-tso explores the difficulty of "knowing *jen*" from either observable performance or inner states, and offers his own unique interpretive contribution.

Hsieh on *Jen* in the *Analects*

In the course of his extensive commentary on the *Analects*, Hsieh expresses the centrality and unfathomability of *jen* as an equation with the Tao, in these words:

> Now as for *jen* being Tao, it is not only that no one can list all the examples; in practicing it no one can do it fully; and it is also difficult to describe.[12]

Hsieh makes three points in his identification of *jen* and Tao. First, the aspects of *jen* are more than can be listed.[13] Second, as an ideal for human character and conduct, *jen* transcends all possible manifestations, such that no one is able to fully reach it in practice. Thirdly, *jen* defies adequate description. Hsieh amplifies this third point by saying, "[T]he more learned one's words are, the more one has departed from *jen*." These three features of *jen* point to a sense of ultimacy, which in turn justifies its correlation with Tao. These features are among the background assumptions of Hsieh's comments on other *Analects* passages, particularly those that highlight the difficulty of "knowing *jen*."

In *Analects* 6:26, Confucius's disciple Tsai Wo is recorded as asking Confucius, "If a person of *jen* were told there was another person of *jen* in a well, would he go and join that person?"[14] Hsieh's comment includes the following:

> Tsai Wo personally received admonishment from the Sage, yet he still suspected the presence of mind [*yung-hsin* 用心] of the person of *jen*; thus we can believe *jen*'s being difficult to know.[15]

That is to say, even being educated by the Sage in person was no guarantee that one would really be able to understand what *jen* is all about. In the following sections, several possible avenues for understanding *jen* will be explored, beginning with exemplary or paradigmatic figures. A second approach, also represented in the *Analects*, is to characterize *jen* in terms of observable qualities of character or action. This proves to be more difficult than it might seem. A third avenue is through a process of inner reflection, and this leads to Hsieh's own unique contribution on the problem of "understanding *jen*."

Exemplary Figures

Given that *jen* is not easy to define, the most direct route to understanding it might be to find an exemplar, someone who embodies that quality of being and acting. The most obvious and appropriate example for Confucius's disciples, both immediate and long-range, would naturally be the Master himself. However, Confucius is recorded as specifically rejecting such epithets for himself. In *Analects* 7:34, the Master says, "How dare I claim to be a sage or a person of *jen*?"[16] Thus, even though their Teacher was for them the greatest exemplar of *jen*, the disciples were not able to elicit such a self-description from him.

If the Master would not explain *jen* in terms of his own conduct, then perhaps some other figure could provide an example, one closer to the disciples' own level of attainment. There are several *Analects* passages discussing the conduct of various disciples or other figures, whether or not they are *jen*. Confucius responds with demurrals that highlight the question of how it is possible to recognize *jen* in the conduct of others.[17]

In 5:19, the disciple Tzu-chang asks about the conduct of two political figures, Ling Yen Tzu-wen and Ch'en Wen-tzu. After Confucius praised them as "*chung*" 忠 (loyal, in the sense of always doing one's best) and "*ch'ing*" 清 (pure), respectively, Tzu-chang asked whether they were *jen*. Confucius gave a reply in both cases which Hsieh reads as "We cannot yet know *jen* therein."[18] In Hsieh's view, the problem was that "one who had the appearance of a generous temperament would also be able to do [the things Tzu-chang was praising]." He continues that it was not that Confucius considered the two men to be "not-*jen*" (*pu-jen* 不仁), but only that he was afraid Tzu-chang would understand purity and doing one's best, but would fail to understand *jen*.

In 6:7, Confucius comments that besides Yen Hui, the other disciples attain *jen* only in fits and starts. Perhaps for this reason, when asked whether his disciples Tzu-lu, Jan Ch'iu, or Kung-hsi Hua (Ch'ih) were *jen* (5:8), Confucius cites their capabilities but withholds judgment on their being *jen*. Hsieh's explanation is that while it cannot be denied that the three disciples have *jen* as a component of their character, as an overall evaluation the three are not up to it. The reason he gives for Confucius's not approving them as "*jen*" is that Confucius was careful in discussing the Tao, not like "the reckless and unsystematic [opinions] of the philosophers [*chu-tzu* 諸子]."[19] In this instance, Confucius's reticence in awarding the designation "*jen*" can itself be understood as a manifestation of *jen*, according to his teaching on being cautious in speaking (*Analects* 12:3).

Knowing *Jen* by Specific Qualities

As another approach, the disciples sometimes try to pin down a definition of *jen* in terms of specific qualities of character. In *Analects* 14:1, Hsien (Tzu-ssu) asks whether "standing firm against the temptation to press one's advantage, to brag about oneself, to harbour grudges, or to be covetous" would qualify as *jen*. The Master replied that all these may be called "difficult" but he didn't know about their being *jen*. Hsieh's comment, once again, is that these qualities "do not necessarily not proceed from *jen*; however they are not sufficient to show the root of *jen*. The Sage's saying 'I don't know' is not considering them to be not-*jen*."[20]

Analects 1:3 provides an opportunity to reason toward *jen* in reverse, by clarifying traits that are far from *jen*. In 1:3, Confucius says that "cunning words" and "an ingratiating face" are rarely *jen*. However, Hsieh comments that even such a *via negativa* understanding of *jen* is also difficult:

Knowing that which is far from *jen*, one can also know *jen*. But as for "cunning words" and "an ingratiating face," knowing them is also difficult.[21]

After saying that those cunning and ingratiating features are also hard to know clearly, he refers to classical examples in the *Li-chi* and *Odes* wherein the words "*ling*" 令 and "*ch'iao*" 巧, translated by Lau as "cunning" and "ingratiating," respectively, have positive connotations instead of critical (see his full comment in appendix 1). He points out that petty persons are often blunt and direct rather than artful (*ch'iao*) and harsh in their expressions rather than pleasing (*ling*), and closes by citing *Analects* 8:4 as the standard:

> If one is able to know that ". . . by speaking in proper tones [*ch'u tz'u-ch'i* 出辭氣], one can avoid being boorish and unreasonable," then one is able to know this. This is appropriate for learning, profound thinking, and energetic inquiring; it cannot be conveyed with words.[22]

In sum, Hsieh cross-references the *Analects* passage on which he is commenting with other central texts of the Confucian tradition, and then draws an intratextual parallel with what for him is a favorite text, *Analects* 8:4, the dying words of Tseng Tzu. As Hsieh says, the serious student is meant to think and inquire diligently, to understand the meaning for oneself (*tzu-te* 自得).

According to Hsieh, even the positive attributes adduced by Confucius himself in explanation or illustration of *jen* do not guarantee an understanding of *jen*. The problem is that although Confucius has given several descriptions of conduct or attitude to serve as signposts of *jen*, in the final analysis they ought not to be confused with *jen* itself. Hsieh wrestles with this problem in an extended commentary on *Analects* 1:2, pointing out that it must be said of each of these attributes, "in the end it is not *jen*." The passage is here cited in full:

> For example, ". . . respectfulness, tolerance, trustworthiness in word, quickness and generosity" (*Analects* 17:6) as *jen*—if one does not know *jen*, then one will merely stop with knowing "respectfulness, tolerance, trustworthiness in word, quickness, and generosity." [Likewise in the case of the passage on] ". . . overcoming oneself and returning to ritual" (*Analects* 12:1) as *jen*—if one does not know *jen*, then one will simply stop with knowing "overcoming oneself and returning to ritual." "When abroad behave as though you were receiving an important guest, when employing the services of the common people behave as though you were officiating at an important sacrifice" (*Analects* 12:2); this is only to be particularly orderly in one's conduct, how can we see it as being *jen*? "The mark of one who is *jen* is that he is loath to speak" (*Analects* 12:3); this is merely to be particularly cautious in speaking, how can we see this as *jen*? Yu-tzu's discussion of *jen* [in *Analects* 1:2] is also like this. One

who is filial and brotherly is close to *jen*, however filiality and brotherly respect are not *jen* [per se].[23]

In this comment, Hsieh has gathered together many of the Confucian sayings that characterize *jen*, and argued that they are not to be confused with *jen* itself. It is not enough, he implies, to simply latch onto Confucius's descriptive statements; each person must ponder them to know that toward which they point.

Reflecting on Filiality

In the quoted comment on 1:2, Hsieh notes that filiality and younger-brotherly respect are likewise only "close to *jen*." Yet he proceeds to argue that filial piety is an especially salient starting point in coming to know *jen*:

> For discussing *jen*, nothing is better than the human heart-and-mind.
> As for what is not artificial in the human heart-and-mind, nothing is
> as good as serving parents and following [obeying] elder brothers.[24]

It is significant that Hsieh mentions the problem of artificiality here because, especially in a highly ritualized society, the genuine or authentic sprouts of *jen* may easily be obscured. He goes on to cite a comment attributed to Confucius in the *Chuang-tzu* to the effect that a child's love for his or her parents cannot be dispelled from the heart-and-mind. He then adduces the forms of filiality from the *Li-chi*, which are observed even in the countryside, noting that while people in country localities cannot simply be considered as already possessing the Tao, to think that they cannot enter the Tao is also improper. This is because, "Whether filiality and brotherly respect can be taken as *jen* and can enter the Tao lies in between being mindful [*nien* 念] and not being mindful."[25]

The right balance of thoughtfulness, in turn, depends on how attentive one is to the heart-and-mind expressed through the forms of filiality and brotherly respect. The issue is how to "catch the traces" of *jen* in one's own experience. So Hsieh recommends reflection on one's heart-and-mind in serving parents:

> If one really wants to know *jen*, then it is in diligent practice, exam-
> ining oneself, and investigating what my heart-and-mind is like at the
> time of serving parents and following elders. To know this heart-and-
> mind is to know *jen*.[26]

The genuine sense of filiality, Hsieh implies, is experienced as natural (*tzu-jan-erh-jan* 自然而然), not out of obligation, nor even out of a conscious sense of propriety. It is in reflecting back on such experience that it is possible to know *jen*, by catching the trace of *jen*. It is almost literally catching or finding the traces of a trail, for the landscape of one's psycho-emotional life may be so ambiguous, and conventional consciousness so full of cultural clichés and selfish desires, that to find a real root or basis of authenticity is much more difficult than might be imagined.

In other words, reflecting on one's own filial piety and respect for elder siblings provides a point of orientation in the search for traces of being *jen*, in terms of one's own experiential landscape. If this recommendation were merely to be self-conscious in performing the proper ritual, then Chu Hsi's criticism that Hsieh's approach just leads to nervous anxiety would be valid and telling.[27] However, what Hsieh recommends is rather a subsequent reflection on what the heart-and-mind actually was in those moments of particular service.

This discussion of "knowing *jen*" began with objective observations of possible human exemplars and has moved to an introspective or reflective mode. Having considered Hsieh's handling of the challenges of understanding *jen* in the *Analects* text, in the next section I will turn to his specific suggestion for characterizing *jen*.

Jen as Chüeh (Awareness, Sensitivity)

Hsieh Liang-tso's most important contribution to Confucian thought, following Ch'eng Hao's lead, is his interpretation of *jen* as *chüeh* 覺. The Chinese character "*chüeh*" includes the verbal meanings "to awaken," "to be conscious of," "to be aware of," and "to be sensitive to." Awakening includes the body and the heart-and-mind on a continuum, so that there is also a connotation of "alertness." Jörg Bäcker translates "*chüeh*" into German as "*Bewußtsein*" and "*Bewußtheit*."[28] Hoyt Tillman uses the translation "consciousness," as do some other authors, but points out that the denotation of "consciousness" privileges Chu Hsi's "cognitive" interpretation of *chüeh* (see later discussion).[29] There is also a specifically Buddhist usage, to translate "*bodhi*" (enlightenment). This Buddhist provenance was one reason for the controversy surrounding Hsieh's use of "*chüeh*," the issue of the extent to which Hsieh's interpretation of *jen* was leaning too far in the direction of Buddhist thought.[30]

The word "*chüeh*" is found once in the *Analects* (14:31), on the worthiness of one who does not anticipate deception or bad faith but yet is first to *be aware* of them. In his comment on this passage, Hsieh remarks that one who commits the error of anticipating attempts at deception and bad faith does not yet know "how the first to be aware are first to be aware" (LYCI 7B/26a). He likens the ability to be aware to stepping on frost and knowing how deep the ice will be.[31] Such awareness would seem to be a kind of intuitive perception of the actual situation, rather than any kind of calculating wariness. Indeed, self-protective wariness would be an impediment to being genuinely aware.

One of Hsieh's clearest statements characterizing *jen* as *chüeh* is in his comment on *Analects* 12:2 and 12:3. In this comment, Hsieh links together two main aspects of *jen* in terms of "aliveness" and "awareness":

> The heart-and-mind having that of which it is aware [*hsin yu suo chüeh* 心有所覺] is called *jen*. In the case of *jen*, the heart-and-mind and affairs are one. The seeds of grasses, trees, and the five grains are called "*jen*." The name is derived from their being alive. Being alive, there is something of which they are aware. The inclination of the four limbs to numbness is called "not-*jen*." The name is derived from not being sentient [*chih-chüeh* 知覺, knowingly aware or conscious]. Not to be sentient is to be dead. When affairs produce sensations [*kan* 感] and one follows them, responding to them with [the four emotions of] delight, anger, sorrow, and joy, as for fully transforming in responsive interaction, one who is not sentient will not be able to do it.[32]

Hsieh uses both awareness (*chüeh* 覺) and vitality (*sheng* 生) as constitutive images for *jen*. These two images are also brought together in an important saying from the *Shang-ts'ai yü-lu*:

> What is the heart-and-mind? It is *jen*. And what is *jen*? What is living is *jen*, what is dead is not-*jen*. These days when someone's body is numb and does not feel pain and itch, it is called not-*jen*. The seeds of peaches and apricots that can be planted and grow are called peach-*jen* and apricot-*jen* (=kernels) because they have living vitality.[33]

By holding together these two primary descriptions of *jen*, as living and as sensitivity and awareness, Hsieh indicates that his understanding of *chüeh* is as a dynamic, relational field of awareness that is identified with the life impulse itself.

Three Realms of Sensitivity

In exploring further the implications of Hsieh's concept of *jen* as *chüeh*, three interwoven "realms" of sensitivity can be discerned. Naturally *jen* refers primarily to the realm of human relations, but in *Tao-hsüeh* thought *jen* is also extended to include the realm of all things (*wan-wu* 萬物). In the particular insight of Ch'eng Hao and Hsieh Shang-ts'ai, both the realm of human relations and the realm of all things are based on sensitivity rooted in the vital connection between one's own body and heart-and-mind. These three "realms" will be discussed in turn.[34]

Sensitivity of Heart-and-Mind and Body

Hsieh's comments referring to numbness of the four limbs as "not-*jen*" recall Ch'eng Hao's citing of medical terminology characterizing numbness or paralysis as lack of *jen* (*pu-jen* 不仁).[35] In the *Internal Classic of the Yellow Emperor*, "*pu-jen*" is a common designation for numbness and lack of sensitivity (not feeling pain and itch, hot and cold).[36] Indeed, bodily awareness of pain and itch as opposed to numbness and paralysis is one of Ch'eng Hao's favorite metaphors for the quality of *jen*.[37] This bodily awareness would include not only the acute awareness of actual pain and itch but also the immediate latent potential to feel pain and itch at any moment. The paradigm can be extended to the general sensitivity of the body, which is in a constant state of awareness even in the midst of other activities.[38]

Ch'eng Hao and Hsieh can be understood as saying more than simply employing this medical usage as a metaphor for the extended implications of *jen*. Both literal and metaphoric "forming of one body" are included, indeed correlated. It is the extension of this corporeal sensitivity and awareness outward that is the process of manifesting *jen*.[39] Hsieh's specific interpretation of *jen* as *chüeh* (awareness, sensitivity) clearly grows directly from this understanding of his teacher.

Considering the heart-and-mind and body as a particular "realm" or level of awareness need not imply a Western-style dichotomy between mind and body.[40] In Hsieh's perspective, the moment of insight in knowing *jen* is based on the unity of heart-and-mind and body in awareness. There is no separation posited here between bodily awareness and the heart-and-mind's awareness, because *chüeh* in its various meanings entails a psychosomatic unity. The opposite of *chüeh* in this sense is numbness or paralysis of both the body and heart-and-mind. The paradox is that while *jen* is "extremely difficult to describe,"[41] it is yet as integral to one's own experience as the inner sense of touch, the vital awareness of one's own limbs. Or perhaps, this integrity itself is a principal source of the difficulty of thematizing *jen*.

When asked how to make effort (*kung-fu* 功夫) in seeking *jen*, Hsieh replied that one could either emulate Yen Hui and work on seeing, hearing, speech, and conduct (*Analects* 12:1) or follow Tseng Tzu's suggestion and work on expressions, gestures, words, and tones (*Analects* 8:4). These actions or expressions of *jen* relate to Hsieh's basic image of bodily awareness:

For example, if one greets people and does not follow what comes forth from the heart-and-mind, that is to have no sensation of pain and itch. As long as one preserves the heart-and-mind of receiving a great guest or assisting at a great sacrifice, one "knows pain and itch."[42]

Certain bodily actions, such as "producing words and tones" (*ch'u tz'u-ch'i* 出辭氣) manifest one's internal quality externally and become paradigmatic for the development or "seeking" of *jen*. For this reason, ritual forms play a vital role in the practice of manifesting *jen* and expanding the one-body relation outward. The key is for the heart-and-mind to be "present"; therefore Hsieh says that if one can preserve the heart-and-mind of seeing an important guest or assisting at a great sacrifice, then that is "knowing pain and itch." In principle, there is no split between psychic and somatic, but in practice the synergy or unity of the two aspects of a person is a goal to be achieved.[43] In this regard, ritual cultivation of the body, including the discipline of "quiet-sitting" (*jing-tsuo* 靜坐), is at once the training of the heart-and mind, since the two are synergistically one.

Jen *as Sensitivity in Human Relations*

As has been taught in the Confucian tradition at least since the time the *Analects* was collected, the most central understanding of *jen* is in the realm of human relations and interpersonal ties, symbolized by the traditional etymology of "person" and "two."[44] Indeed, it may be precisely because it was the commonsense assumption of the discourse, that there are relatively few passages in either Hsieh's *Analects* commentary or the STYL that explicitly reflect on this realm or level of *jen*. In a sense, all discussion of *jen* pertains also to human relations.

The understanding of *jen* in human relations is both broadened and made more intimate by the interpretive idea of "forming one body," with the connection of sensitivity and awareness as its mode and meaning. Hsieh comments on *Analects* 1:4 that unless one recognizes that "others and myself are one" (*jen yü chi wei-i* 人與己為一), one will not be able to live up to the teaching of the passage, including the injunction to put into practice the transmission that one has received.

As the ground of rightness, propriety, wisdom, and trustworthiness, *jen* provides the standard for right human relations.[45] As discussed earlier, among human relations Hsieh placed special emphasis on filiality as a locus for knowing *jen*. This vital awareness within the family group, beginning with the primordial ties of parent-child and among siblings, is then extended outward toward an ever-widening circle of human relatedness. It is *jen* that overcomes the false barrier between self and others, and the effort of overcoming that limited self is the key to manifesting and experiencing *jen* in interpersonal relations. This insight can be further extended to the realm of all things (*wan-wu*).

Sensitivity Toward All Things

Ch'eng Hao taught that *jen* forms one body with Heaven, Earth, and the myriad things.[46] He emphasized that the identification (*t'ung-t'i* 同體) extends to everything and not only to other human beings or human phenomena. It is only humans, however, who can be conscious of and respond to this identification.

Several aspects of cultivating the proper relationship between oneself and things (*wu* 物 and *wo* 我) appear in Hsieh's *Analects* commentary. For him, the aim of Confucian learning is, as Ch'eng Hao said, to realize "forming one body with things without differentiation" (*hun-jan yü wu t'ung-t'i* 渾然與物同體). However, the process of cultivation toward that ideal also requires clarification of one's "allotment" in contradistinction to the flux of things and affairs. On *Analects* 7:11, Hsieh comments that the Sage truly knew "the allotments of things and myself" (*wu-wo chih fen* 物我之分), because he had "no intention and no necessity" when it came to going forward to serve or retiring and staying out of sight. In other words, the Sage knew that serving or not serving depended on external circumstances, and did not let it affect his sense of personal integrity.

For the person of *jen*, as Hsieh comments on *Analects* 4:2, difficult circumstances are recognized as separate from the affairs pertaining to oneself; one does not make the mistake of confusing oneself with things:

> Therefore, one who is not *jen* indeed has not understood "myself" [*wo* 我] as being "myself." Since "myself" has already been lost, then they take things to be "myself" [*i wu wei wo* 以物爲我]. Taking things to be "myself," how could one avoid fancying and detesting?[47]

In other words, one who is not-*jen*, inhumane and apathetic, is bound up with preferences and possessions and thus not able to meet circumstances with equanimity. The person of *jen*, conversely, is able to know "myself" as "myself" and not become confused with things. This implies not confusing one's own integrity with all the preferences and predilections that arise through contact with the things of the world. "Taking things to be myself" is to be without a firm life compass in one's own reflective awareness, and therefore to be confused and carried away by likes and dislikes.

As well as unity between oneself and all things, Hsieh remarks on the unity of human and Heaven. He comments on *Analects* 14:35, "Heaven and humans, things and myself, above and below, originally do not have two [separate] principles."[48] However, there is a disposition of separating things and oneself that stands in the way of realizing this unity. This disposition of separation, which Hsieh calls "*wu-wo chih hsin*" 物我之心 (a subject/object split), has to be overcome. In commenting on *Analects* 8:4, Hsieh attributes the goodness of Tseng Tzu's dying words to the point that "'when a person is about to die,' there is no disposition of separation between oneself and things; therefore, 'their words are good.'"[49] On *Analects* 1:10, Hsieh comments that "one who has the disposition of separating oneself and things is certain not to be deferential [one of the Sage's qualities]."[50]

Thinking of cultivation in terms of one's attitude toward others, as in the phrase quoted by Tzu-kung, "poor without being obsequious" (*Analects* 1:15), is for Hsieh a sign of still thinking in terms of mutual opposition between oneself and things (*wu wo hsiang-tui* 物我相對). If, rather, one is "poor yet joyful," that is to have one's bearings within oneself.[51] Hsieh also refers to the disposition of separation in a passage from the preface to his commentary, quoted earlier:

> When one's [discrimination between] things and self [*wu-wo* 物我] is too deep, [and] in one's breast there is a lance and sharp spear (that is, a deep sense of separation and defensive resentment), then in reading of what is called the reciprocity which can be practiced for one's whole life (*Analects* 15:24), can one really know the taste of it?[52]

From these passages it is clear that by "*wu-wo*" Hsieh means a kind of defensive self-protection that distorts one's relations with other persons as well as with things. From Hsieh's point of view, the perception of separation is in fact a misperception, a not-seeing, not-being-aware, not-*jen*. What stands in the way of vital awareness is a false sense of oneself and of others, a kind of perceptual grid or cluster of dispositions that keeps one from experiencing essential unity with the world.

For this reason, authentic relationship actively based on valuing is the key; genuine awareness is the overcoming of *wu-wo* false-consciousness. What I would call the relational "landscape of awareness" is thus not a privatized world of subjective feelings; rather, it is a shared landscape comprising real relationships and responses. Humane awareness, as receptivity and true resonance, is the way of experientially "forming one body with all things" (*i wan-wu wei i-t'i* 以萬物爲一體). The implication is that rather than an egoistic expanding of the self to include things, the desire to realize *jen* (*ch'iu-jen* 求仁) already assumes that one is an integral part of the *wan-wu* 萬物, both responsive and responsible to the cosmos. This humane awareness allows the relational vectors of all things to freely stream into one; as Mencius said,

"[A]ll things are completed in me."[53] Far from being a mood of self-sufficiency, it is founded on the realization of integral relatedness. Hsieh's sense of *chüeh*, then, refers not simply to "awareness of connection," but also to the vital connection itself.[54] That is to say, *jen* as *chüeh* is "the sensitivity that forms one body."

Jen and Reflection

Hsieh's understanding of *jen* in terms of *chüeh* was strongly criticized by Chu Hsi. Chu understandably thought that Hsieh was confusing *jen* and *chih* 智 (knowing, wisdom), since Chu himself understood *chüeh* as an aspect of *chih*. In the diagram of his *Jen-shuo* 仁說, Chu makes a special point that *chih-chüeh* belongs in the category of *chih* rather than *jen*.[55] However, if Hsieh's gloss of *jen* as *chüeh* is taken seriously, it would suggest that other nuances of *jen* also inform what Hsieh means by *chüeh*, such that for him *chüeh* could not mean simply a cognitive process. Rather, it is clear from the whole tenor of Hsieh's comments that understanding *jen* as *chüeh* is fundamentally experiential. In this light, it even appears that Chu Hsi is the one who subordinates *jen* to *chih* epistemologically, by placing primary emphasis on intellectual analysis.

There is one point in his commentary where Hsieh does connect *chüeh* and knowing together. On *Analects* 8:9, he comments,

> As for ritual and music, rules and measures, there are none that are not preserved in the mysterious Tao. Indeed, the Sage and the common people share in following them. The common people only do not know, that's all. For those engaged in learning, in addition to ritual and music, rules and measures, they on their own have an area of awareness. This is what is called "knowing."[56]

Thus, Hsieh's understanding of *chüeh* is better approached not through an either/or dichotomy between *jen* and *chih* but through a sense of commonality between them.

Analects 6:23 represents the most extensive direct comparison between being *jen* and being *chih* (wise), between the person of *jen* finding joy in mountains and the person of *chih* finding joy in water. Hsieh's comment at this point is that *jen* and *chih* harmonized together are called "sage" (*sheng* 聖).[57] He continues that in cases other than that of the Sage, *jen* and *chih* would have one-sidedness, with different inclinations and accomplishments. Hsieh then relates these two to movement and quiescence, amplified with passages from Lao-tzu's *Tao-te ching* 道德經.[58] To extend the evocative imagery of *Analects* 6:23, when the steadfastness and longevity of the mountain (*jen*) and the swift transparency of running water (*chih*) coincide, that is the incipient manifestation of the mountain cascade (*chüeh*).

As personal experience and reflection, "knowing *jen*" is similar to "knowing flavor," as in Confucius's saying: "There is no one who does not eat and drink, but there are few who can really know flavor."[59] Knowing *jen* has a similar kind of immediacy and intimacy. But "knowing flavor" is not quite the same thing as tasting; it appears that "knowing flavor" requires a reflecting process. In this process, words themselves may be a barrier, as Hsieh points out in his comment on *Analects* 12:2, 3:

> Being able to devote oneself to this task [of seeking *jen*], then *jen* can be understood [while] forgetting about words. Not being able to devote oneself to this and instead desiring to seek *jen* with words, this is analogous to not eating and never knowing the taste.[60]

The experiential taste developed in such reflection then becomes a kind of feedback or encouragement in "seeking *jen*," through whetting one's appetite, so to speak. This reflective sense of "knowing *jen*" also ties in with *wan-wei* 玩味, savoring the text (see chapter 2, above). Both refer to knowing through participation, that is, through experience over time.

In terms of the issues debated between Fingarette and Schwartz, from Hsieh Liang-tso's perspective on *jen* both "inner" and "outer" are provisional: *jen* is present precisely when the distinction is forgotten or overcome. Though the *Tao-hsüeh* Confucians focused much of their interpretive attention on what are generally considered to be "inner dimensions," the heart-and-mind (*hsin* 心) and the nature (*hsing* 性), in the perspective developed here these are seen to be located truly when the separation between self and others, inner and outer, is overcome. As shown in the *Analects* example of genuine filial piety, this *jen* awareness is relation-specific. "Knowing *jen*" is thus a process of personal reflection on the vital connection or bond itself, manifested as relational awareness.

In *Analects* 20:3, the last verse in the book, Confucius says that one has no way of knowing people unless one is able to "know words" (*chih-yen* 知言). Mencius would later say that "knowing words" was something he himself was especially able to do. In his comment on this passage, Hsieh links together knowing *jen*, knowing people, and knowing words:

> The Sage ". . . worries about not knowing people." Some say that in learning one ought to know oneself and that's all; why be in a fit over knowing others? This is not so! Humane people can surely be treated as intimates. On the other hand, not knowing people, how could one

know what a person of *jen* is like? . . . Only one who "knows words" can know them.[61]

As Hsieh presents it, "knowing words" is a kind of art and skill of discerning the character behind the words, and hence of "knowing people," which is a major human task at all levels of society. Those who are good judges of character will be able to orient themselves in the social environment, and wisely choose subordinates and friends. For social interaction as well as personal cultivation, *jen* is the essential key; therefore, the Confucian *Analects* is a text with far-reaching implications.

The issue of "knowing *jen*" is also key to recognizing authenticity in transmission. This is so because *jen* as sensitive awareness and as vital generativity is integral to authentic transmission in the Confucian tradition—both to "content" and to "process." Such authenticity is not a matter primarily of intellectual conformity but of filial engagement with scripture and tradition, in earnest personal reflection. These issues will be discussed in relation to Hsieh's legacy in the following chapter.

CHAPTER FOUR

Authentic Transmission and Humane Learning

Another Look at Chu Chen's Memorial

James T. C. Liu has called attention to the 1136 memorial by Chu Chen introduced in chapter 1 as the first formal statement in an official document of the concept of "*Tao-t'ung*" 道統, the orthodox transmission of the Way.[1] Liu has a point in that several elements manifested in Chu Chen's memorial did become part of the concept of the *Tao-t'ung* as "a single lineal transmission of exclusive orthodoxy."[2] The lineal transmission from Confucius to Tseng-tzu to Tzu-ssu to Mencius (incidentally grouping the Four Books as a set) and the hiatus of more than a thousand years until the Ch'eng brothers are all clearly stated in the memorial. The actual term "*Tao-t'ung*" does not appear, though, so Wing-tsit Chan concludes that "although the idea was present, the term [*Tao-t'ung*] was not."[3]

There are important differences, however, between Chu Chen's memorial and the later concept of *Tao-t'ung*. For one thing, the Tao is identified in the memorial as "the Tao of Master K'ung" without connecting it explicitly to the sage-kings of high antiquity, as Chu Hsi would later do. Further, although there is a single line from Confucius to Tseng Tzu to Tzu-ssu to Mencius, the first-generation disciples of the Ch'eng brothers, Hsieh, Yang Shih, and Yu Tso, are treated even-handedly as inheritors of the authentic transmission. Chu Chen does make a plea for the son of his own teacher, but there is not yet an exclusive sense of one and only one authentic lineage. After all, Chu Hsi, whose exclusive views on the "one authentic lineage" of *Tao-t'ung* would later have such impact, was only six years old in 1136.

In light of the preceding chapter's discussion of Hsieh's understanding of *jen* as sensitivity and awareness, it can be seen that the central concern of the *Tao-hsüeh* fellowship has been very well expressed by Liu:

> With them, the concern for education acquired a much deeper meaning than before. Education should develop consciousness, awareness, and sensitivity . . . a gradual "greening" of moral transformation.[4]

57

Liu's observation of the connection between education or learning (*hsüeh*) and "consciousness, awareness, and sensitivity" is supported by a canonical reference found in Huang K'an's classical commentary on *Analects* 1:1:

> Learning [*hsüeh*] is awakening [*chüeh*], becoming aware and enlightened. It refers to using the Tao of the former kings to guide human situations and dispositions, causing oneself to be aware and enlightened, getting rid of the false and choosing the true, and accumulating and completing the virtue of a *chün-tzu*.[5]

Thus, it appears that before the issue of transmission in *Tao-hsüeh* came down to the question of exclusive *Tao-t'ung* lineages, there was an overall sense in common that resonated with Hsieh's specific insights.

Maintaining the Transmission: Two Lineages

Tillman discusses some opposition to the *Tao-hsüeh* group and their claims, presented in court shortly after Chu Chen's memorial. He gives the impression that Chu Chen's memorial occasioned this opposition, but it is more probable that other factors were involved as well, especially since Chu Chen's rather mundane request for an official post for Hsieh Liang-tso's son Hsieh K'o-nien was granted. On the other hand, it could be argued that the emperor's granting of Chu Chen's request would have been perceived by those concerned as signifying at least tacit acceptance of the basis of his argument, thus acquiescing in the general *Tao-hsüeh* claim.

"*Tao-hsüeh*" became a highly charged and partisan term at the center of bitter controversy during the lifetime of Chu Hsi. It became an epithet for "fake learning" (*wei-hsüeh* 偽學) that spuriously claimed sole possession of the truth.[6] One scholar-official's memorial referred to the *Tao-hsüeh* fellowship's claim to have revived a lost transmission as "wild, strange, immoral, and vile."[7] Later, however, "*Tao-hsüeh*" rose again to a connotation as positive as it had been pejorative. It was eventually affixed as the defining term for what became the mainstream of Neo-Confucian orthodoxy by its usage as an organizing category in the *Sung-shih* 宋史 (History of the Sung Dynasty), compiled during the succeeding Yüan period.[8] In the *Sung-shih*, "*Tao-hsüeh*" was used primarily to single out an orthodox teaching lineage (*cheng-ch'uan* 正傳) in a separate chapter from the "forest" of Confucian scholars (*ju-lin* 儒林).[9]

A standard account of the early phases of transmission within *Tao-hsüeh* traces two lines from the Ch'eng brothers through the two most important disciples, Hsieh and Yang Shih.[10] In an early statement of this two-lineage schema, Chen Te-hsiu 真德秀 (1178–1235), another leading Sung Confucian, wrote in his *Reading Journal*,

> The learning of the two Ch'engs was inherited by Yang Shih, who transmitted it to Lo Ts'ung-yen (1072–1135), and Lo in turn transmitted it to Li T'ung (1093–1163), who finally transmitted it to Chu Hsi. This was the legacy of one school.
>
> Hsieh Liang-tso transmitted it to Hu An-kuo (1074–1138), who transmitted it to his own son Hu Hung (1106–61), who in turn transmitted it to Chang Shih (1133–80). This was the legacy of another school.[11]

As given by Chen Te-hsiu, Chu Hsi's lineal connection to the Ch'eng brothers was as a third-generation follower of Yang Shih (for a different view, see the next section). Chu Hsi, however, did not base his teaching authority on that lineage but claimed to have inherited the transmission directly through his study of the Ch'eng brothers. Indeed, Chu Hsi believed that carefully sifting the records of the Ch'engs' teaching compared quite favorably with seeing the Ch'engs in person, as a basis for arriving at a clear understanding.[12] Thus, Chu's systematic reasoning took precedence for him over the "synaptic" lineal connection with one's direct teachers.

Later, Huang Tsung-hsi 黃宗羲 (1610–95) and others who compiled the monumental *Sung-Yüan hsüeh-an* 宋元學案 (Record of Sung and Yüan Scholars, SYHA) returned to an emphasis on scholarly lineage. They were opposed to the special designation "*Tao-hsüeh*," which had had the effect of making other leading Sung thinkers, such as Lu Chiu-yüan 陸九淵 (Hsiang-shan 象山, 1139–93), appear as second-class Confucians.[13] Huang also opposed the tendency on the part of many scholars to give automatic preference to Yang Shih among the Ch'eng disciples because his line supposedly eventuated in Chu Hsi. Countering this trend, Huang Tsung-hsi objected to using subsequent events and figures as the criteria for ranking the Ch'eng disciples:

> Some who speak about it say that the Tao-nan [道南 i.e., Yang Shih] group led in three generations to Master Chu who completed Confucian teaching, and so we ought to rank [Yang] Kuei-shan above [Hsieh] Shang-ts'ai. Without knowing the whole merits, how can one [simply] go by the later people in making comparisons?[14]

Instead, Huang put forward his own conclusion: "Among the top disciples of the Ch'engs, I myself take [Hsieh] Shang-ts'ai to be the best."[15]

Hsieh and the Hu-Hsiang school

From the formal point of view of the connection between teacher and disciple, the key link in the development of the Hunan ("Hu-Hsiang" 湖湘) school of Neo-Confucian teaching was between Hsieh and Hu An-kuo 胡安國 (1074–1138). There has been some controversy about this link.[16] Yet, as Zhu Hanmin (Chu Han-min) points out, the fact that Hu An-kuo was one of the two original recorders of the STYL gives strong indication for considering him as a disciple of Hsieh, since the task of recording the contents of a teacher's sayings was usually taken up by a direct disciple.[17] However this connection is interpreted, it is clear that Hu An-kuo held Hsieh in high regard. Hu An-kuo's nephew Hu Hsien 胡憲 (1082–1162) notes that when he was with Hu An-kuo in Ch'ang-sha, Hunan, in 1107, Hu An-kuo often remarked on the efficacy of Hsieh's teaching.[18] As Zhu puts it, scholars agree that Hu An-kuo gained much of his learning from Hsieh, and so Hsieh was the primary intermediary between the learning of the Ch'eng brothers and the Hu-Hsiang (Hunan) school.[19] Therefore, it is legitimate to consider Hsieh as forebear of the Hu family learning, and likewise the Hu-Hsiang school as a continuation of Hsieh's teaching lineage.

In this light, it is also interesting to note that Hu Hsien, (Hu An-kuo's nephew and student), was one of the early teachers of Chu Hsi.[20] In his "Record of Deeds" for Hu Hsien, dated the seventh of the seventh month, 1178, Chu Hsi signs himself as Hu Hsien's disciple (*men-jen* 門人).[21] As given in SYHA 48, Chu Hsi's pedigree includes being a second-generation transmitter of Hu An-kuo. If so, that would make him also an intellectual descendant of Hsieh Liang-tso.

In addition, Chu Hsi was spurred on by his teacher Li T'ung 李侗 (Yen-p'ing 延平, 1093–1163) to take Hsieh's thought seriously. As Chu Hsi recorded in the *Yen-p'ing ta-wen* 延平答問 ([Li] Yen-p'ing's answers to [his student Chu Hsi's] questions), Li T'ung considered Hsieh's words to be "extremely good to savor" (*chi-hao wan-wei* 極好玩味).[22] It was with such encouragement that Chu Hsi chose to edit the *Shang-ts'ai yü-lu* as his first major scholarly project. Even toward the end of his life, Chu Hsi acknowledged that it was the learning of Master Hsieh that had gotten him started.[23]

A Problem of Sources

It seems clear that *jen* was at the heart of the learning which Chang Shih 張栻 (Nan-hsüan 南軒, 1133–80), the culminating figure of the Hu-Hsiang school, inherited from Hu Hung 胡宏(1106–61, Hu An-kuo's third son). As Tillman writes,

> Perceiving the youth's (i.e., Chang Shih's) sincerity and capacity, Hu Hung taught him about humaneness (=*jen*). Chang Shih withdrew to reflect and wrote a letter about [*jen*] ... Chang thereafter wrote a long essay on [*jen*], the "Record of Admiring Yen-tzu" (*Hsi Yen lu*).[24]

Tillman continues, describing the centrality of this particular essay, the "Record of Admiring Yen-tzu," in Chang Shih's personal cultivation. With reference to this crucial writing, Tillman notes that "there is a problem regarding Chang's writings as they have come down to us." He explains,

> When Chu [Hsi] finalized the editing and wrote the preface to Chang's collected short writings in 1184, he omitted some of Chang's early writings—including the "Record of Admiring Yen-tzu." Especially given Chu's own testimony to the importance of the "Record of Admiring Yen-tzu," it is as surprising as it is unfortunate that Chu excised these texts from Chang's collected works.[25]

There is no way to know exactly what the reasons were for Chu Hsi's failure to include these writings when he edited Chang's literary collection (*wen-chi* 文集), but it is surely regrettable that such a significant link in the development of the learning of *jen* as Chang's "Record of Admiring Yen-tzu" has not survived.

Chu Hsi's famous essay "*Jen-shuo*" 仁說 (Discussion on *Jen*) was developed in discussion and debate with Chang Shih and the Hunan school. In this context, there was an important exchange of letters between Chu Hsi and Chang Shih, in which the pros and cons of Hsieh's understanding of *jen* as sensitivity (*chüeh*) or conscious awareness (*chih-chüeh*) was one of the main issues. Unfortunately, though Chu Hsi's reply is found in his own literary collection, Chang Shih's letter to Chu Hsi on the theory of *jen* as *chih-chüeh* was not included by Chu Hsi in Chang's *wen-chi* and is no longer extant.[26]

Chang Shih also wrote a "*Jen-shuo*," but there is an anomaly regarding it. In Chu Hsi's literary collection, there is an introductory note appended to his "*Jen Shuo*" to the effect that Chang Shih's "*Jen-shuo*" was erroneously considered in one edition to be by Chu Hsi.[27] In addition, one of Chu Hsi's most prominent disciples, Ch'en Ch'un (1159–1223), considered that Chu had authored two "*Jen-shuo*." Therefore, Liu Shu-hsien has suggested that the "*Jen-shuo*" in Chang Shih's literary collection was actually written by Chu Hsi and then deliberately attributed to Chang Shih:

The *Nan-hsüan wen-chi* (Collection of Literary Works of Master Chang Shih) was completely compiled by Chu Hsi. He deleted all letters and essays that did not conform to his own line of thought and regarded them as Chang Shih's immature work of early years. Is it possible that [Chang] Nan-hsüan never revised his early draft [and that] Chu Hsi wrote another "Jen-shuo" based on his agreement with Nan-hsüan, included it in the *Nan-hsüan wen-chi* as Nan-hsüan's own work, and published it as such[?][28]

Liu's argument was offered in response to an essay by Satō Hitoshi, and was in turn rebutted by Wing-tsit Chan.[29] Here it will just be noted that this is another anomaly in the record of Chang Shih's teaching, and further evidence that the historical eclipsing of the Hunan school by Chu Hsi and his followers, whether deliberate or accidental, does not necessarily imply its being intellectually superseded. The fact that the extant version of Chang Shih's "*Jen-shuo*" has been confused with Chu Hsi's suggests that to some scholars at that time it seemed not to represent the Hunan view. Given the lack of subsequent defenders of the Hunan approach, it may not be warranted to consider Chang Shih's text as simply his capitulation to Chu Hsi's views. In other words, without the supporting documents in the form of Chang Shih's earlier essays and his critical letters to Chu Hsi, it is probably a misreading to consider Chang's treatise as in essential agreement with Chu's.

Even in Chang Shih's text as it stands, there is evidence of some continuity with Hsieh's line of thinking. As Tillman puts it,

> How far Chang would go to accommodate Chu also had limits. In his treatise, Chang did not renounce Hsieh Liang-tso's concept of [*jen*] as consciousness [*chüeh*], but his statement (that a person of [*jen*] had consciousness without confusion) was expressed in such a way as not to confront Chu.[30]

However, Chang's apparent defeat in the debate with Chu Hsi meant that the Hu-Hsiang school as an independent branch quickly disappeared after Chang's death in 1180. Tillman offers the following comment:

> Accepting Chu's characterization of Hunan ideas as having been inherited from Hsieh Liang-tso, Chang was unable to establish his roots in Ch'eng Hao's philosophy. Instead, he followed Chu in looking to Ch'eng I for textual authority.[31]

This comment neatly sums up Chu's forensic skill in detaching Hsieh's ideas from those of his teacher, Ch'eng Hao.

It may certainly be said that Chu Hsi's systematic structuring of the intellectual resources of *Tao-hsüeh* was a major "entrepreneurial" achievement.[32] Nevertheless, the degree of dominance of Chu Hsi's line of thought was in part an accident of history, in that he outlived his major rivals and became a rallying point for the whole of the *Tao-hsüeh* movement. Conversely, the Hu-Hsiang school as a lineal tradition seems to have dissipated after the death of Chang Shih. However, these alternative resources remained part of the collective memory of the Confucian tradition and there were resonances of the "Hunan perspective" down through the later ages of Confucian reflection. Zhu Hanmin lists several major figures as later inheritors of the Hunan perspective, but for our purposes here the most important was the late nineteenth-century philosopher, reformer, and Chinese patriotic martyr T'an Ssu-t'ung 譚嗣同 (1865–1898). T'an's work provides a fitting way to thematize the perspective developed in this book.

Jen-hsüeh as a Theme

In 1897, T'an Ssu-t'ung wrote a major essay entitled "*Jen-hsüeh*" 仁學.[33] Writing at a time of political, cultural, and spiritual crisis in China, T'an drew together ideas and precepts from Confucian, Buddhist, Christian, and modern Western sources to argue vigorously for the centrality of the Chinese cultural tradition in the task of human salvation. T'an's "*Jen-hsüeh*" represents an attempt to come to terms with modern Western culture and Christianity on the basis of traditional Chinese cultural resources. His central understandings of *jen* have roots going back at least to the eleventh century. In expounding the basic thesis that *jen* is "interconnectedness" (*t'ung* 通) that forms one body, T'an draws on the central analogy in Ch'eng Hao's and Hsieh's teaching on *jen*, between physical numbness or paralysis and not-being-*jen*:

> When something touches our body, we feel the contact; when the contact is heavy, we feel irritation and pain . . . Those who are suffering from paralysis, however, cannot feel, as their electric wires have been damaged and are no longer able to pass messages to the brain; the body, though one, is as if divided into different (alien) regions. That is why physicians regard paralysis as not-being-*jen*.[34]

In this passage, T'an brings then-current scientific concepts to bear in explaining the mechanism by which awareness is transmitted. T'an's analogy between *jen*, understood as felt interconnectedness, and electricity or electric fields combines traditional organic and modern mechanistic understandings of the world.

T'an used the nineteenth-century scientific concept of "ether" (*i-t'ai* 以太) as an explanation for the medium of sensitivity, and thus as one of the specific components of his conceptual bridge between "*jen* learning" and "scientific learning." Even though this concept of "ether" may no longer have persuasive power, it is intriguing to consider the possibility that T'an was working from a genuine insight. If, as Yuasa suggests, the unity of heart-and-mind and body is a personal achievement (see chapter 3), then perhaps a unity between these two kinds of learning is also something to be achieved.

A possible key to bringing unity among different kinds of knowing is T'an's point that *jen*, as sensitivity, is the precondition for knowing and understanding. T'an makes this point as one of his opening desiderata, saying that "wisdom is generated from *jen*."[35] There is a direct link here with my earlier discussion in chapter 3 of the relationship of *jen* to *chih* (knowing). Thus, one of the most important nineteenth-century Confucian thinkers was drawing on insights traceable to Ch'eng Hao and especially to Hsieh Liang-tso in the eleventh-century. Moreover, the urgency with which T'an sought to incorporate the intellectual challenges from the West and to defend the core value of *jen* on a new footing is reminiscent of the task that faced the eleventh-century *Tao-hsüeh* thinkers, and is also prescient for Confucians today.

The phrase "*jen-hsüeh*" harks back immediately to T'an's essay,[36] yet as Benjamin Schwartz has noted, "The history of an idea may be more than the history of the term with which the idea ultimately comes to be identified."[37] As the preceding discussion has shown, developing a personal apprehension of *jen* was central to the aim and process of learning in the Ch'eng school. It is fitting, therefore, to characterize this emphasis in learning as "*jen-hsüeh*." From this point of view, the designation "*jen-hsüeh*" can be extended historically to include the Ch'eng school, particularly Ch'eng Hao and Hsieh, with further roots in the teachings of Confucius in the *Analects*. Thus, even though it was not one of the actual terms of their self-definition, "*jen-hsüeh*" is an appropriate designation for Ch'eng Hao, Hsieh, and others who shared their ultimate concerns.

It has been customary to analyze the Neo-Confucian tradition into two separate lines of transmission, *li-hsüeh* 理學 ("the learning of principle"), sometimes termed the rationalistic school of Ch'eng I and Chu Hsi, and *hsin-hsüeh* 心學 ("the learning of the heart-and-mind"), sometimes termed the idealistic school of Lu Hsiang-shan and Wang Yang-ming 王陽明 (1472–1529). However, some modern scholars have called this picture into question. Wm. Theodore de Bary has shown that the concerns of the "learning of the heart-and-mind" were central also for the followers of Chu Hsi.[38] From another point of view, Mou Tsung-san's 牟宗三 reconstruction of the early Neo-Confucian movement also critiques the simple *li-hsüeh/hsin-hsüeh* dichotomy.[39] In light of these recent reconsiderations, it may be appropriate to offer *jen-hsüeh* as a designation that can be understood to include the major emphases of both *li-hsüeh* and *hsin-hsüeh*. Chu Hsi's own definition of *jen*—namely, as the principle or pattern of affection and the virtue of the heart-and-mind—nicely demonstrates this coordination.[40]

The usage of the theme "*jen-hsüeh*" here should be distinguished from another way in which the phrase has been used. In one chapter of his 1937 schematic book *Sung-hsüeh kai-yao* 宋學概要 (*Essentials of Sung Learning*), Hsia Chün-yü divides the major Sung Confucians into various "factions" (*p'ai* 派) of "*jen-hsüeh*" according to their differing characterizations of *jen*.[41] Hsieh's interpretation of *jen* as *chüeh* figures prominently in Hsia's outline as one of the major options.[42] Hsia then lists Hsieh's disciple Tseng T'ien and five other figures as representing this faction: Chang Chiu-ch'eng, Hu Shih, Hu Ta-yüan, Yang Chien, and Fang Feng-ch'en. In Hsia's usage, "*Jen-hsüeh*" means simply "theories of *jen*" and is paralleled by other chapters on various theories of human nature (*hsing*) and the heart-and-mind (*hsin*).

Although Hsia Chün-yü used "*Jen-hsüeh*" narrowly to refer to a component of Sung learning, some recent writers have employed it quite generally as a term for Confucius's own project, as in Tu Wei-ming's article entitled "K'ung-tzu jen-hsüeh chung ti Tao, hsüeh, cheng" 孔子仁學中的道，學，政.[43] The modern Chinese philosopher and historian Hsü Fu-kuan 徐復觀 has written, "The learning of Confucius is precisely *Jen-hsüeh*."[44] This general usage of *jen-hsüeh* provides a backdrop against which the specific shape of Neo-Confucian *jen-hsüeh* can be discerned.

It was surely the learning of Confucius that the *Tao-hsüeh* thinkers most sought to inherit. Hsieh, as well as other Ch'eng disciples, paid particular attention to the *Analects* and made it a touchstone for their personal cultivation. Thematically, "*Jen-hsüeh*" marks the sense of continuity and kinship that Hsieh and the other members of the Ch'eng school felt with the circle of Confucius's own disciples. From this point of view, Hsieh's insight on the problem of "knowing *jen*," far from being an idiosyncratic opinion, is recognizable as an authentic attempt to get to the heart of the tradition, the kernel of humanity. In this light, the thematizing of this particular line of concern as "*jen-hsüeh*" should not be seen as proposing another faction beside the others, but rather as pointing out the particular shape given by Ch'eng Hao and Hsieh to an issue that is central to all of Confucian learning.

Jen-hsüeh and "Humane Learning"

"Humane learning" would be an acceptable, almost literal, translation for "*jen-hsüeh*." However, the English phrase "humane learning" has its own connotations and history, so that the pairing of these two phrases produces a kind of "matching significance" (*ko-i* 格義).[45] For its modern usage, the primary definition of "humane" given in the *Oxford English Dictionary* (OED) is as follows:

> Characterized by such behavior or disposition towards others as befits a [human being] . . . Marked by sympathy with and consideration for the needs and distresses of others; feeling or showing compassion and tenderness towards human beings and the lower animals; kind, benevolent.[46]

This sense of what it means to be humane correlates well with what *jen-hsüeh* as learning seeks to develop and disclose.

There is, however, a further meaning of "humane," also given in the OED as follows:

> Applied to those branches of study or literature (*literae humaniores*) which tend to humanize or refine, as the ancient classics, rhetoric, and poetry.[47]

In this sense, it may be objected that "humane learning" is not appropriate in the Confucian case because of its connotation (with the cognate "humane letters") of becoming "cultured." Peter Bol has highlighted the clashing claims of "*wen* 文 (culture) vs. Tao 道," particularly as articulated by Ch'eng I.[48] Ch'eng I did not want his students to waste their energy doing *wen* (literary pursuits); Hsieh voices a similar sentiment.[49] However, the subtle implication of "culture" in "*jen-hsüeh*" as "humane learning" is not unwarranted. Even though *wen-hsüeh* 文學 (cultured studies), and particularly the writing of poetry, were criticized by some in the Ch'eng school as distracting from the true aim of learning, the course of learning they advocated not only assumed literacy but required intimate familiarity with the classic scriptural texts. Indeed, as members of the *Tao-hsüeh* fellowship saw it, the very posterity of the classical humane culture (*ssu-wen* 斯文) was at stake.

In the terms suggested by Hsieh, the learning of *jen* as an ongoing personal endeavor leads to increased awareness of and sensitivity to the full range of one's human situation, embedded not only in a network of human relations that in principle cannot exclude anyone but also in a cosmos infinite in extent and in complexity. *Jen* is the basis of authentic learning, because unless there is personal engagement and some recognition of commonality, the result would be dehumanizing. This sense of *jen-hsüeh* as humane learning may thus provide a conceptual bridge or rapprochement between two traditions in the West, the Renaissance and the Reformation, that have often been seen as mutually exclusive or antagonistic. *Jen* as "humane" is not developed over against "divine," but rather, according to the *Tao-hsüeh* thinkers, *jen* is also characteristic of the heart-and-mind of Heaven-and-Earth. Conversely, the learning through which one becomes truly cultured is precisely that based upon the deepest springs of the religious life.

In sum, "*jen-hsüeh*" signifies that *jen* is both the content and the norm of authentic transmission in Confucian humane learning. Hsieh Liang-tso, as disciple and teacher of the early *Tao-hsüeh* movement and as a unique contributor to the ongoing Confucian project of "understanding *jen*," holds a special place in that authentic transmission. One aim of this book has been to explore that place within Hsieh's immediate context, and then to extend his insights toward the present.

As Hsieh says in his comment on *Analects* 1:1, "friends come from afar" (*p'eng tzu yüan fang lai* 朋自遠方來) include not only one's contemporaries but also those "among the ancients who were 'first to discover this common element in my heart.'"[50] This interpretation of the *Analects* passage constitutes an invitation to "seek for friends in history." The classical injunction that "those who are first aware then awaken others" (*hsien-chüeh-che chüeh hou-chüeh-che* 先覺者覺後覺者) is applicable on the historical (vertical) axis as well as on the contemporary (horizontal) one. It means that the "awakening" of those in the past has a seed quality to stimulate the awareness of those who come after. For those today who would take up Confucian-style humane learning as a religious quest, Hsieh may be an authentic companion.

Humane Learning as Religious Quest

Warrants for Authentic Transmission

In the integrity of his wrestling with his teachers' instruction, in his savoring of the scriptural and traditional resources for personal cultivation, and in the incisiveness of his own interpretive accomplishment (*tzu-te* 自得), Hsieh by all accounts passed a crucial Confucian test of authentic transmission: he applied what he had received and did not pass on what he had not practiced (*Analects* 1:4). The question of authentic transmission with respect to Hsieh can now be placed in the context of the comparative issues raised in the introduction. In the closing section of his *Jen-shuo*, Chu Hsi argued that Hsieh's gloss of "*chüeh*" 覺 or "sensitivity" for *jen* 仁 was inadequate because it did not account for certain scriptural passages (e.g., *Analects* 6:23), and because it did not square with a particular saying of Ch'eng I, whom Chu took to be the authoritative interpreter of the tradition. In terms of the reasonable analysis of experience, Chu worried that Hsieh's "*chüeh*" would lead to confusion, and perhaps into unconscious or unwitting Ch'an.[1]

A defense of the authenticity of Hsieh's position would be based upon these same considerations. In terms of scripture and tradition, Hsieh's *Analects* commentary is a manifestation of exegetical reasoning, interpreting a scriptural text in light of the text itself, supported by other texts understood as belonging to the same traditional canon. In addition to Hsieh's interpretive insights on specific passages, his commentary taken as a whole represents a significant example of the exegetical reasoning that was foundational to the systematic development of Neo-Confucian thought. For further examples of Hsieh's exegetical reasoning, see his comments on *Analects* chapters 1 and 2, translated in full in appendices 1 and 2. In terms of reason and experience, it can be said that Hsieh treats experience in a nuanced way as a source for understanding *jen*. By emphasizing the reflective process as directed toward actual practice, he does not allow the intellective element to overly dominate the process of personal cultivation. His position on sensitivity is best understood when it is recalled that Hsieh himself was engaged in a continuous discipline of practice, including quiet-sitting.

In general, the Tao-hsüeh Neo-Confucians treated the *Analects* as scripture, in the sense of an authoritative, even revelatory text for thought and practice.

Hsieh and Chu were also very much concerned with tradition, both the tradition of interpretation and the tradition of ritual practice.[2] And they were centrally concerned with the relation of reason and experience, as expressed in their distinctive positions on the relation of *jen* and *chih* 知 discussed in chapter 3. Thus we can observe that the terms of argument between Hsieh and Chu manifest the fourfold pattern of warrants set out in the introduction: scripture, tradition, reason, and experience.

Widening the Theological Circle

Based upon these four warrants, the question of authentic transmission in humane learning can now be recognized as a "theological" issue, in at least three senses. The first is a matter of descriptive definition: granting that the set of "theological" warrants can be taken comparatively, this yields a comparative description of theological reflection that is inclusive of both theistic and non-theistic traditions. Theology, then, can be characterized as constructive reflection based on scripture, tradition, reason, and experience in the context of committed concern for authentic transmission. The concern of Hsieh and Chu for authentic transmission in Confucian *jen-hsüeh* 仁學 (humane learning) is thus an example of non-theistic theological reflection.

Because they were working with a similar pattern of resources and warrants, the Neo-Confucians' understanding of their own task is closer to the self-understanding of Christian theologians than to modern Western philosophers. Thus, the thinking of the Sung dynasty Neo-Confucians can be better understood on analogy with Christian theologians than with modern philosophers. By the same token, the task of Christian theology appears in a new light when understood as a subspecies of a discipline that thinkers in other traditions, including the Confucian, have also been practicing. Thus, a second sense in which the authentic transmission of *jen-hsüeh* is a theological issue, still on the descriptive level, is that this Confucian case contributes to further understanding of the patterns and processes of theological reasoning in general.

In this regard, one way in which Confucian resources can contribute to theological method can be seen by drawing out the implications of the issue of *jen* and *chih*, discussed in chapter 3. Taking Hsieh's side of that issue, if knowing is secondary to being *jen* and "knowing *jen*" is therefore always a second-order reflection on practice, then the core of Confucian theological reflection is located in experiential embodying, not in systematic elaboration. When theology is understood as an activity with a strong basis in personal cultivation, it appears that the deepening and broadening process of the person is also the deepening and broadening of the dimensions of reality that she or he can plumb.

As noted in the introduction, considerable comparative work has been and is being done on the phenomena of scripture in various religious traditions. Further comparative work on the other three warrants, particularly reason and experience, will ramify the comparative description of theology developed here. On the question of how this comparative understanding of theology might affect the work of constructive theologians, this model would suggest that "theologians" in different traditions can learn from one another, as working with the same kinds of resources, warrants, and concerns.

In order to work together, there would have to be a widening of the canons of scripture, tradition, reason, and experience. A major impediment to such widening appears to be precisely the concern for authentic transmission that shapes and bounds the theological endeavor at every point. Even though cross-influences among religious traditions are readily identifiable throughout the history of religion, the issue of authenticity most often divides. Whether or not shared concern for authentic transmission, across profound differences over content, can be a foundation for mutual respect and even common cause is a key issue for the currently unfolding theological exchange.

It is here, I think, that the Confucian understanding of humane learning has a particular contribution to make. It seems to be a perspective from which the other great theological traditions can the more readily be understood as engaged in a common task, namely disciplined reflection on learning to be human. This point, it should be clearly understood, is not intended to be reductionistic. The religious traditions of the world have profound, and profoundly different, understandings of what it means to be human. All, however, intend to enhance human life, and in ways that strengthen rather than diminish the human capacity for humane sensitivity.

Historically speaking, recognized authenticity in transmission has required regeneration of the tradition. The claim of the Ch'eng brothers to have recovered the authentic transmission is not invalidated by their innovations; indeed, it is corroborated by their ability to re-create the excitement of Confucius's disciples in the circle of their own followers. Today, such excitement may perhaps be stimulated by a widened awareness of common theological concern, as the regenerative basis for ongoing authentic transmission.

The third sense in which Confucian *jen-hsüeh* can be considered as theological moves across an imaginary line from descriptive to constructive.[3] To offer one's own assessment of the theological significance of humane learning is, in a way, to continue the line of inquiry raised by Matteo Ricci and James Legge, discussed in the introduction. As it was for Ricci and Legge, such assessment is not simply theoretical but also engaged. Venturing one's own constructive suggestions for the further development of these insights is an ineluctable task from a Confucian perspective, but one that will only be sketched lightly here.

A Religious Rhapsody on *Jen*

No doubt, "*jen*" would not be included in a short-list of "Chinese words for God." There is, however, a formal similarity between "knowing *jen*" as it has been discussed in this book and "knowing God" in the Western theological traditions, in that neither of these is a simple "knowing that." In each case the possibility of knowing is recognized as already conditioned by, given by, that which would be known. Like the theological ultimate(s) of the Western traditions, *jen* is not under the control of human knowledge; rather, *jen* is itself the foundation of authentic knowing. In this light, as noted in the discussion of Hsieh's characterization of *jen* as Tao, the "difficulty" of speaking about *jen* is a sign of its transcendent character.

It has been the Confucian faith and experience that the true nature of *jen* is revealed in the scriptural record of the *Analects*, properly interpreted and practiced. In Tao-hsüeh, the locus of concern has moved through a process of reflection, from action to the incipient springs of action in thought and feeling, with an emphasis on subjectivity and the inventory of personal consciousness. Nevertheless, this interiority, symbolized by the discipline of quiet-sitting, is always fundamentally connected with the basic Confucian emphasis upon integral relations with others and with the ten-thousand things.

In traditional Confucian terms, the full realization of personal cultivation in humane learning is expressed as the "unity of Heaven and human" (*t'ien-jen* ho-i 天人合一). *Jen* itself can be understood as precisely this unity, or that which makes such unity possible.[4] In the line of thinking developed here, the bond of unity between Heaven and human would be best described as humane awareness and sensitivity. Tu Wei-ming remarks that "it is in the sensitivity of the mind—its ability to feel and to care—that the creative potential of human beings truly lies."[5] For both Hsieh and Chu Hsi, the creative potential in human beings is understood as a manifestation of the heart-and-mind of Heaven and Earth (*t'ien-ti chih hsin* 天地之心) for generation and regeneration (*sheng-sheng* 生生). To say that *jen* is the commonality of Heaven and human is to say that human creativity is based upon sensitivity, which also characterizes Heaven.

If sensitivity as creativity is a manifestation of what in the West has been called the *imago Dei*, that in turn suggests that in the healing process of forming sensitive and humane relations with others and with all things, there are resources available to be tapped beyond the "one-inch square" of one's own heart-and-mind. Further, *jen* as the defining characteristic of the creative source of love, life, and continuity of being suggests an understanding of the divine as the perceptive feeling center of the "one body" of the cosmos, critically aware of the pain and itch in every cell.

To venture beyond traditional phrasing, one could speak of the unity of Heaven and *jen* (*t'ien-jen ho-i* 天仁合一). This new expression would signify that Heaven is present as experienced in the incipience and manifestation of *jen*, that is, *relationally*. Both Chinese characters, *t'ien* 天 and *jen* 仁, can be read imaginatively as composed of "human" 人 and "two" 二, hence "relatedness." To speak of the unity or identification of Heaven and *jen* is to locate the resonance of Heaven within human experiences of relatedness through give-and-take mutuality.

Thus, the potential for further theological reflection on *jen* as sensitivity is not only as a quality to be predicated of a subject, either human or divine. It is also a quality to be predicated of a relation, such that "one body" is formed in and through that relation. This line of reflection on *jen* leads not just to another quality ("humane" or "sensitive") of a divine being but also conversely to a way of talking about divinity as a quality of relations. The locus of sensitivity would thus be the relation itself, reflexively, in a way that also constitutes those in the relation. The profound experience of relationality may then be understood as awareness of the divine, that is to say, the "co-presence" of the divine experienced in relation. In sum, *jen* as sensitivity and awareness that forms one body can be understood as the co-presence of divinity, the "co-presence of God," in and through human relatedness.[6]

Humane Learning Today

A religious quest calls forth the full engagement of one's empathetic sensitivity and critical faculties in earnest thought and practice. Hsieh Liang-tso, in company with his teachers, fellow disciples and following generations, looked upon Confucian humane learning in this way as a personal vocation and quest. The recognition of Confucian humane learning as religious quest is necessary to full historical understanding the rise of the Neo-Confucian Tao-hsüeh movement. It is also an important issue in the contemporary cultural debate, parsing anew the intellectual and spiritual resources of the Chinese past.

Though it has passed through more than a century of vigorous and at times scathing critique, I believe we are witnessing the gradual resurrection of the Confucian tradition in China and elsewhere at the outset of the twenty-first century. This is in part because, as the contemporary philosopher Li Zehou (Li Tse-hou) 李澤厚 points out, Confucian cultural values are increasingly relevant to the global human community; respect, tolerance, and harmony are increasingly indispensable in the quest for a humane civil order in the world.

The global transportation and communication network has vastly extended the potential range of human sensitivity and awareness. In the present time, when the sensory body has been artificially extended through the communications media, it becomes a critical question how to maintain the connection between the vastly extended "body" of input and the capacity of one's heart-and-mind to be moved. Ironically, the increased capacity for sensitivity can have a numbing effect on awareness; the sheer volume of sensory input may contribute to a deadening of the responses and a feeling of helplessness.[7] In this situation, humane learning is therapeutic, a way to restore the healthy balance described as the original heart-and-mind (*pen-hsin, liang-hsin* 本心, 良心).

Humane learning entails critical awareness of one's own relational location. It is not just overwhelming sensitivity to the ills of the world, now made vividly available through mass media, nor is it introspective in the sense of opting out of the relational world. The focus is on awareness of those situations about which one is in a position to do something. In this sense, "physical therapy" for relational "numbness" involves deliberate, sometimes painful stretching, beginning from those who are close at hand.

For deepened sensitivity, perception and relationship become one. This is implied in the Mencian definition, "*jen* is the human heart-and-mind," for what is thus called the heart-and-mind is the field of relational interaction itself. As described by Hsieh, that which stands in the way of experiencing the vital awareness that "forms one body with all things" is a perceptual grid that he calls "*wu-wo chih hsin*" 物我之心, the cluster of dispositions that keeps one from experiencing essential unity with all things. Progress in humane learning would proceed through dismantling those perceptive barriers and restoring full relational health.[8]

Humane learning 仁學 is not a "new" idea; its pedigree has a long history, as this book has tried to document. But it is a *timely* idea today, as we try to come to grips with a globalization process that is propelling us to think and feel as one humanity. To return to one of Hsieh's seminal descriptions of *jen* as sensitivity and vitality:

> What is living is *jen*, what is dead is not-*jen* . . . When someone's body is numb and does not feel pain and itch, it is called not-*jen*. The seeds of peaches and apricots that can be planted and grow are called peach-*jen* and apricot-*jen* (kernels) because they have living vitality.[9]

For the learning of *jen* to have living vitality is, among other things, to manifest the generative properties of thinking. Hsieh's thinking was not only about *jen* topically, but was also a manifestation of *jen* in this sense, and thus has both authenticity and generativity.

In the words of Ernst Troeltsch, "*Wesensbestimmung ist Wesens-gestaltung*": to specify the essence or kernel of the tradition is to *gestalt* it afresh.[10] This is what Hsieh endeavored to do, and is key to the authenticity of his transmission in humane learning. It is also the endeavor of this book, including these closing remarks on present possibilities for extending the living ideas that Hsieh Liang-tso, stimulated by the Ch'eng brothers' teaching, discovered in the *Analects* of Confucius.

Introductory Note

The appendices consist of Hsieh Liang-tso's commentary on chapters 1 and 2 of the *Analects*, as gathered from the *Lun-yü ching-i* (LYCI). The edition used is that of the *Hung-shih T'ang shih ching kuan tsung-shu*.[1] As noted in chapter 2, the LYCI is a composite text, with passages from most of the major early Sung Neo-Confucians following each verse of the *Analects*. It is fairly certain that these passages taken together represent Hsieh Liang-tso's *Shang-ts'ai Lun-yü chieh*.[2]

A noteworthy feature of Hsieh's commentary is his constant use of scriptural citations and allusions, discussed in chapter 2 under the headings of "intertextuality" and "intratextuality." His commentary as a whole is an exercise in exegetical reasoning, interpreting the scriptural text in light of itself, supported by other canonical texts. The commentary is thus interspersed with quotations that have had to be traced individually, in order to understand the authorities and warrants on which Hsieh is relying. This makes for somewhat difficult reading at times. In the translations that follow, these scriptural quotations, especially those from the Five Classics, are often given according to the nineteenth-century renderings of James Legge. The resulting stylistic unevenness gives an authentic feel, for in the original commentary those classical quotations are usually marked only by their archaic grammar and syntax.

As noted in chapter 2, Hsieh's commentary is a sustained engagement with the whole of the *Analects* text, not just selective parts of it. Likewise, this book is based on a complete English translation of Hsieh's entire commentary. However, for reasons of economy, only chapters 1 and 2 of the *Analects* are incorporated here. The choice of these two chapters is governed by the fact that many of Hsieh's most important points are included herein. Moreover, Hsieh's comments on later chapters tend to become briefer, so that the first two chapters of the *Analects* give the fullest play to Hsieh's exegetical skill and imagination.

For convenience of reference, the *Analects* passages themselves are included at the head of each section of Hsieh's comments.[3] In developing my renderings of the *Analects* passages, I have worked from D. C. Lau's widely available and respected English translation.[4] I am also indebted to the recent "philosophical" translation by Roger Ames and Henry Rosemont,[5] and have consulted other English and modern Chinese translations as well. Like Ames and Rosemont, I have endeavored to avoid the unnecessarily exclusive language that afflicts many earlier translations. As the focus here is on Hsieh's comments, rather than on the original *Analects* text as such, I have rendered the passages in a way that accommodates Hsieh's interpretations. For Hsieh, the *Analects* was a received text, and so it is here as well.

Analects Chapter 1

1:1 The Master said, "Is it not a pleasure, having learned something, to practice it at appropriate times? Is it not a joy to have friends come from afar? Is it not the conduct of an exemplary person, to refrain from taking offence when others fail to appreciate your abilities?"[1]

Hsieh said: "Having learned, to practice at appropriate times"[2] means that there is no time when one does not practice. "Sitting as a personator of the deceased" is practicing while sitting; "standing (reverently) as in sacrificing" is practicing while standing.[3] "Adhering to this in moments of haste" is practicing in times of haste; "adhering to this in times of danger" is practicing at the time of danger.[4] In this way, then, virtue [*te* 德] is gathered. Could one not be pleased?

"To have friends come from afar"—they do not have to be from the same hall, together on the mat, or exclusively come to the gates of the same teacher in order to call them friends. Exploring among the ancients, for those who were "first to discover this common element in my heart,"[5] and researching among people today, those whom you believe are really not different from you, all are friends. Could one not have joy?

When the Way is the same, there will be mutual understanding; when it is not the same, there will not be mutual understanding. Between teacher and disciples, there are still times when mutual understanding is lacking; how much more so [in the case of] other people. For this reason, "the finest *shih* 士 [scholar, officer] of a village is in a position to make friends with the finest *shih* in the village; the finest *shih* in a state, with the finest *shih* in the state; and the finest *shih* in the Empire, with the finest *shih* in the Empire."[6] "If only a few people know me, then I am honored."[7] "Refraining from taking offence when others do not know you," means one treats oneself considerately; "isn't it the conduct of an exemplary person?"

"Having learned something, to practice it at appropriate times" is the way to treat oneself; "friends who come from afar" are those who are similar to you; "those who do not know you" are those who are different from you, and if "not offended therein," then one is close to joy. The whole text of the *Analects* for the most part does not go beyond these three. "In the eating of

77

coarse rice and the drinking of water, the using of one's elbow for a pillow, joy is to be found,"[8] and Yen-tzu's "living . . . on a bowlful of rice and a ladleful of water . . . not allowing this to affect his joy,"[9] are all what is called "not taking offence."

1:2 Yu Tzu said, "It is rare for a person whose character is such that he is filial as a son and deferential as a younger brother to have the inclination to transgress against his superiors; it is unheard of for one who has no such inclination to be inclined to start a rebellion. Exemplary persons devote their efforts to the root, for once the root is established, the Way will grow therefrom. Being filial as a son and deferential as a younger brother is, shall we say, the root of *jen*."[10]

Hsieh said: The previous section discusses the main point in learning. This passage discusses the starting point in seeking *jen*.[11] As for *jen* being Tao, it is not only that nobody can list all the relevant examples; in practicing it no one can do it fully; and [even] to describe it is also difficult. The more learned one's words, the farther one has departed from *jen*. Although the ancients have often spoken of it, in the end [what they speak of] is not *jen*. For example, [in the passage where Confucius offers the description] "respectfulness, tolerance, trustworthiness in word, quickness and generosity,"[12] for *jen*—if one does not know *jen*, then one will merely stop with knowing "respectfulness, tolerance, trustworthiness in word, quickness, and generosity." [Another passage takes] "overcoming oneself and returning to ritual"[13] as *jen*—if [one] does not know *jen*, then [one] will simply stop with knowing "overcoming oneself and returning to ritual." [Again, consider] "when abroad behave as though you were receiving an important guest, when employing the services of the common people behave as though you were officiating at an important sacrifice";[14] this is only to be particularly orderly in one's conduct [*ch'ih-shen* 持身]; how can we see its being *jen*? "The mark of one who is *jen* is being loath to speak";[15] this is merely being especially cautious in speaking, so why should we see it as *jen*? Yu-tzu's discussion of *jen* is also like this. Although one who is filial and brotherly is close to *jen*, filiality and brotherly obedience are not *jen*.

For discussing *jen*, there is nothing better than the human heart-and-mind. For what is not artificial in the human heart-and-mind, nothing is better than serving parents and following (deferring to) elder brothers. The *Chuang-tzu* says, "A child's love of its parent is destined: it cannot be dispelled from the heart."[16] From this can be seen the innately good heart-and-mind. Coming to following elder brothers, the innately good heart-and-mind has never been far from it since the beginning of life. Starting with the service of parents and deference to elder brothers and fully expanding these, then in what direction could one go that is not *jen*? Now as for the heart-and-mind of serving parents and following elder brothers, [even] one who does it without clearly making it manifest, who practices but does not investigate, and for the whole of life follows it without knowing it, is still able not to have "the inclination to transgress against superiors [or] to start a rebellion." How much more one who truly accumulates effort, magnifies it over a long time, and makes it full and complete?

Now "informing one's parents [before] going abroad and upon returning, presenting oneself before them,"[17] and "in winter warming (the bed for them) and cooling it in summer, and in the evening adjusting everything (for their repose) and inquiring (about their health) in the morning,"[18] can be taken as being filial. People in the country localities are also able to do these. "Precedence of the old over the young"[19] as well as "walking slowly, keeping behind one's elders"[20] can be taken as acting deferentially (younger-brotherly). People in the country localities are also able to do these. However, it is not proper to [simply] consider people in the country localities as [already] possessing the Way. To think that they will never be able to enter the Way is also not proper. But whether filiality and younger-brotherly deference can be taken as *jen*, can enter the Way, lies in between being mindful [*nien* 念] and not being mindful. Therefore, as regards the Way of *jen*, the ancients[21] still found it difficult to discuss. What they could say was merely this, and that's all. If one really wants to know *jen*, then it is in "diligent practice,"[22] examining oneself, and investigating what one's heart-and-mind is like at the time of serving parents and following elders. To know this heart-and-mind is to know *jen*.

1:3 The Master said, "It is rare, indeed, for a person of cunning words and an ingratiating face to be *jen*."

Hsieh said: Although *jen* is difficult to describe, knowing the way to be *jen*, one can also know *jen*. [The passage saying that] "filiality and younger-brotherliness are the root of *jen*"[23] is a case of this. Knowing that which is far from *jen*, one can also know *jen*. [This passage saying that] "it is rare for one with artful words and a pleasing face to be *jen*" is a case of this.[24] But as for "artful words" and "a pleasing face," knowing them is also difficult. The *Li-chi* (Record of Ritual) says: "What is wanted in feeling is trustworthiness; in words artfulness."[25] The *Odes* praise the virtue of Chung Shan-fu, saying, "Pleasing is his deportment; pleasing his looks."[26] Now, is what the *Li-chi* calls "artfulness in words" also rarely *jen*? Is the virtue of Chung Shan-fu also rarely *jen*? With reference to the Sage, what is called "[the exemplary person] by being modest gives it expression"[27] is also words being artful; "relaxing his expression, he seemed no longer to be tense,"[28] is also a pleasing expression. How can just making one's words and phrases good and one's facial expression apt be directly taken as rarely *jen*? Coming to petty persons, they are often blunt and direct in accusing others—when are their words artful? Although inside they are weak and cowardly, their expression is harsh—when have their expressions ever been pleasing?[29] If so, then what is it that makes for artful words, and what is it that makes for pleasing expressions? If one is able to know "by speaking in proper tones, one can avoid being boorish and unreasonable," [30] then one can know it. This is appropriate for learning, profound thinking, and energetic inquiring; it cannot be conveyed with words.

1:4 Tseng Tzu said, "Every day I examine myself on three counts. In what I have undertaken on another's behalf, have I failed to do my best? In my dealings with my friends have I failed to be trustworthy in what I say? Have I put into practice what I have received?"[31]

Hsieh said: The nine streams [of classical Chinese thought] all came from the Sage.[32] Afterward, the more they were transmitted, the more the true meaning was lost. For example, after Tzu-hsia by the time it flowed to become Chuang Chou, the transmission had departed far from the Sage. Only Tseng-tzu's learning focused his heart-and-mind on the internal, and thus it was transmitted without any corruption. As for one who personally received his instructions and got the point, there was Tzu-ssu. The learning of Tzu-ssu can be seen in the *Chung-yung* (Doctrine of the Mean). Examining the *Chung-yung*, then one can know Tseng-tzu. As for one who heard [the teaching] and got the point, there was Mencius. Examining the book of *Mencius*, one can also see Tzu-ssu. Therefore, what they learned was completely true and completely right like this. What a pity! His commendable words and good deeds were not completely transmitted to [later] generations. For example, there are quite a few affairs of Tseng-tzu which are praised by Mencius but which are not recorded in the *Analects*; thus there must be those which have vanished and been destroyed. Now as for those that fortunately have been preserved, how can we not thoroughly invest heart-and-mind!

As for these three [points in Tseng-tzu's self-examination], they cannot be discussed just in terms of the shallow and nearby. "In undertaking on another's behalf, to do one's best; in dealings with others, to be trustworthy in what one says; in receiving from others, to practice it for oneself"—if we do not truly know that the Way is not divided,[33] and that others and self are as one, how can we be like this? "In undertaking on another's behalf, to do one's best" is not just planning when something is about to happen. It extends to the way one ordinarily deals with others in quiet, thoughtful consideration. As soon as there is something not thorough, then it is not "doing one's best." "In dealings with friends, to be trustworthy in what one says" is not just that one carries out one's words and after that can be considered trustworthy. "Joyfully have gratitude in mutually caring for each other; radiantly have refinement [*wen* 文] in mutually connecting with each other."[34] As soon as there is something that is not thorough, it is not "being trustworthy in what one says." "Transmission" [*ch'uan* 傳] is to obtain something from others; "practicing" is to obtain something from myself. If I "receive transmission and do not practice it" then the Way is the Way and I am I, never able to mutually harmonize and become one. "Taking an axe-handle [in order to] carve an axe-handle, looking askance from one to the other, we may still think the pattern is far away."[35] This is because of taking them to be two things.[36] "Receiving transmission and not practicing," how can I participate in other people's Way? How is that different from "taking an axe-handle to carve an axe-handle"? Only if one practices until very familiar, then the Way and "I" will be one.

Generally in the case of these three, if one is almost to the point of selflessness, then one will be able to do it. This is the highest extension of learning.

1:5 The Master said, "In guiding a state of a thousand chariots, approach your duties with reverence and be trustworthy in what you say; avoid excesses in expenditure and have affection for your fellows; employ the labor of the common people in the right seasons."

Hsieh said: To learn to become a king is an affair that takes a long time. Tzu-lu said, "There are the common people and one's fellow peers, and there are altars to the spirits of earth and grain. Why must one have to read books before one is said to learn?"[37] These words are right. The Master's not according with them was just that it was not the [right] way to treat Tzu-kao.[38] Tzu-kung said, "Were the Master to become the head of a state or a noble family, he would be like the person described in the saying: he has only to help them stand and they will stand, to guide them and they will walk, to bring peace to them and they will turn to him, to set them tasks and they will work in harmony."[39] The Master never became head of a state or a noble family. We know that the way he would lead a principality could be taken to lead the whole empire with its states and families. If he could have gained his intention, he would have practiced it with respect to the central states; not gaining his intention he practiced it among his family members. The way of guiding them is one. How much more [a state of] a thousand chariots! [Since] the ancients who were able to "become ruler over a hundred *li* square" all were able to unify the whole realm and win the homage of the feudal lords,[40] then a state of a thousand chariots can likewise be paid attention to with care. "Approach your duties with reverence and be trustworthy in what you say; avoid excesses in expenditure and have affection for your fellows; employ the labor of the common people only in the right seasons." Though it were [a matter of governing] the whole empire, how could that alone not be thus? "Approach your duties with reverence and be trustworthy in what you say"—that is to be reverent and faithful. "Avoid excesses in expenditure," then you will be able to "have affection for your fellows." "Employ the labor of the common people only in the right seasons" is "the business of the people must be attended to without delay."[41]

1:6 The Master said, "Young people[42] should be filial at home and deferential abroad, sparing of speech and trustworthy in what they say. They should care for the multitude at large but cultivate closeness with those who are *jen*. If there is any energy to spare, devote it to making oneself cultivated."

Hsieh said: This explains that those engaged in learning ought to know what should be put first and afterward. For the people of the world to care for their parents is easy, but to be thoroughly filial is difficult; to serve elders is easy, but to be thoroughly younger-brotherly (deferential) is difficult. One who is able to be thoroughly filial and deferential is able to illustrate the great relations among people, and furthermore is able "to be trustworthy in ordinary speech and careful in ordinary conduct,"[43] and "to extend to the full a natural aversion to harming others."[44] "Cultivating closeness [*ch'in* 親] with those who are *jen*" is in order to complete oneself; then as for "myself," I will be established.[45] Coming to "if you have any energy to spare from such action, devote it to making yourself cultivated," isn't this what is called "taking recreation in the arts"?[46]

1:7 Tzu-hsia said, "I'd grant that those who appreciate excellence more than beauty, who serve their parents to the utmost and offer their persons to the service of their lord, and who are trustworthy in word in dealing with friends, have been well educated even if they say that they have not yet received instruction."

Hsieh said: [The meaning of] "appreciating [persons of] excellence [as though] appreciating beauty" is "like hating a bad smell, like loving a beautiful color."[47] The genuine will [*ch'eng-i* 誠意] of all under Heaven does not change from this.[48] This "loving virtue like loving beauty"[49] can be called the epitome [*chih* 至] of loving virtue. Being able "to exert oneself to the utmost in the service of one's parents" is simply "to discharge the duties of a son."[50] Being able "to offer one's person to the service of one's lord," is simply not to dare to have self-interest [*chi* 己].[51] Being able "to be trustworthy in word in dealing with friends,"[means that] on the part of "myself" there is no cheating. "Closeness [*ch'in* 親] between father and son, duty between ruler and subject, and faith between friends"; if one is able to be like this, then elders will certainly have precedence over juniors and between husband and wife there will certainly be distinct [spheres].[52] "The way that Shun became Shun,"[53] "his example worthy of being handed down for generations,"[54] could it be beyond this? The sage is the epitome of human-relatedness. In this case, saying "has not yet received instruction" does not get to the point. Call this, rather, "does not receive instruction," for isn't this almost being one who "knows by birth"?[55]

1:8 The Master said, "Exemplary persons [*chün-tzu* 君子] who lack gravity do not inspire awe, and will not be firm in their learning.[56] Make it your guiding principle to do your best for others and to be trustworthy in what you say. Do not accept as friend anyone who is not as good as you. When you make a mistake, do not be afraid of mending your ways."

Hsieh said: This section ought to be divided into four matters: "giving oneself gravity," "doing one's best for others and being trustworthy," "having friends as good as oneself," and "correcting errors." Those engaged in learning cannot lack any of these. Among people, who is able "to know from birth"? To be able "to know through learning," or "to know through difficulty" are also good. Who is able "to practice easily and naturally"? To be able "to practice for advantage" or "to practice with effort and difficulty" are also good.[57] This text is not discussing [the case of] one who knows by birth and practices easily and naturally. "Giving oneself gravity," "doing one's best for others and being trustworthy," and "having friends as good as oneself" are matters of learning. "Correcting errors" is a matter of difficulty [*k'un* 困].

"An exemplary person who lacks gravity does not inspire awe, and in learning will not be firm." The *Chung-yung* says, "To fast, to purify, and to be correct in dress [at the time of solemn sacrifice], and not to make any movement contrary to the rules of propriety—this is the way to cultivate the personal life."[58] "To fast, to purify, and to be correct in dress" is only dignity of demeanor; how can it manifest one's personal cultivation? We make ceremonial caps in order to dignify our heads and make shoes in order to add gravity to our feet and to guard against rashness.

"Anciently, [people of rank, *chün-tzu*] did not fail to wear their girdle-pendants with their precious stones . . . When advancing they inclined forward, when withdrawing they held themselves up straight . . . when turning round, they made a complete circle; when turning in another direction, they did so at a right angle."[59] In this way they made it so that "evil and depraved thoughts found no entrance into their hearts-and-minds."[60] [These points of ritual are only] in the area of appearance and clothing, yet are able to transform and nourish [the character] in such a way; how much more are looking, listening, speaking, and acting [in accord with the rites] able to give one gravity?![61] Then, what could make one not be firm in learning? "Having a presence which inspires people to look from afar with awe"[62] is also then a matter of course.

"Doing one's best and being trustworthy [*chung-hsin* 忠信]" is the root of advancing in virtue. This is what is called "completing it by silent meditation, and securing the faith of others without the use of words, depending upon their virtuous conduct."[63] If someone doesn't know this and yet wants to enter virtue, how is that different from [wearing] "linen, fine or coarse"[64] yet wanting to be warm or "inhaling wind and drinking dew"[65] yet wanting to be filled. There is no such principle!

Now unless people are either the most intelligent or the most stupid,[66] all are capable of doing what is good and also what is not good. Thus, can the molding and shaping [of their character] have nothing that waits upon friends to practice? Even with Tzu-kung's worthiness, Confucius still advised him, "You should seek the patronage of the worthy among the counselors [*tai-fu* 大夫] and make friends with the *jen* among the *shih* 士 [scholars or officers]."[67] Indeed, serving the counselors of a declining age and making friends with *shih* of meager formalities, "it is difficult side by side with them to be *jen*."[68]

Unless it be a Sage, who is able not to have any mistakes? Only by correcting them is one a valuable teacher. A mistake is a mistake.[69] "Ch'u Po-yü at the age of fifty knew the error of forty-nine."[70] [That] is also mistakes. But the petty person [*hsiao-jen* 小人] is mistaken in practice [while] the exemplary person [*chün-tzu* 君子] is only mistaken in disposition. What constancy do *jen* and rightness have? Pursuing them is to be an exemplary person; abandoning them is to be a petty person. Also, what constancy do lack of *jen* (inhumanity) and unrightness have? Following them is to be a petty person; abandoning them is to be an exemplary person. The reason that exemplary persons are not afraid of correcting [mistakes] is that they know these not having constancy.

The reason that petty persons are afraid of correcting [mistakes] is that they are complacent toward familiar constancy.[71] Yen Hui is "teacher to a hundred generations,"[72] yet [Confucius] said, "[Hui] doesn't make the same mistake twice."[73] Chi-lu (Tzu-lu) was also teacher to a hundred generations. "When anyone told him he had made a mistake, he was delighted."[74] Hsün Ch'ing once called him a "yokel" [*pi-jen* 鄙人].[75] Indeed, he also made mistakes. How could we take once having made mistakes as harming their being teacher to a hundred generations? To know this is to know that "the mistakes of an exemplary person are like eclipses of the sun and moon"[76]—there is no loss of brightness. But people today, due to once having made mistakes, discard themselves and abuse themselves,[77] and suppose that to the end it is not possible for them to be good. Then coming to those who gloss over [their mistakes] with impressive appearances, this is also foolish.[78]

1:9 Tseng Tzu said, "Conduct the funeral [of your parents] with meticulous care and continue sacrifices to remote ancestors, and the virtue of the common people will return to abundance."

Hsieh said: "The nourishment of parents when living is not sufficient to be accounted a great matter; it is only a proper send-off when they die that can be considered a great matter."[79] Therefore, when human feeling reaches to its highest extreme, it cannot be artificial [*wei* 偽].[80] Making for them outer and inner coffins, burial clothes and coverlets, performing for them the spring and autumn sacrifices—how could the Sage force the people? When someone has a feeling about "foxes' eating"[81] and "the falling of frosty dew,"[82] it is not for the sake of [appearances in front of] others that it is so. Use this to direct yourself, and your virtue will return to abundance; use this to teach the people and the people's virtue will return to abundance.

1:10 Tzu-ch'in asked Tzu-kung, "When the Master arrives in a state, he invariably gets to know about its government. Does he seek this information? Or is it given to him?"

Tzu-kung said, "The Master gets it through being cordial, good, respectful, frugal, and deferential. The way the Master seeks it is, shall we say, different from the way others seek it."

Hsieh said: This section discusses learning having already completed the moral nature. Internal fullness must have radiance manifest and seen outwardly.[83] Indeed, it is "impossible to conceal the genuine";[84] thus it is manifested in the Sage's manner and form. Indeed, if one is coarse, harsh, and emotionally agitated, then certainly one's hair will stand on end and one's cap will be raised up. If one is inflexible, fierce, cruel, and perverse, then one's appearance will be hostile.[85] When it comes to [such people] seeking [information], they certainly try to follow others' [wishes] by being pleasing. It is not possible to enumerate all such [examples]. Be that as it may, when virtue reaches to the point of a Sage, there is certainly the appearance of a Sage. This is like the saying, "The demeanor of the Son of Heaven should be characterized by majesty; of the princes, by gravity."[86] Is not the appearance of the Sage "frank though respectful"?[87] Is it not "affable"?[88] Is it not "moving at ease"?[89] Is it not "universal"?[90] In weakness, not making things insulted, and in strength not making things afraid, how could only "cordial, good, respectful, frugal, and deferential" be sufficient to describe him?

Indeed, it is possible to be pure [*ch'ing* 清], and it is more difficult than cordiality. Cordiality is the expression [*fa* 發] of purity and harmony. It is possible to be harmonious, and it is more difficult than being good [*liang* 良]. Goodness is the expression of ease and directness. Originally not having the heart-and-mind to insult others, how could his appearance be anything but respectful? Originally not having the disposition of wasteful extravagance, how could the application be anything but frugal? Originally not having the heart-and-mind of contending and forcing, how could his actions be anything but deferential? Coming to this point, then he is serene and dignified. How could his serenity not be like spring and his dignity like autumn? How could his demeanor not be observable? How could his awesome manner not leave an impression? How could he not be harmonious and happy? How could he not be solemn and reverent? "Keeping distant from violence" and "keeping distant from boorishness" are not worth mentioning.[91] His appearance and manner being like this, how could the disciples not be able to learn to reach this?

Indeed, one who has the heart-and-mind of wrathfulness is certainly not cordial; one who has the disposition of jealousy and destructiveness is certainly not good; one who has the heart-and-mind of wanting to be above others is certainly not respectful; one who has the intention of impressing others is certainly not frugal; and one who has the heart-and-mind of "[opposition between] things and myself"[92] is certainly not deferential. Thus, "cordial, good, respectful, frugal, and deferential," is it only the Sage who is capable of being so?

Now we have departed from the Sage a long time, [but] imagining his form and appearance according to these five qualities can still cause people to be inspired. "How much more [inspiring] to those who knew him personally!"[93] In the case of the lords of Lu and Wei, even though they were very mediocre and even contemptible, when observing a person like this were they alone able not to be surprised and even incredulous? Were they alone able not to feel close to him and even revere him? How could one who wanted to have achievements in the state not go and consult him?[94] Although he may not have been one who was employed at that time, still he would have been one who was revered at that time. [Thus he said, "Were there affairs of state,] though I am not given any office I would still get to hear about them."[95]

If those engaged in learning have a heart-and-mind toward the awe-inspiring manner of the Sage, they also know the means by which to advance in virtue. So then, someone like Tzu-kung can be said to be good at observing the Sage, and can also be said to be good at discussing virtuous conduct. Could it be that we know only about the Sage through this description? We can also know Tzu-kung through this.

1:11 The Master said, "Observe what a person has in mind to do while his father is living, and then observe what he does when his father has passed on. If, for three years, he does not alter his father's ways, he can be said to be a filial son."

Hsieh said: [In the case Confucius described saying,] "Since your father and elder brothers are still around, you are hardly in a position to put immediately into practice what you have heard,"[96] to "observe what the person has in mind to do" is possible. [In the case described by the saying,] "Establish yourself in the practice of the Way, so as to make your name celebrated in future ages . . . this is the fulfillment of filial piety,"[97] to "observe what the person does" is possible. [With respect to] "for three years, he does not alter his father's ways"—how could he think that the father's ways could not bear change? Indeed, if for three years the worthy handle it, then it is "like a fleeting white horse passing a crevice."[98] At that time [during the mourning period], one is agitated, like searching for something and not getting it, and frustrated, like following someone and not catching up. When sitting, one sees the parent's [shadow] on the wall; while eating, one sees the parent's [reflection] in the broth. With respect to the father's ways being permissible to change or not permissible to change, what respite is there to be concerned about it?[99]

1:12 Yu Tzu said, "Of the results brought about by the rites, harmony is considered most valuable. Of the ways of the Former Kings, this is the most beautiful, and is followed alike in matters great and small. Yet it sometimes will not work. To aim always at harmony without regulating by the rites, because one knows only about harmony, also will not work."

Hsieh said: As for the way of ritual and music, their functions are different yet their substance is the same.[100] They constrain [*fan* 反][101] each other in order to complete each other. As for [the dyadic pairs] Yin and Yang, strong and weak, movement and quiescence, *jen* and righteousness, the cultured and the martial, not one of them is not like this; why should ritual and music alone not be so?[102] Yu Tzu knew to consider "harmony as valuable"; indeed, he has seen something of this. To know this is to know [the meaning of] "the wine was clear . . . yet they did not venture to drink; the meat was dry yet they did not venture to eat."[103] How could it be forcing [people] by harming the nature [*hsing* 性] for drinking and eating? How could "one offering with one hundred bows"[104] or an [offering] bench not being for leaning be [a matter of] forcing [people] by harming the nature for relaxation and being at ease? All the world found it suitable, and later generations were at ease with it. From [King] T'ang to the Chou, for many thousands of years, there was no worry or agonizing consideration about not sharing [in ritual] with the common people and having them be discontent as a result of separation.[105] Father and son had more closeness; ruler and minister had more order; feelings and nature were more abundant; customs were more artless [*tun* 敦]. Is it not that they "considered harmony as valuable" and reached to this?

The grace of the former kings has already weakened and ritual and culture do not come from authentic intentions, but come from forcing oneself. They do not come from according with the innate pattern [*li* 理] but stop with ornaments and appearances. To specialize in such [artifice] is in general like the Chi family's sacrifices.[106] "Although they had a strong appearance and a serious and respectful heart-and-mind . . . [instances of] limping and leaning during the sacrifice" were numerous.[107] I am afraid that such ritualists causing people to have difficulty in this way is worse than [Yüan Jang's] excessive haughtiness and presumptuousness in "squatting while waiting."[108] When it comes to this, the ritual of harmony is already lost.

Since true Confucians have not gained official position, it is not the time for them to institute [the rites]. Moreover, hide-bound scholars [*ch'ü-shih* 曲士][109] are bound to the practice of worldly customs and none is able to discover their [true] source. There are some who suppose [ritual] to be "artificial";[110] there are some who consider it to be difficult in order to discipline the world; and there are some who consider it to be "the wearing thin of loyalty and good faith."[111] Essentially they just discuss trivial derivatives and do not reach to [the intentions of] the former kings. How is this not a case of "[those who] pass my gate but do not enter my house"?![112]

[As for] "followed alike in matters great and small, yet it sometimes will not always work,"[113] [the Sage] was afraid that people would not distinguish. With respect to one bow and one obeisance, amid ascending and descending, the Sage still maintained [grades of] abundance and diminution [of ceremony] therein.[114] How much more in "matters great and small"! So his applying harmony toward counselors of lower rank was necessarily different from that toward counselors of higher rank.[115]

[As for] "knowing about harmony and always aiming at it, without regulating it by the rites," [the Sage] indeed despised such disrespectfulness. How could "dishonor in serving a ruler" and "disaffection among friends" not be due to "frequent [reproofs]"?[116] How could losing regulation among family members not be due to women and children being frivolous? Knowing this, then one knows what is to be regulated. The reason that the Sage's harmony is different from [ordinary] people's harmony is simply that he knows their (that is, ritual and music) having [dyadic] opposition.[117] "Following [ritual] in matters great and small" and "not regulating [harmony] with ritual," therefore equally "will not work."

1:13 Yu Tzu said, "Being trustworthy in word is close to being righteous, in that it enables one's words to be repeated. Being respectful is close to being observant of the rites, in that it enables one to stay clear of disgrace and insult. If, in promoting good relationship with relatives by marriage, a person manages not to lose the good will of his own kinsmen, he is worthy of being looked up to as the head of the clan."[118]

Hsieh said: "Repeat" [*fu* 復] here is like "repeat" in "[Nan Jung] repeated [the lines about] the white jade scepter."[119] When words reach the point of causing people to repeat them, this can be called "good speech." When words are trustworthy, they surely are already good—how much more are they "close to being righteous"! [When they are] trustworthy, this is words being certainly possible to practice. [When they are] righteous, this is words being "consistent with one's station."[120] [When words are] trustworthy and close to being righteous, then for generations they can be a guide for the world. [They will] enable those with understanding in later generations also to be able to nourish virtue. When words reach to having this quality, could there be any that would not [merit being] repeated?

Not to be insulting is called being respectful; "performing in measure" is called ritual.[121] There are those who fear others and do not dare to insult them; this is not necessarily performing in measure. There are those who cherish themselves and do not dare to insult others; this [likewise] is not necessarily performing in measure.

What is "performing in measure"? [For example,] "lifting [the *hu* 笏] and kneeling down, hands cupped together,"[122] [and] "on passing the [ancestral] sacred tablet one must quicken the pace"[123]—this is ritual; this is the way of the minister. What disgrace could there be? "Presenting oneself before one's father's friends" and serving them like one's own father [and] serving "someone double one's age" like one's own father[124]—this is ritual propriety; this is the way of the son. What disgrace could there be? In working, compete to be first; in walking follow behind—this is ritual propriety; this is the way of the younger brother. What disgrace could there be?

What is "not performing in measure"? It is to be highly respectful when it is not someone toward whom one ought to be highly respectful. [In being] highly respectful when it is not someone toward whom one ought to be highly respectful, [if] you grant it to those who are above you, it is like the way of concubines and wives. If you grant it to those who are below you, it is the way of "opening the door for favorites, from whom you will receive contempt."[125] Its beckoning of disgrace is inevitable.

"*Yin*" 因 [relation, cause] is relatives [*ch'in* 親]. Therefore "*yin*" 姻 as in "relatives by marriage" and in "marriage" all follow upon relation. Extending my heart-and-mind of "looking upon all with impartial *jen*,"[126] although "all within the Four Seas are brothers,"[127] this can only be called "generalized caring [*fan-ai* 汎愛]"; it cannot be called "being relatives." What are "relatives"? Linked together by surname, knit together by [sharing] meals, these are the inner [father's side] relatives. The outer [mother's side] relatives are the connections of nephew, maternal uncle, and relatives-by-marriage. For those like this, when they are alive there should be the enjoyment of feasts, and when they die there should be the degrees of mourning clothes. How could it be that other people would be able to imitate the relation that is called "relatives"?

Extending this and expanding it, are there also those who can be treated as relatives? There are. Is it not the ruler who guides me? Is it not the teacher who educates me? Is it not a friend who completes me? These three, although they do not naturally belong [to my family], can be treated as relatives. Excluding these three, are there others who can be treated as relatives? I fear that I will not avoid flattery and being of low esteem. If I am a flatterer of low esteem, how could this be called the way of "having respect for my body."[128] Only when relatives do not lose that [position] by which they are relatives, then afterward is it possible to be looked up to by the clan.

To be trustworthy and not go back on one's word, to be respectful in order to manage one's conduct, to treat [others] as relatives in order to be close to them—from the common people's observing this it can also be called beautiful conduct. But once one enters into an area that is not ritually proper and not righteous, it suitably is enough to beckon disgrace and come in for disrespect. Truly, to seek the Way is not difficult. [If one] wants to avoid these [errors], is it not through learning [that one does so]? Indeed, only through learning is it possible to illuminate goodness.

1:14 The Master said, "An exemplary person seeks neither a full belly nor a comfortable home. Such a person is quick in action but cautious in speech, and goes to those possessed of the Way to be put right. Such a person can indeed be described as loving learning [*hao hsüeh* 好學]."

Hsieh said: In this section, [the meaning] cannot be sought from the [simple] facts; rather we ought to infer from the disposition [*ch'ing-hsing* 情性]. Thus, in earlier generations there once were those who ate birds and beasts uncooked.[129] Yet when it came to the sages' changing it by means of cooking, only then did eating correctly desire its fullness [*pao* 飽]. There once were those who [lived in] "kiln-like huts and caves,"[130] yet when it came to the sages' changing them to palaces and houses, only then did dwelling correctly desire its comfort. How could this have been done by selfish human cleverness? Thus the sages were those who "were divine in the transformations they wrought, so that the people were content."[131]

Why only in the case of those who love learning should there not be seeking fullness or seeking comfort? [Consider] "the way the mouth is disposed toward tastes . . . [and] the four limbs towards comfort";[132] can one escape [common human tendencies] and alone be different from others? This is not so. Confucius, Mencius, Tseng-Tzu, and Yen Hui are the teachers for those who engage in learning; among their affairs are those that can be investigated in this matter. For example: "[Eating] coarse rice and drinking water, using one's elbow for a pillow,"[133] and "a ladleful [of water] to drink, a bowlful [of rice] to eat, living in a mean dwelling";[134] can these be called "not seeking fullness and comfort"? It is not so. This is not having resources, and therefore not being able to make one's circumstances pleasing. If they had had the resources, then they would have done it. [Consider] "on the earlier occasion using [only] three tripods"[135] and "changing the mat when about to die";[136] can these be called not seeking fullness and comfort? These cases of not obtaining [something better] cannot be considered pleasing. Due to "taking their place after the counselors,"[137] these were done. If this is so, then in what do the sages and worthies exceed ordinary people? [It is this:] to say that sages and worthies have the heart-and-mind (disposition) of "seeking" comfort and fullness—that is not appropriate.

"Quick" does not mean "hasty"; the sages are not ones who are hasty.[138] "Quick" does not mean "aggressive"; being aggressive is what the wild do.[139] Now being hasty and being aggressive are things that the sage indeed does not do. But coming to the common people, if they are not [a little] hasty, then they have the weariness of being clumsy and slow and not getting things done; if they don't become a little wild, then they have the worry of not being able to forget about their early ways.[140] In between these two [shortcomings], isn't there only "quickness"?

"Cautious" [*shen* 慎] does not mean "terse" or "silent." When there is something to be said—say it! How can one be terse? How can one be silent? "Cautious" does not mean "to speak haltingly." [It is said of Confucius that] "when speaking with counselors of the upper rank, he was frank though respectful";[141] "at court, he was fluent."[142] What is called for is sternness.[143] When there is something to be said, say it. To speak and moreover be stern, can this be called "cautious"? What caution is there once it leaves the mouth? Leaving aside what is beyond these several cases, it is possible to seek for the principle of being cautious in speaking. However, it is difficult to speak about.

[As for] "going to those possessed of the Way to be put right"—a person who does not have a profound intention to beautify their conduct and personally take up the learning of "inquiring earnestly and reflecting on what is at hand,"[144] cannot do so. Thus, those who lean on the gates and walls of the Sage and who speak mild, submissive words and accommodating words indeed are not few! But they cannot be called people who "go to those possessed of the Way to be put right." Before they have gotten it they want to stop; when it comes to hearing such words they are unable to refrain from idleness until they reach it. [As for] "clasping it firmly as if wearing it on one's breast, and not losing it,"[145] isn't there only the son of Mr. Yen [that is, Yen Hui]? There are those who are able to direct their efforts to these several points,[146] yet when we examine both their diligence and their performance, after all what are they really seeking for? How could one be so, except through the love of learning? If one disregards the example of Yen Hui, there is no way to talk about these things. For we ought to know that after Mencius, there was no further instance of someone resembling this.

1:15 Tzu-kung said, "What do you think of the saying, 'Poor without being obsequious, wealthy without being arrogant'?" The Master said, "That will do, but better still, 'Poor yet delighting in the Way, wealthy yet observant of the rites.'" Tzu-kung responded, "The *Odes* say, 'Like bone cut, like horn polished, like jade carved, like stone ground.' Is this not what you are talking about?" The Master said, "Ssu, only with someone like you can I discuss the *Odes*. Tell such persons something and they will know what its implications are."

Hsieh said: This section teaches that those whose native substance is beautiful ought to learn in order to complete it. "Poor without being obsequious," is not having obsequiousness toward others. "Wealthy without being arrogant" is not having arrogance toward others. These are [still perceived] in terms of the opposition of self and things [*wu wo hsiang-tui* 物我相對]. "Poor yet joyful," is to be poor and yet joyful in oneself. "Wealthy yet fond of the rites," is to be wealthy and yet in oneself fond of the rites. Then what do others have to do with me?

Thus indeed, [Mencius said:]

> Here is a basketful of rice and a bowlful of soup. Getting them will mean life; not getting them will mean death . . . When it comes to these being given after being trampled upon, even a beggar would not accept them.[147]

When someone calls [to a starving person], "Come [and eat]!" with condescending pity, even after apology there are those who would not take the food.[148] When has such a person ever been obsequious toward others? [But] observing his overly scrupulous will, when can he ever have joy? This is "poor without being obsequious" being simply different from "poor yet joyful."

The wealthy are [likely] recipients of ill-will [*yüan* 怨]. If they know the techniques to reduce ill-will, how would they dare to be arrogant toward others? The method to keep one's wealth for a long time is to be satisfied without being excessive. If they are able to know the techniques of keeping wealth, how would they dare to be arrogant toward others? However, their heart-and-mind of loving [only] themselves cannot avoid being stingy. When can such people ever attain to the rites? This is "wealthy without being arrogant" and "wealthy yet fond of the rites" being simply dissimilar.

Tzu-kung was a person who "heard one thing and understood two,"[149] and "[when Confucius] pointed out one corner, he was able to come back with the other three."[150] Therefore, he knew the significance of "Like bone cut, like horn polished / Like jade carved, like stone ground."[151] "Like bone cut, like horn polished," is learning through inquiry; "Like jade carved, like stone ground," is completing virtue. [Confucius] discussed with him about being "poor yet joyful; wealthy yet fond of the rites," and he knew the matters of learning through inquiry and completing virtue. Good, was it not, Tzu-kung's penetration! Ah! His was different from "old Master Kao's interpretation of the *Odes*"![152]

1:16 The Master said, "It is not the failure of others to know your abilities that should worry you, but rather your failure to know theirs."

Hsieh said: It is a principle [pattern] throughout the world that from below looking up to the heights is difficult, while from the heights looking down below is easy. Likewise, for the seventy disciples to know the Master was difficult; for the Master to know the seventy disciples was easy. How could there be exceptions in the way people know each other? As for a great person looking at a petty person, it is like seeing the person's liver and guts.[153] As for a petty person glimpsing an exemplary person [*chün-tzu* 君子], no one sees their scope. Observing from this point of view, is knowing others great? Or is being known by others great? Why not also feel urgent about knowing others? To feel urgent about being known by others—this is what troubles those engaged in learning.[154]

Analects Chapter 2

2:1 The Master said, "The rule of virtue [*te* 德] can be likened to the Pole Star, which commands the homage of the multitude of stars without leaving its place."

Hsieh said: The Pole (North) Star is the pivot of heaven. Because it resides in the center, it is called "the northern pole [*chi* 極]." Because the circumference it establishes is a "home" for the twelve stars (or heavenly bodies), it is called the North Star. In this can be seen "non-acting yet fully acting" [*wu-wei erh wei* 無爲而爲]." Thus, those who govern by virtue (or: excellence) are like it. Learning is to complete oneself; governing is to complete things. Although there is the distinction of inner and outer, at the point when their timing and placement are appropriate, then they are one. One who governs by virtue just extends what "I" have and together with the people accords with it, that's all. Therefore on the part of "myself" there is no toil; on the part of others it is easy to follow. Otherwise, one would in a bustling way take [trivial] things to be the important matter. Subsequently, to be able to make people follow oneself is to be an exemplary person [*chün-tzu* 君子] who dwells in a narrow, dirty alley accumulating *jen* and righteousness.[1] Supposing one suddenly attains all under heaven and is established, one will not necessarily be able to perform the deeds of Yü and Chi.[2] "Treating one's parents as parents and elders as elders" is not necessarily able to bring peace to the world.[3] "Without going beyond one's family, [the exemplary person] can bring education into completion in the whole state"—these words are not necessarily to be believed.[4]

2:2 The Master said, "Though the *Odes* are three hundred in number, they can be summed up in one phrase: "Not swerving from the right path [of thought]."[5]

Hsieh said: The *Odes* are the correct among the dispositions of the people, deriving from the beneficence [*tse* 澤] of the former kings. Once the beneficence of the former kings had run its course,[6] the *Odes* thereupon lost their flow. Coming forth from Ch'u and Han there still were Ch'ü [Yüan] and Sung [Yü], Su [Wu] and Li [Ling]. Among Wei, Chin, Ch'i, and Liang there were still Pao [Chao], Hsieh [Ling-yün], Ts'ao [Chih], and Liu [Chen]. Who can say that in the Spring and Autumn period [the poetic genius] was abruptly lost? But indeed, searching for those "stopping in propriety and righteousness,"[7] there are none. Those who do not "make their heart-and-mind at ease before speaking"[8] are unable to stop in propriety and righteousness. Thus, "Have no depraved thoughts" can be said to sum it up in one phrase.

Exemplary persons do not merely recite the words of the *Odes* but will also examine their dispositions, and not only examine their dispositions but also use them to examine the beneficence of the former kings. Indeed, although laws and systems, rituals and music [of high antiquity] are lost from this time, it is still possible to share in their profound and subtle meanings and transmit them. So, in general, the ways of speaking are "joyful but not wanton,"[9] pensive but not distressed, complaining but not angry, sad but not anxious. As in the Ode "*Lü yi* (Plaint over her lot)," the words do not go beyond saying: "[But] I think of the ancients, / That I may be kept from doing wrong."[10] In the Ode "*Chi ku* (Resenting those above)," the words do not go beyond saying: "Those do the fieldwork in the State, or fortify Ts'ao, / While we alone march to the south."[11] Coming to "Frequently engaging in military expeditions, the great officers were in service for a long time," it stops with: "He has brought on us this separation."[12] "Being away on service, without any period fixed for his return, thinking of his perils and hardships, satirized herein" does not go beyond saying: "Oh, if he be but kept from hunger and thirst!"[13]—that's all. If they are "speaking of the affairs of all under heaven"[14] [or] "extolling the form and appearance of sagely virtue,"[15] certainly without waiting for words this can be known. With respect to themes of anxiety, pensiveness, thinking, and consideration, who is able to delightfully roam without being pressed? This is the reason that Confucius made selections of them. When the one who made the *Odes* is like this, can those who read the *Odes* read them with a depraved heart-and-mind?

2:3 The Master said, "Guide them by edicts, keep them in line with penalties, and the common people will try to avoid trouble but will have no sense of shame. Guide them with virtue, keep them in line through the rites, and they will have a sense of shame, and moreover reform themselves."

Hsieh said: "Guiding" is the means to advise [the people]; "keeping in line" is the means to lead them. Edicts and virtue are prior and after; punishments and rites are outward and inward. Wanting to make their hearts-and-minds good, therefore there are virtue and rites. Wanting to make their conduct correct, therefore there are punishments and edicts. If the ruler "guides them by virtue and keeps them in line with the rites," then it is all right for punishments to be renounced. In the absence of virtues or rites, though punishments and edicts still exist, there is the grief of abandoning [genuine] human relations. When it comes to the point that both virtues and rites, and [proper] punishments and edicts are lost, then there comes the sadness of severity in punishments and edicts. When human relationships are abandoned, then [even] exemplary persons will come to violate rightness. When punishments and edicts are severe, then petty people will come to violate punishments. When exemplary persons violate rightness, those among them who have no shame and escape [punishment] will be many. How much more so in the case of petty people!

2:4 The Master said, "At fifteen I set my heart on learning; at thirty I took my stand; by forty I came to be free of doubts; by fifty I understood the mandate of Heaven; by sixty my ear was attuned; by seventy I could follow my heart-and-mind's desire without overstepping the boundaries."

Hsieh said: This section discusses there being no separation between the refined (final) and the coarse (initial) stages in the Way. It is just that there is a difference in whether or not the time is ripe [*shu* 熟]. Although he begins with learning, it can also be seen that the Sage is "born with knowledge."[16] [Yet] being born with knowledge is what the Sage specifically did not claim [*chü* 居].[17] Compare it with food and drink: at the outset, we already know that they can be relished, and when we have added [various forms of] cooking, and have laid out the seven utensils, and have found them palatable, and have become completely full and satiated, [then] we know the relishing and enjoying and the flavors being both mutually forgotten.[18] Although the beginning and end [of the process] are not the same, when have they ever been two separate things? To "set the heart on learning" is to set the heart on this. "Not overstepping the line (of correctness)" is not overstepping from this. How could there be two separate principles?!

Among these, when there is "taking a stand," then nothing is able to shake or snatch one away, and one is "persevering and firm."[19] When there is "being free from doubts," then one completely encompasses the [intrinsic] patterns of things and has no uncertainty. When there is "knowing the heavenly Mandate," then one knows that there is no distance between that from whence principled patterns come and from whence the nature [*hsing* 性, natural tendency] comes forth.[20] When there is "the ears being attuned," then inner and outer are both forgotten. Arriving at this point, then in the changes of give and take, affairs and things,[21] although one might want to add an intent therein, it is not possible to make any addition; although one might not want to add an intent therein, it is not possible to make any subtraction.[22] Although the heart-and-mind is never lost [*fang* 放],[23] yet it is no coming forth from concentrated attention. Although one has never thought [about it], however one has also never been without thought. Never having been without thought, therefore there is that which one desires. Never having lost [the heart-and-mind], therefore one does not "overstep the boundary."

When the Sage was a youth, he already knew this principle. One whose heart is set [on learning] knows that after his learning, he will be able to be calm and joyful. If one's seeing the Way is not clear, he will have absolutely no reason to be set on learning. Not yet knowing to take learning as his own affair, he will have absolutely no reason to be able to stand. Not yet able to stand, he will have absolutely no reason to be without doubts. When the heart-and-mind is not fully employed, and the nature moreover is not known, how can there be "knowing the Heavenly mandate"? If someone does not know the Heavenly mandate, then he and the Way become two, and he will have absolutely no reason for the ears to be attuned. So then, one who does not set the heart on learning abandons everything. There are some who by talk of the mysteriousness [*miao* 妙] of the Sage allowing the heart-and-mind to go freely, [advocate] not learning and yet being able; the more so we can see their wildness and recklessness.

Now we have already departed quite far from the Sage; for this reason, to know the Way and enter into virtue is especially difficult. Indeed, it is not the difficulty of knowing the lofty and brilliant, but rather that setting the heart on learning is difficult. Today the scholars of the world look at the matter of the Sage's will to learn and consider it only shallow and near at hand. As a result, how could they know: what harm does [his learning] do to his "knowing innately"? What harm [does it do] to his "practicing naturally and easily"?[24] With respect to innate knowledge, how could it be that the Sage knows everything? With respect to practicing naturally and easily, how could it be that he is "a natural" at everything? Having that which he did not yet know, he rightly came to know it through learning. Having that at which he was not yet "a natural," he rightly became natural at it through learning. "Starting from below and getting through to what is up above"[25] is really just like this. If learners are able to "read texts intelligently and discern the meanings," to "seek the company of teachers," and to "select their friends"[26]; [if they] resolutely know to attain the Way and "[not] backslide,"[27] resolutely know not to be shaken or snatched by outside things, and resolutely know not to be misled and enticed by heterodox starting-points [*i-tuan* 異端], [then they] can begin to deserve the name of "setting the heart on learning," and can begin to know the Sage as a youth. As for this, can it but be called "difficult"? [In the case of someone who is] not yet able to be this way, even though they may say, "[My] heart is set on learning," I must say that it is not yet so.[28]

2:5 Meng Yi Tzu asked about filial conduct. The Master answered, "Have no violation." While Fan Ch'ih was driving, the Master told him about the interview, saying, "Meng-sun asked me about being filial. I answered, 'Have no violation.'" Fan Ch'ih asked, "What did you mean?" The Master said, "While they are alive, accord with the rites in serving them; when they die, accord with the rites in burying them; accord with the rites in sacrificial observances for them."

2:6 Meng Wu Po asked about filial conduct. The Master said, "Give your father and mother no other cause for anxiety than illness."

2:7 Tzu-yu asked about filial conduct. The Master said, "Nowadays for a person to be filial means no more than that they are able to provide for their parents. But even hounds and horses are provided for. If there is no reverence, where is the difference?"

2:8 Tzu-hsia asked about filial conduct. The Master said, "What is difficult to manage is the expression on one's face. As for the young taking the burden when there is work to be done or letting the old first enjoy the wine and the food—can that by itself deserve to be considered filial?"

Hsieh said: The four men asking about filial piety were not the same; the Sage discussing with each is quite different. But it cannot be said that the central points are not the same. Indeed, "parents are Heaven." One who does not use the way of serving Heaven in serving parents is not sufficient to be called a filial son.[29] As for the Sage discussing Heaven, one saying is not sufficient to include everything of the heavenly principle [*t'ien-li* 天理], and thus is not sufficient to be the sagely words. Since we have already called it "the heavenly principle," how could there be any distinction of shallow and profound? As for Fan Ch'ih, [Tzu-]yu and [Tzu-]hsia, although they were not "in bed with"[30] the descendants of the Three Houses of Huan,[31] they were not ones whose heart was set on sagely learning. However, in their words they brought up filial piety, which cannot but be called a question close to the point. If the Sage, in answering them, left aside "human nature and the heavenly Way," what else would there be to say?![32]

What is it, then, that is called "human nature and the heavenly Way"? It is caring [*ai* 愛] and reverence. "[When your parents are] alive, serve them according to the rites"; if we put aside caring and reverence, then we will not be able to do it. "Giving your father and mother no other cause for anxiety than illness," "the young taking the burden when there is work to be done or letting the old enjoy the wine and the food when these are available," these are caring. Not like "hounds and horses being provided with food," yet "not shown reverence." Be reverent, then show care. [As for] reverence, is it not "when [your parents are] alive, serve them according to the rites?" "When alive, serve them according to the rites" has been discussed in detail by sages and worthies. I will not repeat it again here.

"When they die, comply with the rites in burying them," is not talking about the beauty of inner and outer coffins and the clothes [of the deceased]. One must be earnest [*ch'eng* 誠] and faithful, and it will be acceptable. "Comply with the rites in sacrificing to them," is not talking about preparing the delicious tastes of all the nine regions. Knowing that if one does not use "the grain of a person of *jen*" to sacrifice to one's parents,[33] they certainly do not enjoy it, then how could using "the grain of a person of *jen*" to sacrifice to parents not be "complying with the rites"?

What is "ritual [*li* 禮]"? It refers to "according with principle (or pattern, *li* 理)". According with principle, then one will "have no violation [*wei* 違]."[34] It was not that Fan Ch'ih was vague and did not know this. His asking the question to the Sage was only that he wanted to make sure of the steps.

"Give your father and mother no other cause for anxiety than illness." The care of a father and mother for their child has no [limit] to which it will not reach. Since they love him, for this reason they are anxious about him. They are anxious in case he is found at fault and gets into danger; they are anxious in case he is laughed at and gets into shame. How much more [are they anxious] about daredevils and fierce fighters! If I am not mindful of this, then there will be "parents not [being able to] forget about me"; there will not yet be my not forgetting about parents. How could that not be unfilial? How could that not be failing to accord with principle? Not according with principle, how could that not be "contrary"? Being contrary, how could that be knowing "when parents are alive, comply with the rites in serving them"?!

"Nowadays for a person to be filial means no more than that he is able to provide his parents with food. Even hounds and horses are, in some way, provided with food. If a person shows no reverence, where is the difference?" This refers to care without reverence. One obsessed with hunting cares for hounds; one who rides in affluence cares for horses. This is the same as "liking a beautiful color";[35] both are the utmost of caring for something. Therefore, Confucius particularly used hounds and horses to explain to him. Caring for one's parents yet not being reverent is still not sufficient to be considered filial. It is truly that "serving parents is like serving Heaven."

"What is difficult to manage is the expression on one's face." This does not mean improperly following the father's orders, merely to make one's facial expression pleasing. Coming to a point when the father has a fault, then "[his offspring] should with bated breath and a bland aspect . . . admonish him."[36] "If the offspring has admonished and is still not listened to, they should follow it with loud crying and tears."[37] Coming to "anticipation of their wishes, carrying out their aims, and instructing them in the Way,"[38] these all, I'm afraid, will do injury to one's expression. "As for the young taking the burden when there is work to be done," they must personally want to bring their effort. "When there is wine and food, letting the old enjoy these," [means when] wanting to remove [the food from the altar],[39] it is necessary to request [to give them] what is given.

2:9 The Master said, "I can speak to Hui all day without his disagreeing in any way, as though he were somewhat dim. However, when I take a closer look at what he does on his own after he has withdrawn, I discover that it throws light on what I said. Hui is not dim at all."

Hsieh said: In the teaching of the Sage, although there are many methods, none is better than answering questions. Mencius once said, "How much more inspiring the Sages must have been to those who were fortunate enough to know them personally!"[40] Indeed, when the words enter and the heart-and-mind penetrates, this is the most close and intimate. However, if one does not reach the point of "not being contrary,"[41] then [this opportunity] is lost; then books have nothing by which to be considered different.[42] This is the reason that Yen-tzu alone was considered "eager to learn."[43] As for "not being contrary," indeed sound and hearing mutually penetrate [and] although it is with the ear that one listens, yet in reality it is with the spirit that one receives. Outside of the Sagely learning, Yen-tzu did not have an iota of selfish intention. Abiding among "looking, listening, speaking, and acting,"[44] firmly clasping [the good] therein,[45] untiring therein,[46] [through] his love [of learning] and diligent [practice], his heart-and-mind was unobstructed [*hsü* 虚]. [Just by] observing in thought the Sage's appearance and manner, he would still get something from it; how much more listening to the Sage's words! Then his "not being contrary" was a necessary [consequence]. As for "when I take a closer look at what he does in private after he has withdrawn from my presence" and thence knowing "Hui is not dim after all," the Sage's meaning indeed is not [literally] like this. The Sage could investigate Yen-tzu's appearance and manner immediately and intimately (literally, between eyebrows and eyelashes); he already knew that Hui was not stupid. This saying was only to prove that the Sage investigated Yen-tzu's conduct in detail. These are not words describing true (that is, literal) facts.

2:10 The Master said, "Look at the means people employ, observe the path they take and examine where they feel at home. How is a person's character concealed from view? How is a person's character concealed from view?!"

Hsieh said: "Look at the means [*i* 以] a person employs" is looking at his conduct; "observe the path [*yu* 由] he takes" is observing his actions; "examine where he feels at home" is examining his disposition [*ch'ing-hsing* 情性]. Although the conduct of the exemplary person [*chün-tzu* 君子] and the petty person are not the same, how could it be so without cause? There must be "means." If we look at the means, then it is possible to observe their understanding. Although the actions of the exemplary person and the petty person are not the same, "who can go out without using [*yu* 由] the door? Why, then, does no one follow [*yu* 由] this Way?"[47] Therefore, the Way includes the exemplary person and the petty person; the path they use is one. From this, it is possible to see the virtue of people. "There are cases of exemplary persons not being *jen*";[48] however, what they feel at home in is *jen*.[49] When has a petty person ever for a whole day not been in the good (that is, not done even one good thing)? However, what they feel at home in is profit. What is essential is the long term; then it is possible to know what they feel at home in. From this, it is possible to investigate people's authenticity [*ch'eng* 誠].

"Look at the means they employ" is looking at their changing affairs; "observe the path they take" is observing their constant affairs; in "examine where they feel at home," what is essential is the long term. As for "the means," it is still possible for a petty person to think and consider doing so; it is also possible to force oneself to reach [a standard]. Coming to "the path they use," then among actions and attitudes, it is difficult to force. Coming to "what they feel at home in," then in the midst of the face and expression there surely will be that which appears; this is especially difficult to force. Tseng Tzu said, "What ten eyes are beholding and what ten hands are pointing to—isn't it frightening?"[50] He is saying that there will surely be indications visible outside. However, one who does not have virtue will not be able to observe people with this way. Therefore, in the case of the exemplary person looking at the petty person, it is "like seeing their internal organs."[51] The source of later generations making the distinctions of nine proofs and twelve outflows also comes from this. Yet how could they be like the Sage, so simple and easy?!

2:11 The Master said, "A person who reviews the familiar and gets to know what is new, is worthy of being considered a teacher."

Hsieh said: In the continuity of new and familiar, it is only the changes of affairs that are not the same. However, observing them from virtue as a unity,[52] no one knows their difference. "Getting to know what is new by keeping fresh in mind what is familiar" is like saying "reaching the greatest height and brilliancy and following the path of the Mean" and "achieving breadth and greatness and pursuing the refined and subtle to the limit."[53] Then, the familiar and the new are not two extremities [*chih* 至]. Since reviewing the familiar does not harm knowing the new, then knowing the new is not so-called "rushing forward."[54] Since knowing the new does not harm reviewing the familiar, then reviewing the familiar is not so-called "not forgetting one's early ways."[55] How could one who [merely] complies with things and follows the tracks [of others] be able to "review the familiar and know the new"? Therefore, [one who is able to do so] "is worthy to be a teacher." As for "the learning supplied by memory of conversation,"[56] how could it be talked about on the same day?!

2:12 The Master said, "An exemplary person [*chün-tzu* 君子] is not a vessel."

2:13 Tzu-kung asked about the exemplary person. The Master said, "An exemplary person puts words into action first and only then follows with words."

2:14 The Master said, "The exemplary person openly associates [with others] but does not collude; the petty person colludes but does not associate."

Hsieh said: The [categories of] good in the world, such as *jen*, wise, sage, and worthy, all have a basic definition; only "exemplary person" cannot be discussed from only one starting-point. "There are four things in the Way of the exemplary person,"[57] which the Master did not claim [*chü* 居],[58] yet to call him a Sage is still acceptable. Confucius also said, "There are cases of exemplary persons not being *jen.*"[59] Thus to call him a worthy is also acceptable. What is essential is that which is preserved, that which is nourished. Indeed, [the exemplary person] "understands what is righteous" and does not "cherish generous treatment," "gets through to what is above," and is not "known in small things."[60] [Since] what they preserve and nourish is like this, to try at once to think of their character as a person, how can it be classified? They must be called "exemplary person"; that is acceptable. At this level, how could it be possible to define such a person as "a vessel"?!

Although what they have is "intelligible without words,"[61] what the exemplary person practices certainly does not have the selfishness of binding and being stingy. Due to it not being possible to define him as a vessel, therefore, [Confucius] said, "is no vessel." Yen [Hui] and Min [Tzu] with regard to "having one aspect of the Sage" were not necessarily superior to Tzu-hsia, Tzu-yu, and Tzu-chang; however, they were complete replicas.[62] Mencius with regard to purity, responsibility, and harmony did not necessarily exceed Po Yi, Yi Yin, and Hui of Liu-hsia; however, he did not learn from those three.[63] For one who knows this, it is possible to understand the principle of "is no vessel."

By virtue of his being "intelligible without words,"[64] therefore [Confucius] said, "He first puts his words into action before allowing his words to follow his action." "First putting his words into action" is putting into practice what he has said. "Afterward [allowing them] to follow it" is putting what he practiced into words. One who is able to reach to "virtue harmonizing the unprincipled and insincere,"[65] although he does not speak of it, yet people all know of his being filial. One who is "[genuinely] able to give away a state of a thousand chariots,"[66] although he does not speak of it, yet people all know of his being upright. Then [when] actions reach to [it] but words do not reach to [it], what harm does this do to his being an exemplary person? As in "without words yet the four seasons run their course,"[67] also what harm does this do to its being Heaven? It is by virtue of their not having the selfishness of binding and being stingy, therefore [Confucius] said [that the exemplary person], "associates [*chou* 周][68] but does not collude [*pi* 比]." The exemplary person does not have selfish likes and does not have selfish dislikes. Not having selfish dislikes, then to whom does he feel close [*ho suo ch'in* 何所親]? Not having selfish likes, then there are none to whom he does not feel close. As with the light of the sun and moon, how could it choose the land and [only] afterward shine on it? Therefore, he makes "associations" and afterward it is possible not to "form cliques." The other is bound in feeling "between moisture and foam," saying "only I and you," that is the affair of children.[69] A stout-hearted knight moreover would not do so. Yet do you say that an exemplary person does so? Knowing this, it is possible to know that the exemplary person does not collude but forms associations.

2:15 The Master said, "If one learns from others but does not think, one will be perplexed; if one thinks but does not learn from others, one will be in peril."

Hsieh said: When wisdom is exalted, then virtue will be even more exalted;[70] "studying below,"[71] then occupations will be increasingly broad. Exalted virtue and broad occupation, although they are not two substances, yet from the viewpoint of one whose internal and external are not combined, they cannot but have two entries [*chin* 進]. "Thinking" is a matter of knowing [*chih* 知]; what is wanted is honor. "Learning" is a matter of practice [*hsi* 習]; what is wanted is humility. Able to practice, but not able to think in order to [get to the] essence [*ching* 精] [of] it, then there is the defect of "practicing but not examining." [72] "The people cannot be made to understand it" [73] is exactly speaking of this. If knowledge reaches to it [74] but one is not able to learn in order to gather it, then there is the fault of "fully exerting greatness and losing wherein one dwells." [75] The Master instructing Chi-lu concerning "the six qualities and six faults" [76] is exactly speaking of this.

2:16 The Master said, "To attack strange starting-points [*i-tuan*, heterodoxy] can do nothing but harm." [77]

Hsieh said: Obscure with respect to small achievements, in the dark about great principles, all are what is called *i-tuan* 異端. However, in the time of (Dukes) Ting and Ai, [78] (their) departure from the former kings was still close. Therefore, their losses also were not yet distant. For the time being preserving them (the *i-tuan*), then was not yet very harmful. [If they] wanted to attack them, then there was no evidence. "Without evidence, they cannot command credence, and not being credited, the people would not follow." [79] This would do harm, than which nothing is greater. I am afraid they could not avoid "pushing the waves and helping the billows [and] loosing the wind to stop a wider burning." [80] Therefore, with respect to "oddities, powers, chaos, and spirits," the Master just did not discuss them, that's all. [81] There was no matter of attacking. If another person once understands my "gate and walls," [82] and is able with good intention to follow me, then with respect to *i-tuan*, how could he wait for my words to judge?! The case of Mencius with respect to Yang [Chu] and Mo [Ti], having no choice but to debate, is different from this. [83]

2:17 The Master said, "Yu, shall I instruct you what it is to know? To know what you [ought to] know, and not know when you [ought] not, that is knowledge." [84]

Hsieh said: Tzu-lu was more courageous than the [other] disciples, and he was accustomed to the boundary [*chi* 際] of life and death. Thus indeed, he had that which greatly exceeded others. However, he gave up his former attitude and roamed in the school of the Sage. His making effort was not more than a period of several years. With that kind of pace [lit., in the case of his speed], then with respect to the Way, how could he not have the fault of strongly

venturing and forcefully choosing? Therefore [Confucius] particularly instruc-
ted him with this [saying].

"Knowing it as knowing it"[85] means what can be known [and] cannot not
be known. "Not knowing as not knowing" means what cannot be known [and]
is not necessary to know. As in "theories of life and death," [and] "the
situation of ghosts and spirits":[86] among the common people, then they are
considered to be unknowable; however, among those engaged in learning
[*hsüeh-che* 學者] if one doesn't know, how could this not be a deficiency?!
The distance of a thousand years, "beyond the six directions,"[87] then [among]
the common people there are those who consider not knowing [about these] as
shameful. Among those engaged in learning, supposing [one] does not know
this, then still what harm does it do to the Way? Examples like this, indeed,
cannot be exhausted with one word. Supposing [one is] able to
discriminatingly understand about this, it may be called knowing what
"preserves the heart-and-mind";[88] it may also be called being able to fulfill "the
heart-and-mind of [knowing] right and wrong."[89] Therefore, [Confucius] said,
"This is knowing."

2:18 Tzu-chang was studying in order get an official's salary. The
Master said, "Listen widely, leave out what is doubtful, and
speak with caution on the rest; then you will make few mistakes.
Observe widely, leave out what is hazardous, and put the rest
into practice with caution; then you will have few regrets. When
in your speech you make few mistakes and in your action you
have few regrets, an official's salary will follow as a matter of
course."

Hsieh said: This is Tzu-chang asking the Master about the learning for seeking
an official career, and the Master instructing him with the Way of seeking an
official career. Some gain it from going to lectures, some gain it from
advantageous friends. All are what is called "hearing."[90] How could others
cheat me?! However, [what I am] not yet able to be at ease with in my heart-
and-mind, all are what is called "doubtful." If doubtful, then "don't speak [of
it]" is permissible. "Seeing" is not the seeing of seeing with eyes, but rather the
seeing of seeing in the understanding. When seeing is not doubtful, afterward
action is not doubtful. Regarding seeing having that [with] which [one] is not
yet at ease, then not to act on it is permissible. Hearing the doubtful and
speaking of it, seeing the hazardous and practicing it, although others do not
blame me, will I alone in heart-and-mind have discontent?[91] "Reproach [*yu*
尤]"[92] is not others reproaching it, but rather self-reproach.

"Use your ears widely [listen much] but leave out what is doubtful," can be without caution. [Confucius] also said, "repeat the rest with caution." "Use your eyes widely [look much] and leave out what is hazardous," can be without caution; [Confucius] also said, "put the rest into practice with caution." These all have a profound meaning. One who merely considers what is close at hand,[93] will they be able to get it? Being able to reach to this is not only "words filling up the world without a mouthful of excess; action filling up the world without ill-will or evil."[94] When you are like this, then if the world does not apply [*yung* 用] goodness, you yourself will apply goodness. How could people overlook you? When there is no heavenly principle, [in the world] then you yourself have heavenly principle, then with spirits listening to it, how could [they] overlook you? This is the reason that there is the Way of necessarily obtaining an official position.

2:19 Duke Ai asked, "What must I do before the common people will submit to me?" Confucius answered, "Raise the upright and set them over the crooked and the common people will submit to you. Raise the crooked and set them over the upright and the common people will not submit to you."

Hsieh said: The ways in the world are two, the crooked and the upright. The dispositions [*ch'ing* 情] in the world are two, liking and disliking, and that's all. Liking the upright and disliking the crooked is the highest disposition in the world. Following what they like is the reason that the people submit to you. Going against what they like is the reason that the people depart. So then, the way of governing the world, the state, and the family is only between raising and setting aside, that's all. Indeed, [the actions of] raising and setting aside are the same [in both cases]; yet [the result], order and chaos, is different. Albeit, from ancient times, the days of order have been few but the days of chaos many. How could it be that other [rulers], in their heart-and-mind, stubbornly wanted to raise the crooked and set them over the upright, thereby opposing the heart-and-mind of the whole world?! Indeed, without the Tao to illumine it, then what you yourself consider to be upright, what you yourself consider to be crooked, will also be various.[95]

2:20 Chi K'ang Tzu asked, "How can one get the common people to be reverent, and to do their best with enthusiasm?" The Master said, "Rule over them with dignity and they will be reverent; be filial and treat them with parental kindness and they will do their best; raise the good and instruct those who are not capable and the people will be imbued with enthusiasm."

Hsieh said: "Reverence, doing their best [*chung* 忠] and enthusing [each other]," although it were the common people of the Three Dynasties, what could be added to this? Those like the Chi family, also how could they know that this way truly can govern the world, the state and the family? What he asked, indeed, was only what was transmitted in old family handed-on customs. These three are all what are in the disposition; how could it be possible to force [them] to be so? "Reverence" has no substantial form [*t'i* 體]; only dignity can gather it. "Doing one's best" is surely there; only filial piety and parental kindness can occupy it. "Enthusiasm" is not forced; cause them to know the good as the good, and indeed [those who] do not wait to be summoned and follow will [consider it] light. These three all cannot artificially be good. Those engaged in learning, though they take this to nurture themselves, it is permissible. Though the common people cannot be made to know this,[96] can they be caused not to come forth according to this way? Therefore, what is called "completing oneself" and "completing things" having two [different] end-points is not possible.[97] As for the later generations merely using models and regulations [*fa-tu* 法度] and rules of conduct to discipline and control the human heart-and-mind, we often see the futility of their techniques.

2:21 Someone said to Confucius, "Why do you not take part in government?" The Master said, "The *Book of History* says, 'Oh! Simply by being filial and friendly to one's brothers a person can have influence on government.' This is also taking part in government; why must I insistently 'take part in government'?"

Hsieh said: "Simply by being a good son and friendly to his brothers" is like saying "Let the father be indeed father, and the son son; let the elder brother be indeed elder brother, and the younger brother younger brother."[98] This is the government of one family. If one state is able to be like this, that is the [proper] government of one state. If the whole world [*t'ien-hsia* 天下] is able to be like this, that is the government of the whole world. How could there be two Ways?! They equally are this Way. If one person applies it, we do not see its accumulating but it becomes much; if the whole world all applies it, we do not see its divisions but they become few. The world is all in chaos, yet oneself alone is ordered; on the part of one of "solitary goodness"[99] managing it, [this] does not harm being the great peace. The world is all ordered, yet oneself alone is not yet ordered, on the part of one whose "burden is heavy"[100] managing it, he still would consider it not sufficient. So, those who discuss government after all have the limitation of self-and-things [*wu-wo* 物我]! To say that "simply by being a good son and friendly to his brothers" is not yet enough to practice government, how could these be the words of one who knows the Way?!¹⁰¹

2:22 The Master said, "I do not see how a person who is not trustworthy in word can be acceptable. When a pin is missing in the yoke-bar of a large carriage or in the collar-bar of a small carriage, how indeed can they be driven?"

Hsieh said: "To have it in oneself is called 'trustworthy.'"¹⁰² "A person who is untrustworthy," then, is [one who] does not have it in oneself. Confucius and Mencius discuss trustworthiness like this. However, from the viewpoint of those who are not engaged in learning, neither will anyone know what is called "having" is having what thing, nor will anyone know "not having" is not having what thing.¹⁰³ Now, moreover, it is discussed with the closeness of form and nature.

The Sage is the apogee of human relations. Although one cannot take "trustworthiness" to describe [the Sage], however from his causal nature [*yin-hsing* 因性] describing him, he also can be said to have this nature. From his "fulfillment of [bodily] form"¹⁰⁴ describing him, naturally he can be said to have this form. The Sage indeed is like this, but as for the multitude of people also, how could they abandon this nature? When have they ever departed from this form? On what basis could they be called "not having"?

It is said, "Looking and not seeing is the same as having no eyes; listening and not hearing is the same as having no ears."¹⁰⁵ Then even if we call it "not having this form," what unacceptability would there be? When one holds onto the heart-and-mind of wanting to harm others,¹⁰⁶ then this is almost having no "natural compassion."¹⁰⁷ When one harbors the heart-and-mind of "boring holes in the wall and jumping over,"¹⁰⁸ then this is almost having no "shame at evil."¹⁰⁹ Even if we call it "not having this nature," likewise what unacceptability would there be?

Heaven gives it, and yet oneself is not able to have it. When [they've] come to this point, [if you] seek their having that by which to be differentiated from "the escape of the soul brings about change"¹¹⁰ (i.e., a wraith), [it is] already rare; is it still possible to call them human? The world thus indeed has the theory of "shades."¹¹¹ Only in the case of such person is it possible to judge them by describing their neither having nor not having (or: neither being nor not being).

[To speak of] "a pin missing in the yoke-bar of a large cart or in the collar-bar of a small cart," [is] picking an analogy which is really not far away.

2:23 Tzu-chang asked, "Is it possible to know what ten generations hence will be like?" The Master said, "The Yin built on the rites of the Hsia. What was added and omitted can be known. The Chou built on the rites of the Yin. What was added and omitted can be known. Should there be a successor to the Chou, even a hundred generations hence can be known."

Hsieh said: Tzu-chang's intention was to say "the distant must be experienced by the nearby." [He] can also be said to be speaking of "thoroughly investigating principle." But intention has its utmost (i.e., limit); therefore, the Sage did not consider it to be so, and also did not consider it not to be so. He directly and freely [elaborated] with his own meaning, that's all. What was the Sage's meaning? He considered that as for those who came before him, already "It is tested by the experience of the Three Kings and found without error."[112] On the part of those who come after him, it also ought to "wait for a hundred generations for a sage [to confirm it] without a doubt."[113] The principle of successive changing,[114] of omitting and adding,[115] comes from fully exhausting, then changing, and with the common people finding it appropriate. Do not say, compile the excesses of Tchou,[116] not one can be successively changed; hand down the posterity of Yao, not one can be decreased or added. Look at that in which its principle resides, what it is like, that's all. From this it is possible to see the Three Kings' diligence [*yung-hsin* 用心]. [In] this, the Sage's attitude with respect to the principle of successive changes, omitting and adding, can be known. As for who would be a successor to Chou, maybe it would be one who uses the sagely to succeed to the sagely? One could not get to know. Maybe it would be one who uses the violent to change the violent?[117] [We] cannot get to know. Does he know the reason for omitting and adding? [We] cannot get to know. Does [he] not know the reason for omitting and adding? [We] cannot get to know. One can only "have its evidence in the common people,"[118] and examine it in the ghosts and spirits.[119] Although at a distance of a hundred generations, if a Sage does things, must it [not] be the same as this? This can be known.

2:24 The Master said, "To offer sacrifice to ancestral spirits other than one's own is obsequious. Seeing what is right, to leave it undone shows a lack of courage."

Hsieh said: [In] this section, even though the meanings of the two parts are different yet in intention they mutually follow. Yin and Yang exchange and there are spirits [*shen* 神].[120] Form and *ch'i* 氣 (vital energy) separate and there are ghosts (ancestral spirits, *kuei* 鬼).[121] One who knows this is wise; one who attends to this is *jen*. Only someone [in whom] *jen* and wisdom are united can institute sacrificial rites. The intention of the sacrificial rites [is this]: for those [to whom it is] permissible [to offer sacrifice], allow people to approach [*ko* 格] them,[122] [and] do not allow people to "treat them as entirely dead."[123] For those [to whom it is] not permissible [to offer sacrifice], allow people to keep them at a distance,[124] [and] do not allow people to "treat them as entirely alive." When treated as entirely alive, their ghosts will be spiritual; when treated as entirely dead, "their ghosts will not be spiritual."[125] Then how could "the situation of ghosts and spirits" not be clear and evident?[126] In the case of those who are neither knowing nor *jen*, they are not sufficient to participate in this; moreover, how could they know about there being ghosts which are not spiritual?

Also, at a time when government and education are lost, ritual and rightness abandoned, then no wonder those who sacrifice to what is not to be sacrificed to are so confused. If the Sage at that time abruptly wanted to speak of it, there was no evidence; if he wanted to order it with ritual, [he had] no position. Out of his worry that was deep and his thought that was far-reaching, what was done was to say that if [they were] able to know which ghosts and spirits were to be sacrificed to and sacrifice to them, then the principles of ghosts and spirits would not be unclear to all under Heaven, and the sacrificial rites would still not be lost [*sang* 喪]. Indeed, the principle of ghosts and spirits not being clear to the world originally comes from sacrificing to what should not be sacrificed to.

This is the way to pray with respect to not being obsequious thereby. Knowing obsequiousness as shameful, and in addition being able to be brave with regard to not doing so,[127] is very near to constant and correct. Therefore [Confucius] continued it with "Seeing what is right, to leave it undone shows a lack of courage."

[As for being] *jen* and also not warlike, indeed there are such among princely families. Then indeed there are cases of knowing reaching to it, yet courage not being able to act.[128] However, how can what we call "seeing" in this [passage] really be [simply] "seeing"?! If it is like their seeing what they are fond of, then how could [they] not be able to be like parents loving an infant. If it is like seeing what they hate (as an enemy), then how could [they] not be able to be like a hawk or falcon following small sparrows. [If they] say [they] are not able do it, I will not believe it. [As for] those who are calmly and non-aggressively[129] *jen*, there are those who are like Wu Yu and are able to resist the sway of rampant illegitimate power [*pa-hu* 跋扈].[130] This can be seen. How much more a person who "looking within finds oneself upright"?[131]

Original Chinese Texts

As noted in chapter 2 of this book, Hsieh's *Analects* commentary has been preserved by Chu Hsi and his students in the *Lunyü ching-i* (LYCI), along with related sayings of the Ch'eng brothers and commentaries by several other Cheng disciples and associates. In the original LYCI text, the passages of commentary by the various authors appear *seriatim* after each verse of the *Analects*. Hsieh's commentary for *Analects* chapters 1 and 2 has been collated and translated in appendices 1 and 2, respectively. The corresponding original Chinese text of Hsieh's commentary is provided here for reference.[1]

1.2

謝曰上章論為學之大體此一節論求仁之方也夫仁之為道非舉之莫能至而語之亦難其語愈博其去仁愈遠古人語此者多矣然而終非仁也如恭信敏惠為仁若不知仁則止知恭信敏惠而已克己復禮為仁若不知仁則止知克己復禮而已門如見大賓使民如承大祭此特飭身而已何以見其為仁者也認此特愼言而已何以見其子之論仁蓋亦如此爾為孝弟者近仁然而孝弟非仁也可以論仁者莫如人心人心之不偽者莫如事親從

1.1

謝曰學而時習者無時而不習如坐則習坐如立則習立如齊則習齊時習也造次必於是顛沛必於是顛沛時習也遠方來非我之所同然後謂之朋自古人先得我心之所同求之今人信其己不異皆朋也能無樂乎有朋自朋之閒有不相知者況它人乎是以一鄉之善士斯得一鄉之善士知我者希則我貴矣人不知而善士斯得天下之善士知天下之子之閒猶有不相知者況今之人不知不慍則其自待者厚斯不亦君子乎學而時習之所以自處也有朋自遠方來同乎己者也人不知而不慍之所也而不慍焉則幾於樂矣論語一經大抵不出此三者飯疏食飲水曲肱而枕之樂亦在其中矣顏子一簞食一瓢飲不改其樂皆不慍之謂也

1.3

謝曰仁雖難言知其所以為仁者亦可以知仁矣若孝
弟為仁之本是也知其遠於仁者亦可以知仁若巧
言令色鮮矣仁是也然巧言令色之亦難禮曰辭
信辭欲巧詩稱仲山甫之德曰令儀令色然所謂辭
欲巧亦鮮仁乎仲山甫之德亦鮮仁也哉至於聖人所謂
孫以出之辭亦巧矣遜顏色怡如也岂至於小人蓋嘗以
好其言語善其顏色直以為鮮仁也豈能知出辭氣可遠鄙倍則
訐以為直矣言何嘗巧雖內荏而色厲焉能知出辭
何者為巧色若能知之矣
知之矣此宜學淺悶而力索不可以言語道也

1.2 cont.

兄莊子曰子之事親命也不可解於心此可見其良心
矣至於從兄則自有生以來良心之所未遠者以事親
從兄而充之則何往而非仁也夫親親從兄之心行之
而不著習矣而不察終身由之而不知者伺能不好犯
必面冬溫凊昏定晨省而充之者亦可以為孝矣闌巷
上作亂況於真積力久攜而充之之者亦可以為孝矣閭巷
能之然而出入則但孝弟閭巷之人亦
能之長幼有序徐行後長亦可以為有道亦可
入道亦不可也但孝弟也可以為弟矣閭巷之人亦
之閭蓋古人猶難言之其可言者此而已若
知此心則知仁矣
實欲知仁則在力行自省察吾事親從兄時此心如何

1.5

謝曰學之為王者事久矣子路曰有民人焉有社稷焉
何必讀書然後為學此言是也然夫子不與之者特非
所以待子羔也子貢謂夫子之得邦家者所謂立之斯
立道之斯行綏之斯來勁之斯和夫子未嘗得邦家也
知其為邦家之道則可以為天下國家矣
國不得志行乎家人其為道一也況千乘乎古人得百

1.4

謝曰九流皆出於聖人其後愈傳而愈失其真如子夏
之後流為莊周則去聖人遠矣獨曾子之學用心於內
故傳之無弊其親永而得之者有子思子思之學中庸
可見也考中庸則知曾子矣閭而得之者有孟子考
子之書可以見子思矣蓋其所學至真至正如此惜
乎其瑰言奇行不盡傳於世如孟子所稱何子之事不
載於論語者甚多則其泯滅者有矣今其幸存者不
孟心乎如此三者未可以淺近論也為人謀而忠與人
交而信傳而習此三者幾於無我則能之是學之至也
此乎為人謀一有不忠矣與人
以處人者一有不盡則非忠矣於人則非特
言而後信也雖然有恩以相愛粲然有文以相接一有
不盡則非信矣以其二物故以異於執柯伐柯他人之
習則道自我自我終之不能相合而
而祝之猶以為遠者以其二物故以異於執柯伐柯他人之
道我何嘗何以異於執柯伐柯則以惟習而熟則道與
我為一矣凡此三者幾於無我則能之是學之至也

1.7 　　　　　1.6 　　　　　1.5 cont.

1.5 cont.

里之地而君之皆可以一天下朝諸侯則千乘之國亦
可以用心矣敬事而信節用而愛人使民以時雖天
下亦何獨不然敬事而信敬而信也節用則能愛人使
民以時民事不可緩也

1.6

謝曰此言學者當知所先後也天下之人愛親爲易盡
孝爲難事長爲易盡孝弟爲難能盡孝弟則能明人之大
倫又能庸言之信庸行之謹充其無欲害人之心而親
仁以成己則在我者立矣至於行有餘力則以學文者
其游於藝之謂乎

1.7

謝曰賢賢易色如惡惡臭如好好色天下之誠意無易
於此此好德如好色亦可謂好德之至也事父母能竭
其力共爲子職而已乎君能致其身不敢有已而斯
朋友交言而有信在我有不欺矣父子有視君臣有義
朋友有信能如此則其長効必能有序夫婦必能有別
矣則舜所以爲舜其法可傳於天下者其能外是乎聖
人人倫之至也此而曰未學不得謂之不學也其亦幾
於生而知之者乎

1.8

謝曰此一段常分爲四事自事忠信友如己改過學者
闕一不可也人孰有生而知之者乎能學而知之困而
知之亦善矣孰有安行之者乎能利而行之勉強而
行之亦善矣此非論生知安行者也自重忠信如己
者學之事也過而改困而學也君子不重則不威學則
不固中庸曰齊明盛服非禮不動所以修身也齊爲
服所以見其修身乎蓋爲冠所以正其首爲
腹所以重其足所以防其躁也古之君子必佩玉逃則
入也夫容貌衣服之間俯仰能移容也而況視聽言動
能自重敬學如之何而不固也則其儼然人望而
亦徐事耳忠信進德之本也所謂默而成之不言而信
存乎德行者也然不知此而欲進德何異希今之學
欲温吸飽飲欲飽無是理矣夫人自不言而信
皆可以爲善可以爲不善則其薰陶冶能無待於朋
習乎以子貢之賢孔子猶以爲其友之賢者友其
士之仁者事襄世之大夫友薄俗之士難與並爲仁
矣自非聖人孰能無過惟其改之爲貴師也過也遂
伯玉行年五十而知四十九之非亦過也但小人過於
行事君子過於情性耳夫仁義亦何常之有蹈之則爲
子舍之則爲小人不仁不義亦何常之有循之則爲小
人舍之則爲君子所以勿憚改者如其無常也而曰
小人所以憚改者安於故常也顏回百世師也而曰
不武過季路亦百世之人告之以有過則喜有過而告其爲百世之
謂之鄙人蓋亦有過矣盍以爲有過而告其爲百世之

1.10　　　　　1.9　　　　1.8 cont.

謝曰此一節論學之既成德性內充必有光輝著見乎
外者蓋誠之不可揜也故以與人儀形明之蓋誠威
慨則必與上衡冠很慢則其容悴悴然將有水者
必以喜隨人如此者不可勝計也然則德至於聖人之
地者其必有聖人之容如天子穆穆諸侯皇皇是也聖
人之容閒閒侃侃非提非揖總總柔而可爲也非剛
不爲物懼其惟溫良恭儉讓足以名之乎蓋清可爲也
而難於溫溫者清和之發也和難之何而不恭本無侮
人之心貌如之何而不泰本無侮
易直之發也本無人之心貌如之何而不泰本無侮
泰之心用如之何而不儉本無競強之心行如之何而
不讓至於此則泰然矣儳然矣其泰然也豈不如秋
儳然也豈不如秋豈不容止可觀豈不威儀可象豈不

謝曰養生不足以當大事惟送死可以當大事蓋人情
之至極而不可以僞也彼有威於狐狸之食霜露之降非爲
聖人豈以強民哉彼有威於狐狸之食
人而然也以此處己則己德歸厚矣以此教民則民德
歸厚矣

師乎知此則知君子之過如日月之食焉無損於明也
今人以當有過而自弃自棄以爲終不可以爲善遂至
於文且飾者亦惑矣

1.12　　　　1.11　　　　　1.10 cont.

謝曰禮樂之道異用而同體相反以相成陰陽也剛柔
也動靜也仁義也文武也莫不如是何獨禮樂不然乎

謝曰有父兄在如之何其聞斯行之觀其志可也立身
行道揚名於後世孝之終也觀其行可也三年無改於
父之道豈以爲父之道不忍改與蓋三年之閒賢者處
之則如白駒之過隙嘗是時皇皇然如有求而弗得望
望然如有從而弗及坐則見親於牆食則見親於羹於
父之道可改也不可改也亦恤乎

和樂豈不莊敬遠暴慢不足道也遠鄙倍不足道也夫
容貌如此諸弟子豈不能學以致乎豈有念慮之心
者必不溫有忮刻之心者必不良有欲上之心者必不
恭有驕人之意者必不儉有物我之心者必不讓則溫
良恭儉讓其惟聖人之乎今去聖人久矣此五者
想見其形容猶能使人興起而況於親炙之者乎借令
顏之也學者有心於聖人威儀之閒亦知所以進德
矣雖不能當時所用猶爲當時之開亦知所以
獨能不親且敬乎欲有爲於一者其能不就而謀之
乎雖不能有心於聖人威儀之閒亦可謂善觀聖人矣
行焉於此豈獨知聖人哉又將以知子貢矣

有子知以和為貴蓋有見於此也此則知酒漿而不敢飲肉乾而不敢食豈非勉以事飲食之性哉一獻而百拜几設不倚豈非勉以事安逸之性哉天下宜其由世安之自唐至周數千載聞無苦心刻意不與民其由難所不安之患父子益親君臣益序情性益厚風俗益敦得非以和致然也先王之澤既衰禮文不出於誠意而出於勉強不出於循理而止於飾貌從事於以臨祭者多矣禮家使人如此之難儒既不得位無制作斯也往往如季氏之祭雖有強力之容肅欽之心破居於以肆之愈出於世俗之習而其能察其源也或以為薄之時曲士又牽於世俗之習而不及先王也豈非過我門而偽者有矣或以為難以強世者有矣或以為忠信之薄者有矣室者欺小大由之有所不行恐其無辨也聖人於人我室者欺小大之語末流而不及先王也豈非過聖人於一拜一揖升降之閒猶有隆殺焉又況小大乎則其用節之蓋惡其瀆也事君之辱朋友之疏豈不以數乎家人之失節豈不以嬻子嘻嘻乎知此則知所節矣聖人之和於大夫者必有異於上大夫矣而和而不以禮節之所以異於人之和者知其有反而已小大由之有和於大夫者必有異於上大夫矣以禮節之故均於不可行也

善也信乎求道非雜欲免斯者其惟學乎蓋惟學可以明也行矣然一入於非禮非義之地適足以招恥辱取不敬其言恭以飭其身親不失其親然後可宗也信不食所尊身之道惟親親以與人同眾人觀之亦可謂美外亦有可親者乎吾恐不免於諂賤也既諂賤矣尚謂友乎成我也其惟君乎治我也其惟親舍此三者之親者乎有之其惟師乎敎我也其惟天賜亦可以親矣戚所謂親親者若是者人可以疑倫也推此而達之亦可之聯外親也謂親親繼之以姓綴之以食內親也甥舅姻婭謂之親何謂親親繼之以姓綴之以食內親也甥舅姻婭心雖四海之內皆兄弟也此特可以謂之汎愛同仁之親也故恭敬而致恭施於在我之上者猶妾婦之道於在我之下者是啟寵納侮之道也其招恥辱必矣因所當恭而致恭而致恭於在我之上者非所當恭也也何恥辱之有何謂不中節非所當恭也非也子道也何恥辱之有見父之執猶事父年長以倍猶事兄也何恥辱之有勞則爭先行則必後禮也臣道未必中節也何謂中節自愛以超禮也必趨禮事父道不敢侮人者有矣未必中節也非也子道也非此其有不可復者乎不悔之謂恭中節之謂恭畏人而為天下者是也義則言之中倫者是也信且近義則可以世行者是也義則言之中倫者是也信且近義則可以

謝曰復當如復白圭之復言至於使人可復亦可謂善言矣言而信固已善也而況於近義乎信則言之必可

1.14

謝曰此一節不可以事求當以情性推之蓋上世當有
茹毛食腥者矣及至聖人易之以烹炰則食正欲其飽
者也當有陶復陶穴者矣及至聖人易之以宮室則居
正欲其安也此豈今人之私智爲哉蓋聖人神而化之使
民宜之於安佚獨與人異乎是不然孔孟曾顏學者之師
也其事有可考者如疏食飲水曲肱而枕之與簞食瓢飲
食在陋巷可謂不求飽且安乎是不然此無財不可以
爲悅者也有財則爲之矣前以三鼎死且易餐可謂不
求斯爲之矣然則聖賢所以過人者安在謂聖賢有求
也求飽安之心則不可爲悅非欲速與事之聚
後斯爲之矣而言豈可簡邪豈可默言之而便正欲
也敏於進取之謂進言之而言豈可簡邪豈可默慎
聖人既言之至眾人無欲速則有遲鈍不及事之聚
不入於狂則有不忘其初之思於斯兩者之間其
乎慎言伺默之謂言之而言意而閭閭在朝廷而便正欲
非嘔嗎之謂與上大夫言而言意既可謂慎乎既一出於口
其腐也言之乎而言意而屬可謂慎乎既一出於口
何者之外可以求慎言之理矣然而難
言也就有道而正焉者爲鶩意於美身爲切問近思之學
者不能如此也蓋倚聖人之門牆說巽言從法言者豈
少哉此未可謂就有道而正焉者未得其欲罷不能及
聞之語而不惰既得之拳拳服膺而弗失惟顏氏之
子乎有能從事於茲數者亦考其用心考其行事泉
何求哉非好學而何當從心考其行事不可以語此矣
當知自孟子以後無復夢夢於此矣

1.15

謝曰此一節論質美者當學以成之也質而無謟者無
謟於人也富而無驕者無驕於人也此物我相對之稱無
也貧而樂貧而自樂也富而好禮富而自好禮者也人
亦貧而於我哉豈一簞食一豆羹得之則生弗得也有所
至於蹴爾而與之乞人也不屑及其嗟來之志何時而
弗食若斯人也何嘗謟於人哉亦何屑及其嗟來之志
亦異高叟之爲詩矣
義如切如磋如琢如磨成德之事善乎子貢之逵也嗚呼其
而好禮而知問學成德之事善乎子貢之逵也嗚呼其
隅而能以三隅反者也故知有如切如磋如琢如磨之
驕與富而好禮者也若斯人者亦何時而中禮邪此當之
心能知邪亦不敢驕於人滿而不溢所以長守
能樂邪能知所以守富之術亦不敢驕於人然其自愛之
知所以損怨之術亦何敢驕於人而樂也富者之府
富而能知所以守富而無謟於人哉而樂也富然怨所以之府
弗食若斯人也何屑及其嗟來之志亦何時而
亦貧而於我哉豈一簞食一豆羹得之則生弗得也有所
謟於人也富而無驕者無驕於人也此物我相對之稱無

1.16

謝曰天下之理自下視高則難自高視下則易如七十
子知夫子則難夫子知七十子則易人之所以相知何
有不然者大人之視小人如見肺肝小人而窺君子莫
見晱域以是親之知人者爲大乎人知者爲大乎誠亦
急於知人乎急於人知此學者之患也

2.1

謝曰北辰天之樞也以其居中故謂之北極以其所建周於十二辰之舍故謂之北辰於此見無爲而爲者爲政以德者如之學以成己政以成物雖有內外之殊及其時措之宜則一也以德爲政者特推吾所有與民由之而已故在我則不勞在人則易從故苟爲不爾將弊弊然以物爲事而後能使民從己者是居陋巷積仁其親長其長未必能爲禹稷之事也親義之君子一旦中天下而立未能平天下也不出家而成於國此語未必信也

2.2

謝曰詩者民之情性之正出於先王之澤先王之澤既熄而詩遂亡其流出於楚漢猶有屈宋燕李魏晉齊梁之間猶有鮑謝陶劉勤謂當春秋之時而遠亡蓋求其言亦將以考其情性非特以考其情性又將以考先其止乎禮義則止乎禮義非易其心而後語者不能則思無邪可謂一言以蔽之矣君子之於詩非徒誦王之澤蓋法度禮樂雖亡於此猶能并與其深微之意而傳之故其爲言率皆樂而不淫哀而不困恐而不怒哀而不愁如緣衣傷己之詩也其言不過曰我思古人伴無斁兮緊敬怨上之詩也其言不過曰土國城漕我獨南行至軍旅起大夫久役止日自貽伊阻佼行無期度思其危難亦風爲不過曰尚無飢渴而已若夫天下之事美聖德之形容固不待言而可知也其與愁憂思慮之作孰能優游不迫也孔子所以有取焉作詩者如此讀詩者可以邪心讀之乎

2.3

謝曰道所以勸之齊所以率之政與德爲先後刑與禮爲表裏欲以善其心故有德欲以正其身故有刑政道之以德齊之以禮雖刑措可也惟無德而刑政猶存爲傷人倫之廢至於并與刑政而亡刑政之苟人倫廢則君子至於犯義刑政苟則小人至於犯刑君子犯義是以無恥而苟免者多況於小人乎

2.4

謝曰此一節論道之精粗無二時熟與不熟有差別耳雖始於學亦可以見聖人生而知之也生而知之特聖人之不居也嘗如欲食焉始則知其可嗜已而加烹飪焉已而設匕箸焉已而可於口已而飽飫厭足已而知嗜好與滋味兩相忘於是矣何嘗有二物哉志於學志於是也亦豈有二理哉其閒有所謂立則物莫能搖而貞固矣有所謂不惑則規矩物理而無疑矣知天命則知理之所自來至於此則酬酢事物之變雖欲加意焉不可得而益雖欲不加意焉不可得而損心雖無思焉而非出於收心雖未嘗放焉亦未嘗無思也未嘗無思故有所欲嘗放故不喻矩未可得而成童時已知有此理焉者知其學而後可以安且樂也若道之不明決無志學之理未知以學爲事決無可立之理惡有知天命者乎不知天命則理心且不盡性且不知豈有知天命者乎不知天命則與道爲二決無耳順之理然則不志於學者舉廢之矣

2.4 cont.

或乃以謂聖人縱心之妙不學而能益見其狂且妄也今去聖人既遠所以知道入德為尤難蓋非知高明之難而志乎學為難也今天下之士視聖人志學之事特以為淺近又豈知何害其為生知乎何害其為安行乎聖人之於生知物物而知之於安行豈非知之有所未而安之有所未安亦當學而知之有所未安之下學而上達正如是爾學者儻能離經辨志親師擇友決知中道可以知豈可以為外物搖奪決知不為異端誘惑始可以當志學之名始可以知聖人為童子時出是可不謂難矣乎未能如此雖曰志乎學吾必謂之未也

2.5 – 2.8

謝曰四人問孝不同聖人語之各異要之非不同也蓋親天也不以事天之道事其親者不足以為孝子既謂之言天也一言不足以該天理不足以為聖言既謂之天理矣何淺深之有哉樊遲游夏雖不在孔門三桓子孫非志於聖學者然其言有及於孝亦不可不謂之切問也聖人對之舍性與天道又烏得而言哉何謂性與天道則聖人不能言也父母唯其疾之憂皆能有養而不敬敬也然則愛敬非孝事之不如犬馬皆能有養而不敬敬也然則愛敬非生事之以禮乎生事之以禮死葬之以禮非謂棺槨衣衾之美也必誠信可矣祭之以禮非

2.5 – 2.8 cont.

謂備九州之美味也知不以仁者之粟祀其親必不享也則以仁者之粟祀其親豈非以禮乎何謂禮順之謂也順理則無違矣違非茫然不知也有問於聖人之者特欲質其目而已父母唯其疾之憂父母之愛其子無所不至惟其疾之是以憂之也以苟嘗取危是所愛也以苟笑取辱是所憂之也而況於好勇鬥很乎苟不念此則親之不忘我者有矣我之所以不忘親者未之有也豈非不順理不順理豈非違也違也違則能有生事之以禮豈非不孝哉今之孝者是謂能養至於犬馬皆能有養不敬何以別乎此言愛之至也故特以犬馬語之者愛馬而不敬猶不足以為孝信乎事親之至於先意愛其親而好色豈以隨之至於有過則色難此非荀於從父之令悅其顏色而已下氣怡色以諫之諫而不聽則號泣以隨之有過則承志喻父母於道皆恐傷其色有事弟子服其勞乃欲躬致其勞也有酒食先生饌欲將徵必請所與也

2.9

謝曰聖人之教雖多術然莫善於答問孟子嘗曰而況於不遠之地則與亡則嘗無以異也此顏子所以獨於親炙之者乎蓋言入心通最為親且切然苟不至為好學所謂不違者豈聲聞相通雖以耳聽而實以神受也顏子於聖學之外無一毫私意留於視聽言動之聞拳拳為孜孜為其好篤其心虛想起觀聖人之形容

2.10

2.9 cont.

猶將有得況於聞聖人之言乎則其不違也必矣所謂
退而省其私然後知囘也不愚聖人之意蓋不如此聖
人於眉睫之間察顏子之形容已知其不愚矣爲此言
者特以是證聖人察顏子之詳非眞實之言也

謝曰視其所以視其行事也觀其所由觀其動作也察
其所安察其情性也君子小人雖行事不同然者必有
因而然者必有以也則可以觀其所以識君子小
人動作雖不同然誰能出不由戶何莫由斯道也故道小
有君子小人其所由一也於此則可以見人之德君
子而不仁者有矣然而所安者仁小人何嘗一日不
於善然而所安者利要其久則可以知其所安於此
可以察人之誠視其所以視其變事也觀其所由觀其
常事也察其所安要之以久也所以在小人猶可以思
慮爲亦可以勉強至至於所由動作態度之間難乎
勉強也至其所安則必有發見者尤所難勉乎
強也嘗子曰十目所視十手所指其嚴乎言此見於外
也然非有德者不能以此道觀人故惟君子視小人如
見其肺肝也後世爲九證十二流之別其源亦出於此
然豈如聖人爲簡且易也

2.12 – 2.14

2.11

謝曰天下之善如仁智聖賢皆有主名特君子不可以
一端論也君子之道四夫子所不居則謂之聖人亦可
又曰君子而不仁者有矣而非小人亦可要其所存
養者如此一想其爲人將何以目之乎其必謂之君
子也此等豈可以器名之乎其所有雖
閔子於聖人之一體未必偹於子夏子游子張然而具體
也孟子於清和未必過於伯夷伊尹柳下惠然而具體
學三子也知此者可以識不器之理矣以其不言而
喻故曰先行其言而後從之先行其言也而
後從之言其所行也能至於德諧頑嚚雖不言而人皆
知其爲孝能諧千乘之國雖不言而人皆知其爲廉則
其所行固無係於言其不言亦何害乎故君子恥其言
行至而言不至何害其爲君子如不言而四時行焉何
不比也彼係情於濡沫之間謂惟予與汝者乃兒女之
不親如日月之光豈擇地而後照乎故周而不比君子
事此士上不爲也而謂君子爲之乎知此者可以知君
子不比而周也

謝曰新故之相因特事變之不同然自一德者觀之莫
知其異也溫故而知新猶言極高明而道中庸致廣大
而盡精微則知新非進取之謂在知新不害其爲溫故
則知新之謂能溫故知新豈徇物踐迹者之所爲乎
不忘其初之謂能溫故知新豈徇物踐迹者之所爲乎
故可以爲師矣與記問之學豈可同日而語哉

2.15

謝曰知崇則德益崇下學則業益廣崇德而廣業雖非
二體然自其內外不合者觀之不可以不兩進也思知
之事也欲其崇學習之事也欲其卑能智矣而不能思
以精之則有習矣而不察之病民不可使知之正謂是
也知及之而不能學以聚之則有窮大而失其所居之
破夫子語季路以六言六蔽正謂此矣

2.16

謝曰隱於小成暗於大理皆所謂異端然當定哀之時
去先王猶近故其失亦未甚姑存之則未甚害也欲攻
之則無徵無徵則弗信弗信則民弗從其害也莫大
焉恐其不免挑波助瀾縱風止燎也彼有一識吾之於
神特不語而已無事於攻也故夫子於怪力亂
善意從我則其於異端豈待吾言而判哉若孟子之於
楊墨不得不辯則異乎此

2.17

謝曰子路勇於學者也彼尤閑於死生之際蓋有大過
人者然故舍故態而遊夫子之門其為功不過數年之間
若是其速則於道豈無強探取之以
此知之為知也可以知不可以知為不知者也不知為
不可知不必知者也如死生之說鬼神之情狀在眾人
則以為幽然而在學者苟不知此豈非闕疑
千歲之遠六合之外則眾人有以不知為愧者吳在學
者儘不知此則亦何恃於道也此者蓋非可以一言盡
也儘能別識於此亦可謂知所存心矣亦可謂能充是
非之心矣故曰是知也

2.18

謝曰此子張以干祿之學問於夫子而夫子語之以干
祿之道也或得之於往訓或得之於益友皆所謂聞也
彼豈欺我哉然未能安於吾心所謂疑也勿言可
也見非見乃見也見乃不疑然後行之不
雖有所未安者不行可也問疑而言則行有
疑於心無懼乎其傜多見闕殆可以無悔
又曰慎行其餘此皆近思近思則可以得之乎
能至於此非特言滿天下無口過行滿天下
若汝如此則用善則人其舍汝乎無怨惡
理則已有天理則神之聽之其舍汝乎有必得
祿之道也

2.19

謝曰天下之道二枉直而已矣直而已悟二好惡而已
直而惡枉天下之至情順其所好人之所以服也逆其
所好人之所以去也然則為天下國家之道特在於舉
錯之間而已故舉錯則同治亂則異然自古治日少而
亂日多彼其心豈固欲舉枉錯直以拂天下之心哉蓋
無道以照之則自以為直自以為枉者亦多矣

2.20

謝曰敬忠以勸雖三代之民何以加此如季氏者亦豈
知此道真可以為天下國家也彼其所問蓋故家遺俗
之所傳耳三者皆情性所有豈可以強為乎敬無體也
惟莊可以聚之忠固有也惟孝慈可以居之勸非強他

2.20 cont.

之疎矣

也使知善之爲善盡有不待詔而從之輕矣此三者皆

不可以僞爲善學者雖以此自養可也民雖不可使知

之其能使不出於此道乎然則所謂成己成物有二致

不可矣後世徒以法度繩墨科持人心者亦多見其術

2.21

謂孝乎惟友于兄弟未足爲政豈知道者之言乎

謝曰孝乎惟孝友于兄弟猶言父父子子兄兄弟弟此

一家之政也豈一國之政也天下能如此一國之政天

下之政也豈有二道哉同是道也一人用之不見其分

而多天下皆用之不見其不同是道也少天下皆亂而已獨治

在獨善者處之不害爲大平天下皆治而已未治在任

重者處之酒以爲不足然則論政者果有物我之限哉

2.22

謝曰有諸已之謂信人而無信則無諸已矣孔孟論信

如此然自不學者觀之亦莫知所謂有者何物也亦

莫知所謂無者何物也今且以形性之近論之聖人

人倫之至雖不可以信言然自其因性言之亦可謂有

是性自其踐形言之自可謂有是形豎人固如此然有

亦豈能舍是性亦何嘗離是形何以謂之無也曰視之

不見與無目同聽之不聞與無耳同則雖謂之無是形

2.22 cont.

小車無軏取嘗實不遠矣

論惟斯人者可以當之以言其非有非無也大車無輗

於遊魂爲變者已希矣可謂之人乎世蓋有魍魎之

可之有天與之而已不能有之以至於此求其有以與

懷穹愈之心則幾於無羞惡則雖謂之無是性亦何不

何不可之有常其操欲害人之心則幾於無惻隱當其

2.23

謝曰子張之意以謂遠必有以驗乎近亦可謂窮理之

言也然意則有盡故聖人之意不以爲然亦不以爲不

暢之以己意而已聖人之意如何以謂在我之後者既

以考諸三王而不謬在我之後者又當百世以俟聖人

而不惑也因革損益之理出於變則變而與民宜之不

謂纂紂之餘一無可因革紹堯之後一無可損益視其

理之所在何如耳於此可以見三王之用心矣此聖人

於因革損益之理可知也繼周者或有以聖繼聖者乎

不可得而知也或有以暴易暴者乎不可得而知也其

知所以損益乎不可得而知也不知所以損益乎不可

得而知也其雖可以徵諸庶民可以驗諸鬼神者雖百

世之遠有聖人作其必同乎此其可知也

2.24

謝曰此一段立義雖異而意則相循陰陽交而有神形
氣離而有鬼知此者為智事此者為仁惟仁智之合者
可以制祀典祀典之意可者使人格之不使人致死之
不可者使人遠之故其鬼神致
死之故其鬼不神則鬼神之情狀豈不昭昭乎若夫不
知不仁者不足以與此亦知鬼有不神者乎而又當
政教失禮義廢之時則非所祭而祭之者宜其紛如也
其愛深思遠之所為則無徵欲秩之以禮則無位
聖人於此時欲驟而語之則無徵能知所喪也豈鬼神
之理未為不明於天下也祀典猶不喪也豈鬼神之理
不明於天下原於非所祭而祭之者以祈於不諂之
焉知諂為可恥而又能勇於不諂庶乎經正矣故繼之
以見義不為無勇也且不盜有如公子家者則知
及之而勇不能行者豈有矣然此之所謂見亦豈真所
謂見哉使其如所好則豈不能如父母之愛赤子使
其如見所譬則豈不能如鶺鴒之逐烏雀謂不能為吾
不信也恂恂仁者有如吳祐而能抗跛厄之威此可見
矣又況於自反而縮者乎

NOTES

Notes to Introduction

1. Both Hsieh and the Ch'eng brothers will be more fully introduced in chapter 1.

2. "*Tao-hsüeh*" 道學 (Learning of the Tao) was the primary designation for this movement during the Sung dynasty, as discussed in chapter 4. "Neo-Confucian" has become a conventional English designation for the movement, though its range of meaning is wider and more ambiguous than that of "*Tao-hsüeh.*" Though there has been some recent scholarly disagreement on the usage of these terms, there is consensus that both of them can properly be applied to the Ch'eng brothers and their circle, and so they are used interchangeably here. For accounts of the beginnings of the Neo-Confucian movement, see the writings of Wing-tsit Chan, Wm. Theodore de Bary, Fung Yu-lan, and Hoyt Tillman listed in the selected bibliography.

3. Many scholars have remarked on the difficulty of rendering the Chinese "*jen*" into English. Some common translations include "benevolence" (James Legge, D. C. Lau), "humanity" (Wing-tsit Chan), "love" (Derk Bodde), and "Goodness" (Arthur Waley). Since exploration of the subtleties of "understanding *jen*" is key throughout this investigation and will explicitly occupy much of chapter 3, for the most part "*jen*" will not be translated. As used in this study, the term "*jen-hsüeh*" (learning of *jen*; humane learning) will be explained in chapter 4.

4. The issue is more complex than simply asking whether "Confucianism" is or is not "a religion." Of that form, Wilfred Cantwell Smith has saliently remarked that it is a question "the West has never been able to answer and China never able to ask." See Smith's *The Meaning and End of Religion* (San Francisco: Harper & Row, 1978), p. 69. However, part of the complexity is that something like that Western question *has* been asked and much debated in modern China. The modern Chinese word "*tsung-chiao* 宗教," originally a modern Japanese translation of the Western concept "religion," has much the same range of usage as the English word "religion," though the root-meanings of its components tend to support Smith's argument ("ancestral-teaching"). This suggests that the problem at hand is largely a modern one for both East and West. As for the term "Confucianism," it should be noted that there is no exactly corresponding Chinese phrase; the indigenous terms would be *ju-chiao* 儒教 (*ju*-teachings) or *ju-chia ssu-hsiang* 儒家思想 (thought of the *ju* school), wherein Confucius is understood as the paradigmatic "*ju*." For an extended discussion of "*ju* 儒*,*" see Robert Eno, *The Confucian Creation of Heaven: Philosophy and the Defense of Ritual Mastery* (Albany: SUNY Press, 1990).

5. Some professional philosophers might demur at this. Nevertheless, the study of comparative philosophy, working with other traditions of thought as well as the Western, is a significant recent development in the field of philosophy. See, for example, David Hall and Roger Ames, *Thinking Through Confucius* (Albany: SUNY Press, 1987), esp. 1–25 and passim.

6. See Mote's foreword to Tu's *Way, Learning, and Politics: Essays on the Confucian Intellectual* (Singapore: Institute of East Asian Philosophies, 1989), xiv. This volume was republished by SUNY Press in 1993.

7. Foreword, xv. In the course of his remarks, Mote points out that he has taken Hsün-tzu as his guide to the genuine Confucian perspective and thinks of Mencius as an "aberration." For their part, the Neo-Confucians made the opposite assessment, following Mencius and relegating Hsün-tzu to a sideline.

8. See Irene Bloom, *Knowledge Painfully Acquired: The K'un-chih chi by Lo Ch'inshun*, (New York: Columbia University Press, 1987), 41.

9. The notion of "good reasons" is developed by Wayne C. Booth in *Modern Dogma and the Rhetoric of Assent* (Notre Dame: University of Notre Dame Press, 1974). See also Tu Wei-ming, "*Jen* as a Living Metaphor in the Confucian *Analects*," in *Confucian Thought: Selfhood as Creative Transformation* (Albany: SUNY Press, 1985), esp. pp. 82–83.

10. See the essays collected in Rodney L. Taylor, *The Religious Dimensions of Confucianism* (Albany: SUNY Press, 1990). Taylor cites Streng explicitly on p. 3, calling his definition "a central element of my work on the religious dimensions of the Confucian tradition." See Frederick Streng, *Understanding Religious Life*, 3rd ed. (Belmont, CA: Wadsworth, 1985), 1–8.

11. Streng 7. See chapter 3.

12. See Tu Wei-ming, *Centrality and Commonality: An Essay on Confucian Religiousness* (Albany: SUNY Press, 1989), 94–5. Tu's whole phrase is "ultimate self-transformation as a communal act and as a faithful dialogical response to the transcendent."

13. For a sustained study of the "three teachings" focused on a particular Ming dynasty figure, see Judith A. Berling, *The Syncretic Religion of Lin Chao-en* (New York: Columbia University Press, 1980). A wealth of examples of cross-fertilization among the three can be found in Liu Ts'un-yan, "The Syncretism of the Three Teachings in Sung-Yüan China," *New Excursions from the Hall of Harmonious Wind* (Leiden: E. J. Brill, 1984), 3–95.

14. For a discussion of a range of views on the "three teachings" during the Sung period, see my "*San-chiao*: Religious Dimensions of Pacific Culture" in *Religion in the Pacific Era*, ed. Frank K. Flinn and Tyler Hendricks (New York: Paragon House, 1985), 95–110. Although it can be argued that the concept of "three teachings" was an elite abstraction from a more complex field, the point is that it was an indigenous Chinese way of framing the matter.

15. See Girardot's article, "Chinese Religion: History of Study," in *The Encyclopedia of Religion*, ed. Mircea Eliade (New York: Macmillan, 1987), vol. 3, 312–23, esp. 313.

16. For a complete translation with Chinese text, see Matteo Ricci, S.J., *The True Meaning of the Lord of Heaven (T'ien-chu-Shi-i)*, translated with introduction and notes by Douglas Lancashire and Peter Hu Kuo-chen, S.J., and edited by Edward J. Malatesta, S.J. (St. Louis: Institute of Jesuit Sources, in cooperation with the Ricci Institute, Taipei, Taiwan, 1985).

17. *True Meaning* 24–25.

18. Ricci's own description of the *T'ien-chu shi-i* as found in *Fonti Ricciane*, ed. Pasquale M. d'Elia, S.J. (Rome: Libreria dello Stato, 1942–1949), vol. 2, 292, and translated by George H. Dunne, S.J. in *Generation of Giants* (Notre Dame: University of Notre Dame Press, 1962), 96–97.

19. Dunne, *Generation of Giants*, 32.

20. See Gernet, *China and the Christian Impact: A Conflict of Cultures*, translated by Janet Lloyd (Cambridge: Cambridge University Press, 1985), 3.

21. That is, the *Analects* 論語, *Mencius* 孟子, and two chapters from the *Li-chi* 禮 記 (Record of Ritual), namely "Ta-hsüeh" 大學 ("The Great Learning") and "Chung-yung" 中庸 ("The Doctrine of the Mean"). See discussion in chapter 2.

22. David E. Mungello, "The Seventeenth-Century Jesuit Translation Project of the Confucian *Four Books*," in Charles E. Ronan, S.J., and Bonnie B. C. Oh, eds., *East Meets West: The Jesuits in China, 1582–1773* (Chicago: Loyola University Press, 1988), 252–72, esp. 260.

23. Legge's Preface to pt. 1 of *The Sacred Books of China: The Texts of Confucianism*, published as vol. 3 of *The Sacred Books of the East* (hereafter SBE), ed. F. Max Müller (Oxford: Clarendon Press, 1879, reprinted Delhi: Motilal Banarsidass, 1978), xiv. Italics are used here to represent emphatic spacing.

24. Legge, prolegomena to his translation of the *Shu-ching* in vol. 3 of *The Chinese Classics* (Oxford: Clarendon Press, 1893–95), 192.

25. Legge, prolegomena to vol. 1 of *The Chinese Classics* (reprinted as *Confucius: Confucian Analects, The Great Learning and the Doctrine of the Mean*, New York: Dover Publications, 1971), 111.

26. Ibid., 99. The homiletic quality of Legge's prolegomena to his translations of the *Analects* and of *Mencius*, it should be remembered, came in the context of his having been accused by his fellow churchmen of "exalting Confucianism." See Lauren Pfister, "The 'Failures' of James Legge's Fruitful Life for China," *Ching Feng* 31:4 (December 1988), 255.

27. Legge wrote of Confucius that "his morality was the result of the balancings of his intellect, fettered by the decisions of men of old, and not the gushings of a loving heart, responsive to the promptings of Heaven, and in sympathy with erring and feeble humanity" (ibid., 110). Perhaps Legge himself, under different circumstances, would have been happy to read the *Analects* as many Confucians have, as reflective of just such a responsive and sensitive heart-and-mind. See later discussion, especially chapter 3.

28. The development of such a cross-cultural notion of scripture is relatively recent, as can readily be seen by comparing the lengthy article entitled "Scripture" by William A. Graham in the *Encyclopedia of Religion* (ed. Mircea Eliade, 1987, vol. 13, 133–45) with the same entry in the *Encyclopedia of Religion and Ethics* (ed. James Hastings, New York: Charles Scribner's Sons, 1924, vol. 11, 276): "Scripture. — See Bible, Infallibility, Inspiration, Revelation."

29. To mention just a few collections, see Ninian Smart and Richard D. Hecht, eds., *Sacred Texts of the World: A Universal Anthology* (New York: Crossroad, 1982); Kenneth Kramer, *World Scriptures: An Introduction to Comparative Religions* (New

York: Paulist Press, 1986); and Andrew M. Wilson, ed., *World Scripture: A Comparative Anthology of Sacred Texts* (New York: Paragon House, 1991).

30. See Wendy Doniger O'Flaherty, ed., *The Critical Study of Sacred Texts* (Berkeley: Berkeley Religious Studies Series, 1979); Frederick M. Denny and Rodney L. Taylor, eds., *The Holy Book in Comparative Perspective* (Columbia, SC: University of South Carolina Press, 1985); William A. Graham, *Beyond the Written Word: Oral Aspects of Scripture in the History of Religion* (Cambridge: Cambridge University Press, 1987); Miriam Levering, ed., *Rethinking Scripture: Essays from a Comparative Perspective* (Albany: SUNY Press, 1989); and Wilfred Cantwell Smith, *What Is Scripture? A Comparative Approach* (Minneapolis: Fortress Press, 1993).

31. John B. Henderson, *Scripture, Canon, and Commentary: A Comparison of Confucian and Western Exegesis* (Princeton: Princeton University Press, 1991), 5–6.

32. Henderson 21.

33. Miriam Levering, "Rethinking Scripture," in *Rethinking Scripture*, 1.

34. See Rodney Taylor's "Scripture and the Sage: On the Question of a Confucian Scripture," in *Religious Dimensions*, 23–37. This essay is also found in *The Holy Book in Comparative Perspective*. In addition to the work of Taylor and others, see Yen-zen Tsai, "*Ching* and *Chuan*: Towards Defining the Confucian Scriptures in Han China (206 BCE–220 CE)," (Th.D. diss., Harvard, 1992). Both Taylor and Tsai argue explicitly for "scripture" rather than "classic" as the appropriate category.

35. See Legge's preface to SBE, vol. 3, xx.

36. The term "*T'ien-chu*," apparently coined anew by a Chinese catechumen, was in use by 1583 in a catechism predating Ricci's treatise. As an indication of the complexity of these "term questions," however, it turned out in subsequent controversy with Buddhists that "*T'ien-chu*" had already been used as a translation for the Sanskrit *devapati*, "master of gods." Nevertheless, "*T'ien-chu*" became the official term for God in Chinese Catholic Christianity. See *The True Meaning of the Lord of Heaven*, 12, 32–35, and Gernet, 26, 217, 292, 108.

37. See *The True Meaning*, 123f. Ricci's translators then give his supporting passages from the *Book of Odes* (*Shih-ching*) according to Legge's renderings, but alter them to translate "*Shang-ti*" as "Sovereign on High" rather than "God."

38. John D. Young, *Confucianism and Christianity: The First Encounter* (Hong Kong: Hong Kong University Press, 1983), 29.

39. See *The True Meaning*, 107ff, 199f. David Mungello points out that in their translation work on the *Four Books*, the Jesuits "spurned" Chu Hsi's commentaries because "[they] found the interpretations of Sung Neo-Confucians to be filled with philosophic materialism, polytheism, or even atheism, which were irreconcilable with the proposed Confucian-Christian synthesis." See Mungello, 264, 254. An example of Chu Hsi's handling of potentially theistic passages is his discussion of a passage in the *Book of Documents* in which King Wen is visited by the Lord (*Ti* 帝) in a dream. Chu says that neither the idea of a formless master nor the popular image of the Jade Emperor is fitting for this *Ti*, and draws the agnostic conclusion that "no scholar can answer this." See *Shu-ching*, "Yüeh-ming" in Legge, *The Chinese Classics*, vol. 3, 250, and *Chu-tzu yü-lei* 朱子語類 (CTYL), 79, Chung-hua shu-chu edition, 2035. Wing-tsit Chan remarks, "What Chu Hsi meant is that we do not know whether there is a

Heavenly Lord, but if there is, he must follow principle." See *Chu Hsi: New Studies* (Honolulu: University of Hawaii Press, 1989), 188.

40. See Legge's *Notions of the Chinese Concerning Gods and Spirits: with an Examination of the Defense of an Essay, on the proper rendering of the words* Elohim *and* Theos, *into the Chinese Language by William J. Boone, D. D.* (Hong Kong, 1852).

41. Legge, preface to *The Yi King* (*I-ching*), pt. 2 of *The Sacred Books of China*, published as vol. 16 of SBE, xx.

42. Legge, preface to SBE, vol. 3, xxv. Throughout this book, "*jen**" will be used to indicate 人 (the two-stroke character for human being), to distinguish it from its cognate "*jen*" 仁 (humane).

43. Legge, prolegomena to *Chinese Classics*, vol. 1, 100.

44. Ibid., 99. The term "*Shang-ti*" had indeed largely lost its former transcendent significance in elite culture by the time of the eleventh- and twelfth-century Confucian revival, and "*T'ien*" (Heaven) was in the process of being transmuted into the phrase "*T'ien-li*" 天理 (Heavenly principle or pattern).

45. Legge remarks that while he sought to determine the meaning of the text on his own, he "soon became aware, however, of the beauty and strength of Chu's style, the correctness of his analysis, and the comprehension and depth of his thought." Preface to *Chinese Classics*, vol. 1, vi.

46. Both Ricci and Legge had strong opponents, and even today there are two major versions of the Bible published in Chinese, differing only in the term used for God.

47. *Towards a World Theology: Faith and the Comparative History of Religion*, (Philadelphia: Westminster Press, 1981), 151.

48. See *A Bibliographic Guide to the Comparative Study of Ethics*, ed. John Carman and Mark Juergensmeyer (Cambridge: Cambridge University Press, 1991). The *Guide* consists primarily of annotated bibliographies of ethically significant texts organized according to a "tradition outline" appropriate to each different tradition, with introductory essays explaining key terms and issues in the tradition. See my "Neo-Confucian religious ethics," chapter 6 of the *Bibliographic Guide*, 195–227.

49. Neville writes, "Theology has outgrown its Christian origins and become a discipline that ought intrinsically to be accountable to public norms for which one's inherited religious tradition makes no *final* difference." See *The Tao and the Daimon* (Albany: SUNY Press, 1982), 12.

50. See George Lindbeck, *The Nature of Doctrine: Religion and Theology in a Postliberal Age* (Philadelphia: Westminster Press, 1984).

51. Hsieh's commentary on the *Analects* evidences complete familiarity with the whole text, dealing with the mundane problems that the text addresses in its "ordinariness" in addition to the directly inspirational passages.

52. See *Towards a World Theology*, passim.

53. *Behind the Masks of God* 36–46.

54. Levering, *Rethinking Scripture*, 1.

55. For an insightful discussion that is helpful in considering reason and experience cross-culturally, see John E. Smith, *Purpose and Thought: The Meaning of Pragmatism* (New Haven: Yale University Press, 1978).

56. Rosemary Radford Ruether, *Sexism and God-Talk: Toward a Feminist Theology* (Boston: Beacon Press, 1983), 12.

57. Thus, such texts as the Bible and Culture Collective's *The Postmodern Bible* (New Haven: Yale University Press, 1995) show various ways of using the contemporary experience of particular groups to restructure biblical interpretation.

58. Arthur Waley, *The Analects of Confucius* (New York: George Allen & Unwin, 1938), 73–74.

Notes to Chapter 1

1. See "Chu nei-han lun K'ung-Meng chih hsüeh ch'uan yü Erh-Ch'eng" 朱內翰論孔孟之學傳於二程 (Secretary Chu discussing the transmission of the learning of Confucius and Mencius to the Ch'eng brothers) in *Tao-ming lu* 道命錄 (Record of the destiny of the Tao) compiled by Li Hsin-ch'uan 李心傳, Ming Hung-chih edition 3/2a–b, and also *Chien-yen i-lai hsi-nien yao-lu* 建炎以來繫年要錄 (Important records chronologically interrelated from the Chien-yen period [1127–1130] onward), also compiled by Li Hsin-ch'uan, 101/12b–13b, *Ts'ung-shu chi-ch'eng* ed., 1660–61, Wen-hai ch'u-pan-she ed., 3246–48, Chubun shuppansha indexed edition, 837–38. Some of this portion of the memorial is translated by Wing-tsit Chan in *Chu Hsi: New Studies*, 321; the last line cited here particularly follows his translation. The memorial is also discussed by Hoyt Tillman in *Confucian Discourse and Chu Hsi's Ascendancy*, (Honolulu: University of Hawaii Press, 1992), 20–21. On Chu Chen, see *Sung-Yüan hsüeh-an* 宋元學案 (Scholarly records of Sung and Yüan, hereafter SYHA) 37, "Han-shang hsüeh-an" 漢上學案.

2. On the Ch'eng brothers, see A. C. Graham, *Two Chinese Philosophers: Ch'eng Ming-tao and Ch'eng Yi-ch'uan* (London: Lund Humphries, 1958: new edition, LaSalle, IL: Open Court, 1992). Graham's pioneering work treats the major concepts in the Ch'eng brothers' teachings and discerns fundamental differences in their ideas. This work has recently been translated into Chinese by Cheng Dexiang (Ch'eng Te-hsiang), a lineal descendant of Ch'eng I, as *Chung-kuo te liang wei che-hsüeh-chia: Erh-Ch'eng hsiung-ti te hsin ju-hsüeh* (Dezhou: Da-hsiang ch'u-pan-she, 1999).

3. The felicitous characterization of *Tao-hsüeh* as a "fellowship" is developed by Hoyt Tillman in *Confucian Discourse*, 2–9.

4. For a concise account of the relations among these five, see the introductory chapter in Hoyt Tillman's *Utilitarian Confucianism*, and also the appendixes to Graham's *Two Chinese Philosophers*.

5. Ch'eng I, "Ming-tao hsien-sheng mu-piao" 明道先生墓表 (Epitaph for master [Ch'eng] Ming-tao) in *Honan Ch'eng-shih wen-chi* 河南程士文集, 11, *Erh-Ch'eng chi* 二程集 (ECC), vol. 1, 640. This translation is indebted to those of A. C. Graham in *Two Chinese Philosophers*, 158 (Graham gives the reference as *Yi-ch'uan wen-chi* 7/7B/6–9) and Peter K. Bol in *"This Culture of Ours": Intellectual Transitions in T'ang and Sung China* (Stanford: Stanford University Press, 1992), 302. The quotation in the last line is from *Mencius* 5A7, repeated in 5B1; see further discussion in chapter 3.

6. Ch'eng Hao died in the sixth month of 1085; see Ch'eng I's record of him in "Ming-tao hsieh-sheng hsing-chuang" 明道先生行狀, ECC, 673.

7. Ch'eng I, "Ming-tao hsien-sheng men-jen p'eng-yu hsü-shu hsü" 明道先生門人朋友敍述序, in *Honan Ch'eng-shih wen-chi*, 11, ECC, 639.

8. The paradigm of a long lost and then recovered transmission of the Tao can be traced back to Han Yü 韓愈 (768–824) and his essay "On the Original Tao [*Yüan Tao lun* 原道論]." For example, see the discussion in Carsun Chang, *The Development of Neo-Confucian Thought* (New York: Bookman Associates, 1957), vol. 1, 97. Subsequently, the focus of this sense of rejuvenation would shift to the two Ch'eng brothers collectively ("Erh-Ch'eng" 二程), and then under Chu Hsi's influence to primary emphasis on Ch'eng I. Indeed, the two brothers came to be referred to as a single persona, "master Ch'eng" 程子, with Ch'eng I dominant.

9. See, for example, Miriam Levering, "Ch'an Enlightenment for Laymen: Ta-hui and the New Religious Culture of the Sung," Ph.D. diss., Harvard University, 1978.

10. See chapter 4.

11. Three of the "Four Masters of the Ch'eng School" 程門四先生 are mentioned in Chu Chen's memorial: Hsieh, Yang Shih 楊時 (1053–1135, master Kuei-shan 龜山先生), and Yu Tso 游酢 (1053–1123, Ting-fu 定夫, master Chai-shan 齋山先生). Yin T'un 尹火享 (1071–1142, master Ho-ching 和靖先生) is often listed as the fourth, although that honor is sometimes given to Lü Ta-lin 呂大臨 (1046–1092).

12. As Satō Hitoshi 佐藤仁 has pointed out, there is no firm evidence for the 1050 date, except to judge from the fact that Yu Tso, who was born in 1053, referred to Hsieh respectfully as an elder. See Satō Hitoshi, "Sha Ryosa 'Rongo kai jo' ni yosete," found in *Kokugo no kenkyū* 10 (Showa 52 [1977]), 77–86. Satō also notes the discrepancy concerning the date of Hsieh's passing away, which is often given as 1103 but now generally recognized as c.1120 or 1121, based on Yang Shih's epitaph for Yu Tso (d. 1123) in which he mentions Hsieh, saying that "within three years the two of them died one after the other." See *Yang Kuei-shan chi* 楊龜山集, 6/117, and also Graham, *Two Chinese Philosophers*, 195n.

The *Sung shih* 宋史 erroneously locates Shang-ts'ai district in Shou-ch'un prefecture, which would put it in modern Anwei province; this is probably a confusion with Hsia-ts'ai 下蔡. Both locations can be found in volume 6, 22–23 of *Chung-kuo li-shih ti-t'u chi* 中國歷史地圖集 (The Historical Atlas of China), edited by Tan Qixiang (T'an Ch'i-hsiang) (Shanghai: Cartographic Publishing House, 1982); see also the local gazetteer for Shang-ts'ai district, *Shang-ts'ai hsien-chih* 上蔡縣志, preface dated the twenty-ninth year of the K'ang-hsi reign [1690].

13. This account of Shang-ts'ai's life is indebted to Wing-tsit Chan's biography of him in *Sung Biographies*, edited by Herbert Franke (Wiesbaden: Steiner, 1976), supplemented by other sources. For office titles and other official terminology, see Charles O. Hucker, *A Dictionary of Official Titles in Imperial China* (Stanford: Stanford University Press, 1985).

14. See STYL, #57. As the phrase "hsiu-ts'ai" referred in Sung times to candidates in the Metropolitan examinations, it may be inferred that in his youth Hsieh had pursued a course of study geared toward the civil service examinations and had met with some success.

15. See SYHA, SPPY edition, 24/8b.

16. The *Shang-ts'ai yü-lu* has been translated into German by Jorg Bäcker in his doctoral dissertation, "'Prinzip der Natur' und 'Sein Selbst Vergessen': Theorie und Praxis des Neokonfuzianismus anhand der 'Aufgezeichneten Aussprüche des Hsieh Liang-tso (1050–1121),'" Rheinische Friedrich-Wilhelms-Universität, Bonn, Germany, 1982, and also into English by Chu Ron-Guey in his M.A. thesis, Columbia University, also 1982. Bäcker's dissertation offers an analysis of "*li* 理 (principle)" as ontological ground, the obstructions of *li* in the self, and the purifying methods of investigating and following *li*, as presented in the STYL. His thematic focus is on heavenly principle (*t'ien-li* 天理) and selfishness, which Bäcker interprets as the "forgetting" of heavenly principle. He also pays some attention to Ch'an Buddhist and Taoist philosophical antecedents.

17. There will be further discussion of Chu Hsi's role with respect to Hsieh's teachings and writings in the last section of this chapter and also in subsequent chapters.

18. Little description of the actual Tao-hsüeh practice of quiet-sitting is given in the sources. As Janine Sawada has noted, in Tao-hsüeh "tangible aids . . . were generally left to the discretion of the individual Confucian scholar. Quiet-sitting and keeping a journal of one's daily progress were two visible approaches to inner cultivation, but they were not prescriptive features." See *Confucian Values and Popular Zen* (Honolulu: University of Hawaii Press, 1993), 165.

19. This incident is included in the influential collection by Chu Hsi and Lü Tsu-ch'ien, *Chin ssu-lu* 近思錄, translated by Wing-tsit Chan as *Reflections on Things at Hand*; see chap. 4, #63, translation, 151.

20. *Chin ssu-lu* 14/21, *Reflections*, 304. Chan gives the reference as from the *Erh-Ch'eng Wai-shu*, but the original source is STYL #65, as recorded by Tseng T'ien.

21. *Chin-ssu lu chi-chieh* 近思錄集解, Shih-chieh shu-chü edition, 341.

22. On "rote memorization," see the "Hsüeh-chi" chapter of the *Li-chi* 18/10, rendered by James Legge, *Li Ki*, vol. 2 (published as SBE, vol. 28), 89–90, as: "He who gives (only) the learning supplied by his memory in conversations is not fit to be a master."

23. "Trifling with things and losing purpose [*wan-wu sang-chih* 玩物喪志]" comes from *Shu-ching* 25, "Lu ao" (The Hounds of Lu); compare Legge's translation, *Chinese Classics*, vol. 3, 348–49.

24. The description of this incident translated here is found in the *I-Lo yüan-yüan lu* (Record of the Origins of the I-Lo School [of the Two Ch'engs], ILYYL) 9/4a, which in turn cites *Hu-shih ch'uan chia-lu* (Family Record of the Hu Transmission). A shorter version is found in STYL #102.

25. "The heart-and-mind of natural compassion [*ts'e-yin chih hsin* 惻隱之心]" is described as the beginning (*tuan* 端) of *jen* in *Mencius* 2A6; see Lau, 82–83. So central was *jen* in Ch'eng Hao's teaching that he identified his disciple's feelings of shame with the beginning of *jen*, rather than the beginning of *yi* 義 (dutifulness or rightness) as in the *Mencius*.

26. This continuation of the incident is found only in the longer *I-Lo yüan-yüan lu* account (ILYYL 9/4a). The term "*hua-t'ou*" 話頭 (in some editions replaced by *yü-t'ou* 語頭) recalls Ch'an Buddhist usage.

27. Quoted in STYL #19, Kinssei kanseki sokan edition (KKS), 18. The KKS reprints a 1756 manuscript from Japan. Sectioning is nearly uniform among the several extant editions of the STYL (see bibliography). The translation here follows Wing-tsit Chan, "Neo-Confucian Philosophical Poems," *Renditions*, 4 (Spring 1975), 11.

28. STYL #19, KKS, 17. The reference is to *Analects* 11:26, in which Confucius's disciple Tseng Tien lyrically expresses his "heart's desire" for enjoying river bathing and chanting poetry in the spring season, and Confucius heartily rejoins "I'm with you." In addition to Chan's discussion of these poems in *Renditions*, see William Theodore de Bary, *Learning for Oneself* (New York: Columbia University Press, 1992), esp. 43–52.

29. STYL #19, KKS, 18. The allusion is to *Mencius* 7A13, "for he transforms whomever he passes by [*suo-kuo-che hua* 所過者化]." Here, as elsewhere, Chu Ron-Guey's translation of the STYL has been a helpful resource.

30. See STYL #13, KKS, 11.

31. *Tso-chuan*, in the fourth month of the first year of Duke Ai (494 BCE). See Legge, *The Chinese Classics*, vol. 5, 793 and 795. The phrase is also found in *Mencius* 4B20 (Lau 131) as referring to the way that King Wen treated the people.

32. See [Kuang-hsü] Fu-kou hsien-chih 扶溝縣志, 5/32a.

33. See Hu Yin, "*Shang-ts'ai Lun-yü chieh* hou-hsü" (Postface to Hsieh Liang-tso's *Explanations of the* Analects), in *Fei-jan chi*, 19/7b–9a; SKCS 1137/540–41.

34. There are conflicting records concerning the chronology of Hsieh's service; for example, the chart of officials in the Ying-ch'eng local gazetteer *(Kuang-hsü Ying-ch'eng chih)* lists Hsieh as Magistrate *(ling* 令*)* during the Yüan-fu period (1098–1100), one of two noteworthy magistrates during the entire Sung. But this dating conflicts with that found in the commentarial record *(chuan)* in the same gazetteer, which places his service in Ying-ch'eng after his imperial audience with Emperor Hui-tsung in 1101.

35. Hu An-kuo had responsibility for the Hupei circuit during the fourth year of Chung-ning (1105), which also places Hsieh's service in Ying-ch'eng after 1100. See Satō Hitoshi, 77, citing the record of Hu An-kuo's life by his nephew and son by adoption, Hu Yin.

36. This was recorded by Hu An-kuo's nephew Hu Hsien (1082–1162) in "Hsieh Hsien-tao yü-lu pa," found in *Shang-ts'ai hsien-chih*, 14/80a.

37. On this discrepancy in chronology, see note 30.

38. *Mien-ch'ih hsien chih* 3/18a–b. Chu Ron-Guey places this service after Hsieh's service in Loyang. If so, it would mean that Hsieh visited Ch'eng I on several different occasions and that the visit recorded in the *Mien-ch'ih hsien-chih* is separate from the account of Hsieh's visiting after a year's separation.

39. *Sung shih* 428, Tao-hsüeh 2; 12732. The Northern Sung capital, called Tung-ching or Pien-ching, was located on the site of modern K'ai-feng in Honan. Wing-tsit Chan gives the date of this audience as 1104, but this seems to conflict with the episode about the reign-title, which logically would have occurred during the time the reign-title was in force (1101–02).

40. *Kuang-hsü Ying-ch'eng chih* 8/2a. The praise about his expecting to have no legal cases alludes to *Analects* 12:13.

41. See SYHA 24/1a.

42. See SYHA 24/1a–b. Satō Hitoshi (78) doubts the veracity of this account.

43. For a detailed study of Wang An-shih's "new policies" when he was chief minister, the philosophy and political idealism behind them, and the subsequent controversies they sparked, see James T. C. Liu's *Reform in Sung China: Wang An-shih (1021–1086) and His New Policies* (Cambridge, MA: Harvard University Press, 1959).

44. Liu, *Reform in Sung China*, 10.

45. Hsieh's quotations from the commentaries of Wang An-shih and his son Wang Fang, as well as the admiration expressed for the elder Wang in STYL, would seem to indicate that in spite of the polemics surrounding Wang's "new policies," Hsieh respected their scholarship. See chapter 2.

46. *Tao ming lu* 3/2a–b.

47. See Chu Hsi, comp., *I-Lo yüan-yüan lu* 9/2a.

48. Ch'ao Pu-chih, "Pa Hsieh Liang-tso suo shou Li T'ang ch'ing-chuan ch'ien-tzu wen" (Colophon to a thousand-word precious seal character writing of the T'ang dynasty collected by Hsieh Liang-tso) in *Chi-le chi* 33/23b; SKCS 1118, 654. See the chapter on Ch'ao in Peter K. Bol, "Culture and the Way in Eleventh Century China," Ph.D. diss., Princeton University, 1982.

49. "Hsieh Shang-ts'ai yü-lu hou-hsü," in *Hui-an hsien-sheng Chu Wen-kung wen-chi* (CWKWC) 75/3a; see also the KKS edition of STYL, 89.

50. CTYL 104, 2615; this translation differs somewhat from that found in Chan, *New Studies*, 15.

51. "Hsieh Shang-ts'ai yü-lu hou-chi," in CWKWC 77/14a–b; see the KKS edition of STYL, 94, and also the SYHA supplement.

52. See Chan's annotation in *A Sung Bibliography/Bibliographie des Sung*, edited by Etienne Balazs and Yves Hervouet, (Hong Kong: Chinese University Press, 1978), 222.

53. *Sung wen-chien* 92/9a–12b, SPTK edition. See *A Sung Bibliography*, 439–40. Hsieh's preface is also found in the SYHA, chapter 24, probably based on the *Sung wen-chien* text. In addition, it is found in *Ching-i k'ao* 經義考 (Investigations of Meanings in the Classics) compiled by Chu I-tsun 朱彝尊 (1629–1709).

54. See discussion in chapter 2.

55. Hu Yin, "Shang-ts'ai Lun-yü chieh hou-hsü," found in *Fei-jan chi*, SKCS edition, 19/7b–9a.

Notes to Chapter 2

1. Steven Van Zoeren, *Poetry and Personality: Reading, Exegesis, and Hermeneutics in Traditional China* (Stanford: Stanford University Press, 1991), 151. Specifically, Van Zoeren refers to "the criticizing and loosening of traditional and institutional authority over interpretation [and] a renewed and deepened engagement with the classics [themselves]." He points to the promulgation of block-printed editions of the Confucian canon in the tenth century as paving the way for the new interpretive developments of the succeeding two centuries and as a parallel to Reformation era events (156–57).

2. *Scripture, Canon, Commentary*, 11. In the same passage, Henderson offers the following caution:

> The extent to which the Sung Neo-Confucians reoriented Confucianism in their time should not go unrecognized. And indeed it has not, especially by modern historians of Neo-Confucian thought who, like Burckhardtian historians of the Renaissance, sometimes take their subjects' reformationist rhetoric a little too uncritically.

3. In these terms, *Tao-hsüeh* interpreters were primarily involved with the "philosophical" approach. See Gardner, *Chu Hsi and the Ta-hsüeh*, 9:

> The "critical" approach sought to determine the authenticity, authorship, or reliability of a classical text or its commentaries. The "programmatic" approach focussed on ancient institutions, systems, or moral values described in a classical text and argued for their applicability to the current situation. The "philosophical" approach saw in the Classic an explanation of the cosmos and man's relationship to that cosmos, or of man's inner source of morality.

4. See *Poetry and Personality*, 153–55, 277 n.7.

5. In *Government Education and Examinations in Sung China* (151), Thomas H. C. Lee offers this comment on the "exposition of the classics" (*ching-i* 經義) style of official examinations that Wang had implemented:

> The idea was to test the ability of candidates in putting classical knowledge into effective use in argumentation . . . The stress this style laid on familiarity with the Confucian classics and more or less imaginative reading of these texts contributed in a certain unmistakable way to the rise of the so-called "Sung School" of classical learning, which was part of the Neo- Confucian movement.

6. The Four Books comprise the *Analects* (*Lun-yü* 論語), the *Mencius* book (*Meng-tzu* 孟子), and two chapters from the *Li-chi* 禮記 (Record of Ritual), the "Great Learning" (*Ta-hsüeh* 大學) and the "Doctrine of the Mean" (*Chung-yung* 中庸).

7. See Daniel Gardner, *Chu Hsi and the Ta-hsüeh*, 3, and also Wang Mou-heng, *Chu-tzu nien-p'u* 4A, 176–78.

8. For example, Daniel Gardner writes in *Learning to be a Sage* (39), "with Chu Hsi, the Four Books came to displace the Five Classics as the central texts in the Confucian tradition." See also Gardner's *The Classics During the Sung (Chu Hsi and the Ta-hsüeh)*, as well as Wing-tsit Chan's seminal essay, "Chu Hsi's Completion of Neo-Confucianism," *Etudes Song: In Memoriam Etienne Balazs*, 2nd ser., 1 (1972), 59–90.

9. See Chu Hsi, "Kuo-chao chu lao hsien-sheng Lun-Meng ching-i kang-ling" 國朝諸老先生論孟精義綱領 (An Outline of the Essential Meanings of the *Analects* and *Mencius* according to the Elder Masters of our Dynasty), 2a, in *Chu-tzu i-shu* 朱子遺書 (Surviving Works of Master Chu), I-wen yin-shu kuan edition, vol. 7. See also the translation in Henderson, 18.

10. STYL #20.

11. *Poetry and Personality*, 214. In the course of his discussion, Van Zoeren makes an overly literary criticism of the STYL text, analyzing two sections as "two versions of the same saying," as though Shang-ts'ai talked about Ch'eng Hao's reading of the *Odes* only once.

12. *Yi-shu*, 22A/*Erh-Ch'eng chi*, 279, responding to a question by Chang Po-wen (my translation). This passage is partially included at *Chin-ssu lu* 3/36; see translations in Wing-tsit Chan's *Reflections on Things at Hand*, 103, and Van Zoeren, 215.

13. Hsing Ping's work was later (from the 1190s on) included in the *Shih-san ching chu-shu* 十三經注疏 (Commentary and Explication of the Thirteen Classics). See *A Sung Bibliography*, edited by Yves Hervouet, 41. The annotation is by Ichikawa Yasuji, translated by B. Albertat. See also Van Zoeren, 157 and 278, n.18.

14. Ho Yen includes comments by K'ung An-kuo (fl 130 BCE), Pao Hsien and a Master Chou (both fl. in the Kuang-wu period, 25–57 CE), Ma Jung (79–166), Cheng Hsüan (127–200), Ch'en Ch'ün (third cent.), Wang Su (195–256), and Chou Shang-lieh (third cent.), as well as his own opinions. See Hsing Ping's preface, 1a, and also Legge's prolegomena to *Chinese Classics*, vol. 1, 19.

15. Ichikawa in *A Sung Bibliography*, 41.

16. See James T. C. Liu, "How Did a Neo-Confucian School Become State Orthodoxy?" 501f. See also his *China Turning Inward*.

17. For an examination of Chu Hsi's sources, see Otsuki Nobuyoshi, *Chu-tzu ssu-shu chi-chu tien-chü k'ao* (Taipei: Student Book Co., 1976). Dennis A. Leventhal has prepared a helpful chart giving a statistical breakdown of the 502 quotations in the LYCC. See Dennis A. Leventhal, "Treading the Path from Yang Shih to Chu Hsi: A Question of Transmission in Sung Neo-Confucianism," *The Bulletin of Sung and Yüan Studies* #14, 1978, 50–67.

18. *Chu-tzu nien-p'u* (65) gives the date of the completion of the LYCC as the sixth month of 1177, when Chu Hsi was in his forty-eighth year. However, Ch'ien Mu argues that this was only the first draft and that Chu Hsi later made many changes. He cites a passage from *Chu-tzu yü-lei* 朱子語類 (Classified Conversations of Master Chu, CTYL) 19, recorded sometime after 1189, in which Chu says that ten years earlier he had circulated the LYCC among friends and local people published it without his knowledge while it still had many unsettled places. See *Chu-tzu hsin hsüeh-an*, IV, 200–201.

19. The full name of the compilation, encompassing both the *Analects* and the *Mencius*, is *Kuo-ch'ao chu lao hsien-sheng Lun-Meng Ching-i* 國朝諸老先生論孟精義 (Essential Meanings of the *Analects* and *Mencius* by the Old Masters of Our Dynasty); it was also known as the *Chi-i* 集義 (Collected Meanings). See *Chu-tzu nien-p'u*, 46.

20. The other five are Fan Tsu-yü (1041–98), Lü Hsi-che (c. 1036–c. 1114), Lü Ta-lin, Hou Chung-liang (fl. 1100), and Yin T'un.

21. *Chu-tzu yü-lei* (CTYL) 19, Chung-hua shu-chu edition, 441. The *Analects* text and the various commentaries upon it were much discussed between Chu Hsi and his disciples. Many of these conversations are included in the CTYL, especially in *chüan* 20–50 on the *Analects*, arranged verse by verse.

22. The *Hung-shih T'ang shih ching kuan ts'ung-shu* was compiled during the Ch'ing dynasty by Hung Ju-k'uei (洪汝奎) and published in the *Kuang-hsü chung jing Hung-shih kung shan-t'ang ji-ch'eng* 光緒中涇洪氏公善堂集成.

23. CTYL 115, 2783, recorded by Lin K'o; translation modified from that of Wing-tsit Chan in *Chu Hsi: New Studies*, 14. Hsieh Hsien-tao 謝顯道 is the courtesy name for Hsieh Liang-tso (Shang-ts'ai).

24. CTYL 120, 2887. The translation follows Wing-tsit Chan, *New Studies,* 16.

25. In the Ch'ing dynasty work *Ching-i k'ao* 經義考 (Investigation into the Meanings of the Classics) compiled by Chu I-tsun 朱彝尊 (1629–1709), Hsieh's *Lun-yü chieh* 論語解 is listed as "not seen," rather than "extant" or "lost," suggesting that by then at least it was probably though not definitely lost. Wing-tsit Chan also notes that "Hsieh's commentary is no longer extant," *New Studies,* 29, n.7.

26. In the LYCI, several *Analects* passages are broken into sections, thus giving rise to a higher number of passages than usually given for the *Analects.*

27. See *Sung wen-chien* (SWC) 92, Kuo-hsüeh chi-pen tsung-shu (KHCPTS) edition, vol. 181/11, 1234–36.

28. See the prefatory note to Yu Tso's "Lun-yü tsa-chieh" 論語雜解 in *Yu Ting-fu hsien-sheng chi* 游定夫先生集 1/1a.

29. These comments are intended to indicate an appreciation and critical response to John Henderson's notion of "commentarial strategies." See *Scripture, Canon, and Commentary,* chapter 5.

30. These favorite passages are Tseng Tzu's dying words about a serious countenance, proper expression, and speaking in proper words and tones (8:4), and Confucius's saying that in learning he starts from below and reaches what is above, and that only Heaven understands him (14:35).

31. For a careful description of the political factions surrounding Wang An-shih, see James T. C. Liu, *Reform in Sung China: Wang An-shih (1021–1086) and His New Policies* (Cambridge, MA: Harvard University Press, 1959).

32. The saying is found in *Analects* 7:16; translation modified from Lau, 88.

33. "子曰: 攻乎異端，斯害也已." This reading of the passage hinges on the gloss, given by Hsing Ping (2/3b), of "*kung*" 攻 (to attack) as "*chih*" 治 (to order, to study). Concerning Hsieh's alternative understanding of the passage, see his full comment on *Analects* 2:16 in appendix 2.

34. In the LYCC, Chu Hsi uses only those comments by Hsieh and others that fit his own systematic interpretation. Thus, it can be said that there is a figure/ground reversal between Hsieh's comments as they are recorded in the LYCI, and as they are utilized selectively by Chu Hsi in the LYCC.

35. Hsieh's preface to the STLYC, as found in the *Sung wen-chien* version, KHCPTS, vol. 181/11, 1235.

36. *Analects* 9:11, Lau 97. Although the play on the English word "hard" does not exist in the Chinese originals, the underlying point of similarity still holds, that the more earnest the effort the more one encounters the difficulty.

37. SWC version, 1235. This assertion and the long passage leading up to it were omitted in the version of Hsieh's preface that Chu Hsi included in the LYCI collection.

38. SWC version, 1235; also found in other versions.

39. The phrase "encounter-dialogues" comes from John McRae's description of Ch'an Buddhist *yü-lu* 語錄 collections. See John R. McRae, *The Northern School and the Formation of Early Chan Buddhism* (Honolulu: University of Hawaii Press, 1986).

40. SWC 1234.

41. SWC 1234.

42. Compare Henderson's discussion (134) of the commentarial assumption of clarity/obscurity, noting "the apparent paradox that the classics are easy yet difficult, plain yet obscure."

43. SWC 1234.

44. *Odes* III.i.V.3, Legge's translation, *Chinese Classics*, vol. 4, 293; also "Doctrine of the Mean" 12, Legge's translation, *Chinese Classics*, vol. 1, 392.

45. *Odes* III.i.I.7, Legge's translation, *Chinese Classics*, vol. 4, 286; an alternative translation is: "The doings of the supreme Heaven have neither sound nor smell" ("Doctrine of the Mean" 33, Legge's translation, *Chinese Classics*, vol. 1, 433).

46. Alternatively: One who knows that "there is something hidden" and "there is nothing hidden" are not two—if we abandon his book, wherein can we see him?

47. SWC 1236.

Notes to Chapter 3

1. See Tu Wei-ming 杜維明, "*Jen* as a Living Metaphor in the Confucian *Analects*," *Philosophy East and West*, vol. 31, no. 1 (January 1981), reprinted in *Confucian Thought: Selfhood as Creative Transformation* (Albany: SUNY Press, 1985), 81. Tu notes Herbert Fingarette as an exception to this consensus.

2. See Eno, *The Confucian Creation of Heaven*, 66.

3. Arthur Waley, *The Analects of Confucius*, 28.

4. Herbert Fingarette, *Confucius: The Secular as Sacred* (New York: Harper & Row, 1972), 40. The specific case to which he refers is *Analects* 4:4, read as saying that the person whose intent is set on *jen* has no hatred (dislike, *wu* 惡), when juxtaposed with 4:3, saying that only the person of *jen* knows how to like and dislike others.

5. "*Jen* as a Living Metaphor" 85.

6. Fingarette 43. The eschewing of psychologizing is also a theme in David Hall and Roger Ames, *Thinking Through Confucius* (Albany: SUNY Press, 1987).

7. See Max Weber, *The Religion of China* (New York: Free Press, 1968 [1951]), esp. 226–38.

8. In this regard, Fingarette's more general studies of human performance, for example in *Self-Deception* (New York, 1969), are helpful in putting his treatment of Confucius in perspective. See also the discussion of Fingarette's work in Stephen A. Erickson, *Human Presence: At the Boundaries of Meaning* (np: Mercer University Press, 1984), 55–67.

9. Benjamin I. Schwartz, *The World of Thought in Ancient China* (Cambridge: Belknap Press of Harvard University Press, 1985), 74.

10. Schwartz 75.

11. Schwartz 80.

12. This passage is part of Hsieh's comment on *Analects* 1:2. For the full comment, see appendix 1.

13. The examples of *jen* are such that "no one could raise all of them [*chü chih mo neng sheng* 舉之莫能勝]." Other translations of this phrase are possible, but this one seems to best fit the context.

14. The translation here is modified from that of D. C. Lau (Penguin, 1979). Unless otherwise noted, citations from the *Analects* follow Lau's translation.

15. LYCI 3B/29a.

16. In the alternative account given in *Mencius* 2A2, Mencius explains that Confucius did not "presume" (*chü* 居) sagehood.

17. Passages in which Confucius says that he "does not know" about someone being *jen* could also be interpreted as a kind of rhetorical denial that the person is *jen*. For example, see Yang Po-chün, *Lun-yü shih-chu*, especially 43–44, on *Analects* 5:5, 5:8. But that is not how Hsieh reads these passages.

18. "*Wei chih yen te jen*" 未知焉得仁. LYCI 3A/19a. D. C. Lau, on the other hand, renders Confucius' response as "he cannot even be said to be wise, how can he be *jen*?"

19. LYCI 3A/7b–8a.

20. LYCI 7B/2a.

21. LYCI 1A/8a.

22. LYCI 1A/8b.

23. LYCI 1A/6a.

24. LYCI 1A/6a–b.

25. LYCI 1A/6b; "*tsai nien pu nien chih chien*" 在念不念之間. The valence of *nien* here is quite different than in much of Buddhist teaching, as Hsieh describes:

> The Buddhists regard the nature [*hsing* 性] as the sun and thoughts [*nien*] as clouds. That one perceives the nature by removing thoughts is analogous to revealing the sun by dispersing clouds. What the Buddhists try to eliminate is exactly the matter we Confucians must concern ourselves with. (STYL #41/36, following Chu Ron-Guey's translation, 145.)

26. LYCI 1A/6b.

27. For example, the discussion of Hsieh's comment on *Analects* 1:2 preserved in the *Chu-tzu yü-lei* 朱子語類 (CTYL 20/477) includes the following:

> [I, Huang Kan] asked, "Mr. Hsieh said, 'At times when I serve parents and follow [obey] my elder brother, I examine what this heart-and-mind is like; knowing this heart-and-mind then one knows *jen*,' how is this saying?" [Chu Hsi] answered, "It is just these words that get people all worried; the two Teachers (i.e., the Ch'eng brothers) have never said things like this."

See also my later discussion of Chu Hsi's *Jen-shuo* 仁說.

28. Jörg Bäcker, passim.

29. Tillman 77.

30. As for any direct connection between Hsieh and Ch'an Buddhist masters, the most that Kusumoto Bun'yu could adduce is a sort of "guilt by association" argument

based on contacts recorded of Hsieh's fellow disciples Yang Shih and Yu Tso. See his *Sōdai jugaku no zen shisō kenkyū* 宋代儒学の禅思想研究, 288–93.

31. An apparent allusion to *I-ching* 易經, K'un 坤 hexagram, line 1; see Wilhelm-Baynes 13.

32. LYCI 6B/8b. One of the challenges in translating this passage is to avoid an overly "subjective" reading of "*chih-chüeh*" 知覺, the usual modern Chinese equivalent of the English word "consciousness." Here, "that of which it is aware" (*you suo chüeh* 有所覺) can be understood, I believe, as referring at once to the subjectively apprehended sensation or feeling and to the source object with which the sensation represents interaction. It is an explicitly interactive notion of perception; as Hsieh says, "In the case of *jen*, the heart-and-mind and affairs are one."

33. STYL #6/4; see Chu Ron-Guey's translation, 48.

34. A suggestive modern account of these three realms of human life is found in *Exposition of the Divine Principle* (New York: HSA-UWC, 1996), 32–36.

35. For example, *Erh Ch'eng i-shu* 2a, in *Erh Ch'eng chi* (ECC), 15.

36. The idea seems to be that the flow of *ch'i* 氣 is somehow blocked or unbalanced between Yin and Yang. For an example of this diagnosis, see Chou Feng-wu and Chang Ts'an-chia, *Huang-ti nei-ching su wen yü-shih* 黃帝內經素問語釋 (An Explanation of the Language of the *Simple Questions on the Yellow Emperor's Internal [Medicine] Classic*), chapter 34, 341–42:

> Ch'i Po said, "When *jung-ch'i* 榮氣 [related to blood] is deficient [*hsü* 虛], then [the flesh] is numb [*pu-jen* 不仁]; when *wei-ch'i* 衛氣 [vital essence, defensive energy] is deficient, then [the limb] cannot be used. When both are deficient, then [the limb] is both numb and paralyzed, and the flesh is afflicted; the human body and will do not respond to each other. Prognosis: death.

This passage is rendered somewhat differently by Ilza Veith in *Huang Ti Nei Ching Su Wen: The Yellow Emperor's Classic of Internal Medicine*, 252.

37. A. C. Graham explains, "Not to feel a disinterested sympathy with others is to lose the consciousness that they are one substance with oneself. It is like numbness in a limb—a simile which recurs frequently in Ming-tao's sayings and which in unattributed sayings can be taken as almost certain evidence that he is the speaker." See *Two Chinese Philosophers*, 98.

38. For an insightful phenomenological discussion of the kinds of awareness associated with the body, see Drew Leder, *The Absent Body* (Chicago: University of Chicago Press, 1990), passim. See also Drew Leder, ed., *The Body in Medical Thought and Practice* (Boston: Kluwer, 1992).

39. The modern Chinese "*ma-mu pu-jen*" 麻木不仁 (apathetic, insensitive, unfeeling) preserves this correlation between physical and affective numbness.

40. As Tu Wei-ming notes in "A Chinese Perspective on Pain" (147): "The well-known modern Western dichotomy of body and mind is quite alien to the traditional Chinese mode of thinking." See also Hall and Ames, *Thinking Through Confucius*, 20: "In the polar metaphysics of the classical Chinese tradition, the correlative relationship between the psychical and the somatic militated against the emergence of a mind/body problem."

41. Ch'eng Hao in *Erh-Ch'eng i-shu* 2a; ECC, 15.

42. STYL #33/33–34; Chu Ron-Guey's translation, 80–81.

43. On the unity of mind-and-body as an achievement, see Yuasa Yasuo, *The Body: Toward an Eastern Mind-Body Theory*, passim.

44. "*Jen*" 人 and "*erh*" 二. Recently raised questions concerning the historical accuracy of this etymology do not alter the fact that it was the presumed etymology of "*jen*" 仁 for most of later Chinese intellectual history.

45. On *jen* as the ground of the other primary virtues, see Ch'eng Hao's "*Shih jen p'ien*" 識仁篇.

46. See *Erh-Ch'eng i-shu* 2A; ECC, 15. This passage is included in the "*Shih-jen p'ien*."

47. LYCI 2B/2a; "fancying and detesting" implies being fettered by one's own likes and dislikes.

48. LYCI 7B/30a.

49. LYCI 4B/5b.

50. LYCI 1A/22b. If one's sense of self is formed over against others, one cannot easily flow with the patterns of human-relatedness.

51. LYCI 1A/32b.

52. Preface, SWC version, 1235. The longer passage in which this remark appears was discussed in chapter 2.

53. "*Wan-wu chieh pei yü wo*" 萬物皆備於我, *Mencius* 7A:4. The phrasing here suggests a relational sense of "completed by me," as well as the microcosmic sense of "complete in me."

54. Hsieh's comments on the issue of self and things can be fruitfully compared with those of Su Shih; see Peter K. Bol, "*This Culture of Ours*," esp. 276–81.

55. CTYL 105, 2633. See also chapter 4.

56. LYCI 4B/12b.

57. It is worth recalling that "*sheng*," customarily translated as "sage," is the highest level of human attainment. As such, "*sheng*" is used as a Chinese translation for "saint," "sacred," and "holy."

58. LYCI 3B/25b.

59. "Doctrine of the Mean" 4; see Chan, *A Source Book*, 99. See also "Great Learning" 8 (Chan 90), which is cited by Hsieh on *Analects* 12:2, 3.

60. LYCI 6B/9a.

61. LYCI 10B/8a.

Notes to Chapter 4

1. James T. C. Liu, "How Did a Neo-Confucian School Become the State Orthodoxy?" *Philosophy East and West*, vol. 23, no. 4 (October, 1973), 490–91, n. 14. "Tao" is capitalized here even though Prof. Liu does not do so.

2. Liu, 490, n.15.

3. "The New *Tao-t'ung*," in Wing-tsit Chan, *Chu Hsi: New Studies*, 321. Chan maintains that it was Chu Hsi who coined the term "*Tao-t'ung*" in the 1189 preface to his *Chung-yung chang-chü* 中庸章句 (Arrangement and Commentary on the

"Doctrine of the Mean"). For Chan, this was one of Chu Hsi's major contributions to "the completion of Neo-Confucianism."

4. Liu, 490, n.15.

5. Huang K'an 皇 侃, *Lun-yü i-shu* 論語義疏 (Elaboration of the Meaning(s) of the *Analects*) 1/1a, *Ku-ching chieh hui-han*, 1847.

6. See Conrad Schirokauer, "Neo-Confucians Under Attack: The Condemnation of Wei-hsüeh," in John W. Haeger, ed., *Crisis and Prosperity in Sung China* (Tucson: University of Arizona Press, 1975), 163–98.

7. See Tillman 21; the official was Ch'en Kung-fu (1076–1141).

8. See T'o T'o, et al., *Sung shih* 宋史, *chüan* 427–29, biographies section 186–88, Chung-hua shu-chü edition, esp. 12709–10, for the official statement of how the Ch'eng-Chu school recovered the Way. For a narrative account of the rise of *Tao-hsüeh*, see Wm. Theodore de Bary, *Neo-Confucian Orthodoxy and the Learning of the Mind-and-Heart* (New York: Columbia University Press, 1981), and James T. C. Liu, "How Did a Neo-Confucian School Become the State Orthodoxy?"

9. In the course of a bibliographic article on the *I-lo yüan-yüan lu* 伊洛淵源錄, Wing-tsit Chan notes, "The *Sung-shih* biographies of the men concerned are based on this work, and its division into the two groups . . . made the partisan spirit official." See *A Sung Bibliography*, 223.

10. As will be seen, this schema is different from, and does not necessarily imply, the later interpretation of Neo-Confucian thought which divides it into a Ch'eng-Chu/Lu-Wang dichotomy (discussed later). For a detailed study of Yang Shih, see Melanie Alison Jameson, "South-returning Wings: Yang Shih and the New Sung Metaphysics," Ph.D. diss., University of Arizona, 1990.

11. Chen Te-hsiu, "Hsi-shan tu-shu chi 西山讀書集," SKCS edition 31/44b–45a. See Mao Huaixin, "The Establishment of the School of Chu Hsi and Its Propagation in Fukien," in *Chu Hsi and Neo-Confucianism*, 503–20. See also Zhu Hanmin, *Hu-Hsiang hsüeh-p'ai yüan-liu* 湖湘學派淵流 (On the Origins of the Hu-Hsiang School), 23–24. On Chen Te-hsiu's contributions to the acceptance of *Tao-hsüeh* as state orthodoxy, see Tillman, *Confucian Discourse*, 241–45.

12. See CTYL 18/678.

13. On Huang Tsung-hsi's criticism of the category "*Tao-hsüeh*," see Julia Ching's introduction to her selected translation of Huang's *Ming ju hsüeh-an* 明儒學案, *The Record of Ming Scholars*, 7. Thomas A. Wilson has done an extensive study of the formation of orthodoxy as a political question, via the major anthologies of Sung Confucian writings. See his *Genealogy of the Way: The Construction and Uses of the Confucian Tradition in Late Imperial China* (Stanford: Stanford University Press, 1995).

14. Huang Tsung-hsi, comment in "Shang-ts'ai hsüeh-an 上蔡學案," *Sung-Yüan hsüeh-an* 宋元學案 (SYHA) 24/1b.

15. SYHA 24/1b.

16. As edited by Ch'üan Tsu-wang and Wang Tze-ts'ai, the SYHA describes Hu An-kuo as a *chiang-yu* 講友 (friend in learning, that is, a peer) of Hsieh, and also of Yang Shih and Yu Tso, and a disciple (*men-jen* 門人) of two other Confucian scholars. But it also lists Hsieh's disciple Chu Chen as Hu's *chiang-yu*. Ch'üan notes that later

Confucians placed Hu under Hsieh's line but says that they are mistaken, and Wang adds a reason: "[Hsieh] Shang-ts'ai did not receive [Hu] formally as a disciple." SYHA, 34; 9/110.

17. Zhu Hanmin 27.

18. See Hu Hsien, "Hsieh Hsien-tao yü-lu pa 謝顯道語祿跋" in *Shang-ts'ai hsien-chih* 上蔡縣志, 14/80a.

19. Zhu Hanmin 28. Furthermore, there were also intricate ties between Hsieh and other members of Hu An-kuo's prominent scholarly family. Hu Yin 胡 寅 (1098–1156), Hu An-kuo's eldest son by adoption from his brother's family, wrote the postface to Hsieh's *Analects* commentary; Hu Hsien 胡 憲 (1086–1162), Hu An-kuo's nephew and student, wrote a foreword to the STYL; Hu Hung 胡 宏 (1106–1161), Hu An-kuo's third son, had a complicated affinity with Hsieh's thought; and Hu Hung's cousin and student Hu Shih 胡 實 (1136–1173) and his nephew and student (Hu Yin's son) Hu Ta-yüan 胡大遠 both accepted Hsieh's most important and controversial contribution, namely his teaching on *jen* as *chüeh*.

20. As Conrad Schirokauer writes, "Hu Hsien was a follower of An-kuo's teachings and during his university years secretly read the writings of the Ch'eng brothers, which were then proscribed." See his article "Chu Hsi and Hu Hung," in *Chu Hsi and Neo-Confucianism*, 482. When Chu Hsi was fourteen, his father Chu Sung (1097–1143), just before passing away, expressed the wish that Chu Hsi study with three friends, Liu Tzu-hui (1101–1147), Liu Mien-chih (1091–1149), and Hu Hsien. See SYHA 43, "Liu-Hu chu-ju hsüeh-an."

21. "Chi-hsi hsien-sheng Hu kung hsing-chuang" in CTWC 97:16a–18b.

22. Chu Hsi, Yen-p'ing ta-wen (Yen-p'ing Li hsien-sheng shih ti-tzu ta-wen) 1/34b, Kinsei kanseki sokan edition, 98.

23. See Chu's memorial inscription written in the winter of 1191 for a temple honoring Hsieh, "Te-an fu Ying-ch'eng hsien Hsieh hsien-sheng ts'u chi." CTWC 80/4b–5b. Chan (*New Studies*, 14) translates one of the closing sentences, "As a youth, I foolishly made up my mind to study. My interest was aroused by the theories of the Master." It is noteworthy that in this record, Chu praises Hsieh's discussion of *jen* as "*shih-li*" 實理 ("real principle" or "pattern of reality") while omitting his most important gloss on *jen*, namely *chüeh*.

24. *Confucian Discourse* 45.

25. *Confucian Discourse* 46–47, emphasis added.

26. See Wing-tsit Chan's essay "Chu Hsi's 'Jen-shuo'" in *New Studies*, 171. Hoyt Tillman also notes this "unfortunate loss" and tries to compensate for it. See *Confucian Discourse*, esp. 70–81.

27. Chan, *Source Book*, 593, and *New Studies* 173f.

28. Liu Shu-hsien 劉述先, "Further Examination of Chu Hsi's 'Treatise on *Jen*,' the Concept of the Great Ultimate, and Orthodox Tradition of the Way—Reflections on Participating at the International Conference on Chu Hsi [in Chinese]," in *Shih-hsüeh p'ing-lun* [Historical Tribune], no. 5 (January 1983), translated by Wing-tsit Chan, *New Studies*, 176–77.

29. Satō's essay is found in *Chu Hsi and Neo-Confucianism*, 212–27. Chan's rebuttal of Liu's article is found in *New Studies*, 177.

30. *Confucian Discourse* 80.

31. *Confucian Discourse* 81.

32. Peter Bol has characterized Chu Hsi as "the most influential thinker and intellectual entrepreneur since Hui-yüan." See his review of Daniel Gardner's *Learning to Be a Sage: Selections from the Conversations of Master Chu, Arranged Topically* in *Journal of Sung-Yuan Studies* 22, 210.

33. On Tan's *Jen-hsüeh*, see Chan Sin-wai, trans., *An Exposition of Benevolence: The Jen-hsüeh of T'an Ssu-t'ung* (Hong Kong: Chinese University Press, 1984), and Douglas David Wile's "T'an Ssu-t'ung: His Life and Major Work, the '*Jen Hsueh*,'" Ph.D. diss., University of Wisconsin, 1972. See also Hao Chang, *Chinese Intellectuals in Crisis: The Search for Order and Meaning (1890–1911)* (Berkeley: University of California Press, 1987).

34. *An Exposition of Benevolence*, section 3, 73, slightly modified. The original analogy as drawn by Ch'eng Hao and expanded by Hsieh was discussed in chapter 3.

35. "*Chih-hui sheng yü jen*" 智慧生於仁 is point #10 of the introductory definitions; cf. *Exposition*, 62, 238.

36. Indeed, T'an may have coined the term, as his essay is the only identification for "*jen-hsüeh*" in the standard dictionaries, Morohashi and Chung-wen Ta tz'u-tien.

37. *The World of Thought in Ancient China*, 176.

38. See Wm. Theodore de Bary, *Neo-Confucian Orthodoxy and the Learning of the Mind-and-Heart* (New York: Columbia University Press, 1981) and *The Message of the Mind in Neo-Confucianism* (New York: Columbia University Press, 1989).

39. A major interpretive re-evaluation of "orthodoxy" in the lineage of *Tao-hsüeh*, particularly of the place of the Hu-Hsiang scholars, was initiated by Mou Tsung-san in *Hsin-t'i yü hsing-t'i* 心體與性體 (The Substance of the Mind and the Substance of Human Nature), (Taipei: Cheng-chung Book Co., 1969), 3 vols.

40. The defining phrases are "*ai-chih-li*" 愛之理 and "*hsin-chih-te*" 心之德. "*Ai*" is translated here as "affection" rather than "love" because "love" is a highly charged and multivalent word in English, sharing significant common ground with "*jen*." Thus, David Wile translates the title of T'an Ssu-t'ung's essay as "The Learning of Love."

41. See "Jen-hsüeh chih nei-jung chi ch'i p'ai-pieh" (The Content and Separate Factions of the Learning of Jen), in *Sung-hsüeh Kai-yao* (Essentials of Sung Learning) (Shanghai: Shang-wu yin shu kuan, Min-kuo 26 [1937]), 162–208. Hsia's work is helpful in highlighting the centrality of *jen* in the concerns of leading Sung Confucians, since it has often been overshadowed by attention to newly important terms in Sung thought, such as *li* 理 and *ch'i* 氣.

42. Hsia makes an interpretive error in treating Hsieh's teaching only in relation to Ch'eng I and not Ch'eng Hao.

43. Found in *Chung-kuo che-hsüeh*, number 5, 17–32, and in *Chung-kuo wen-hua ti wei-chi yü chan-wang*, 19–36. An English equivalent, "The Way, Learning, and Politics in Classical Confucian Humanism," was published as Occasional Papers, no. 2 (1985) by the Institute of East Asian Philosophies, Singapore, and reprinted in *Way, Learning, and Politics: Essays on the Confucian Intellectual* (Albany: SUNY Press, 1993). I would simply like to note that I do not find "humanism" to be an apt translation for "*jen-hsüeh*," for reasons suggested in the next section.

44. See Hsü's essay "Shih Lun-yü ti 'jen'—K'ung-hsüeh hsin lun" in his collected volume *Chung-kuo ssu-hsiang shih lun chi hsi-p'ien* (Taipei: Shih-pao wen-hua ch'u-pan-she, 1982 [Min-kuo 71]), 355.

45. Reminiscent of the process by which Buddhist teachings came to be indigenized in China, "*ko-i*" might be translated "match-ing meanings," in the sense of a dynamic "wrestling match" with ideas.

46. OED 1345. According to the OED, "humane" was originally the same word as "human." The spelling "humane" remained for "human" until the early eighteenth century (see OED, Compact Edition, 1345); cf. *jen* 仁 and *jen** 人. Representing one type of this older usage, the phrase "Humane and Divine learning" occurs, in which the first term meant "relative to man as distinguished from God." See Samuel Purchas, *Pilgrimage* 1613 (1614 edition, 320), OED 1345. In 1709, with the older usage, Alexander Pope wrote, *Ess. Crit.* 527, "To err is humane, to forgive divine." There is an interesting comparison with *Analects* 4:7, "Observe the errors and you will know *jen*"; D.C. Lau reads *jen* as *jen**: "Observe the errors and you will know the man." Even after the two words "humane" and "human" became differentiated, their meanings were and are closely interrelated; in 1841 Trench wrote, "It is just in man to be merciful . . . to be humane is human." *Parables* viii (1877 edition), 159, cited in OED, 1345. This recalls the Confucian definition, found in both "Doctrine of the Mean" and *Mencius*: "*Jen* is [the distinguishing characteristic of being] human" (*jen-che, jen* yeh* 仁者人也) *Chung-yung* 20; see also *Mencius* 7B16. The two cognate words also appear as adjective and noun, as in *Mencius* 1B15, "This is a humane human" (*jen-jen* yeh* 仁人也).

47. OED 1345. In this sense, the phrase "humane learning" is attested by 1701: "To learn Humane Learning; that is to say, to understand the Greek Poets and Orators and to write well in that Tongue." Jean Le Clerc, *Lives of the Primitive Fathers*, translated 1701, 174, cited in OED 1345.

48. See Peter K. Bol, "Culture and the Way in Eleventh-Century China," Ph.D. diss., Princeton, 1982, and also his *"This Culture of Ours,"* esp. chapter 9.

49. See STYL #90: "Few students who first learn *wen* can reach the Tao. Even extensive reading will bring jeopardy to oneself. Therefore Ming-tao taught me, 'My worthy friend, when you read books, be cautious in not becoming entangled in the ink.'"

50. *Mencius* 6A7, Lau 164; the original text has "The sage is . . . ."

Notes to Conclusion

1. The Neo-Confucians had learned much from Buddhist meditation practices, as evidenced by their emphasis on reflection and the practice of quiet-sitting. So Chu felt that if one were not "careful," one might drift unawares toward the Ch'an (meditation) schools of Buddhism. Indeed, as Miriam Levering has documented, scholarly Buddhist teachers in Chu's time, such as Ta-hui Tsung-kao, were making a concerted effort to win over Confucian literati.

2. Hsieh specialized in the *Li-chi* in his studies, while Chu also worked on the ritual classics and compiled his own guide to family rituals, known as the *Chu-tzu chia-li* 朱

子家禮. Chu's text has been translated and discussed by Patricia Ebrey in *Chu Hsi's Family Rituals* (Princeton: Princeton University Press, 1991). In related work, Ellen Neskar has examined the specific rituals associated with shrine veneration of the *Tao-hsüeh* figures. See Ellen G. Neskar, "The Cult of Worthies: A Study of Shrines Honoring Local Confucian Worthies in the Sung Dynasty (960–1279)," Ph.D. diss., Columbia University, 1993.

3. As A. C. Graham has put it, "We, like the Chinese, fully engage with the thought only when we relate it to our own problems." See the author's preface to *Disputers of the Tao*, ix.

4. This point was suggested by Prof. Meng Peiyuan 蒙培元 of the Chinese Academy of Social Sciences in Beijing, in personal conversation.

5. Tu Wei-ming, "Hsiung Shih-li's Quest for Authentic Existence," reprinted in *Humanity and Self-Cultivation*, 246.

6. As I have tried to suggest, Confucian humane learning is open to transcendence. It does not participate in the humanism/theism split that has come to characterize Western thought. Thinking about humane learning in this way can be helpful in overcoming a great divide in Western intellectual culture.

7. In an image developed by Richard R. Niebuhr, the modern situation for human sensitivity appears as the plight of "radial man," who is beset by sensory signals from around the globe. In Niebuhr's words, "Our electronic global nervous system relentlessly transmits the anger, fears, and hopes of every emerging nation and pent-up ghetto to the sleepless mind of the radio listener." See his *Experiential Religion*, preface.

8. On this point, there is an intriguing similarity between the Confucian notion of awareness and some observations on awareness and the "middle zone barrier" made by the Gestalt psychologist Fritz Perls. See Perls, *The Gestalt Approach and Eye Witness to Therapy* (n.p.: Science & Behavior Books, 1973), esp. 129–130, and James Lynwood Walker, *Body and Soul: Gestalt Therapy and Religious Experience* (Nashville: Abingdon Press, 1971), 184.

9. STYL #6/4; see Chu Ron-Guey's translation, 48.

10. For a methodological discussion of Troeltsch's maxim, see Michael Pye, "Comparative Hermeneutics in Religion," in *The Cardinal Meaning*, 9–58. According to Pye's note (16, n.19), the original quotation is found on p. 431 of Ernst Troeltsch, "Was heißt 'Wesen des Christentums'" ("What Does 'Essence of Christianity' Mean?"), in *Gesammelte Schriften*, 2 (Tübingen 1913), 386–451; first published in *Die Christliche Welt*, 1903. An English translation of Troeltsch's article is found in *Ernst Troeltsch: Writings on Theology and Religion*, trans. and ed. Robert Morgan and Michael Pye (Atlanta: John Knox Press, 1977), 124–179.

Notes to Introduction to Appendices

1. See chapter 2, the section on "Gathering Hsieh's Commentary."

2. Some of the entries in the LYCI include additional sayings attributed to Hsieh that are also found in and presumably taken from the *Shang-ts'ai yü-lu*. These separate sayings have not been included in this appendix, because they are not part of his commentary per se.

3. I have followed standard sectioning of the *Analects* chapters.

4. D. C. Lau's translations of *Analects* 1–2 are found in *Confucius: The Analects*, translated with an introduction by D. C. Lau, (London: Penguin Books, 1979), 59–66.

5. Roger T. Ames and Henry Rosemont, Jr., *The Analects of Confucius: A Philosophical Translation* (New York: Ballantine Books, 1998).

Notes to Appendix 1

1. The phrase "conduct of an exemplary person" translates *"chün-tzu"* 君子, used adjectivally here (*chün-tzu*-like).

2. Practice (*hsi* 習) includes both specific learned actions and habitual attitudes.

3. These phrases are from *Li-chi* "Chü-li, shang" 1/4. (Passages from *Li-chi* are cited according to the Harvard-Yenching Series index, reprinted as *Li-chi yin-te* by Shanghai ku-chi ch'u-pan-she, 1983). See also Legge, *Li Ki*, vol. 1 (published as SBE vol. 27), 62. Legge notes that in the Chou rituals, "the representatives of the dead always sat, and bore themselves with the utmost gravity."

4. Citing *Analects* 4:5; in context, "this" (*shih* 是) stands for *"jen"* in these phrases. In the second phrase, *"tien-p'ei"* 顛沛 has been rendered as "stumbling" (Lau), "tottering" (Waley), "wandering and suffering hardship" (*tien-p'ei liu-li* 顛沛流離) (Yang), and "seasons of danger" (Legge). The general idea is that in urgent or desperate moments one still remains within the realm of *jen*.

5. *Mencius* 6A7, Lau 164; the original text has "The sage is . . . ."

6. *Mencius* 5B8; see Lau 158. The *shih* were a social stratum in ancient China between the high official class and the common people, including scholars, apprentices, and minor officers.

7. *Lao Tzu* 70. Although there are textual difficulties with this passage, Hsieh is following a common reading. See Chu Chien-chih, *Lao-tzu chiao-shih*, in the Hsin-p'ien chu-tzu chi-ch'eng series, (Beijing: Chung-hua shu-chu, 1987 [1984]), 281.

8. *Analects* 7:16, Lau 88.

9. *Analects* 6:11, Lau 82.

10. A variant reading for this passage, replacing 仁 with 人, is sometimes given: "the root of a person's character." Hsieh clearly takes the passage as discussing *jen* 仁.

11. *Ch'iu jen chih fang* 求仁之方, or: the direction in which to seek *jen*.

12. *Analects* 17:6, Lau 144.

13. *Analects* 12:1, Lau 112.

14. *Analects* 12:2, Lau 112.

15. *Analects* 12:3, Lau 112, modified.

16. *Chuang-tzu* 4,1.40; Graham 70, slightly modified. This saying is attributed to Confucius.

17. *Li-chi,* "Ch'ü li" 1, 12; see Legge, *Li Ki*, vol. 1, 68.

18. *Li-chi,* "Ch'ü li" 1, 10; Legge, *Li Ki*, vol. 1, 67. "For all sons it is the rule: in winter, to warm (the bed for their parents), and to cool it in summer."

19. *Mencius* 3A4, Lau 102; see also *Li-chi* 6/8.

20. *Mencius* 6B2, Lau 172, modified.

21. That is, Confucius and his disciples.

22. "*Li-hsing*" 力行," *Chung-yung* 20; see Chan, *Source Book*, 105.

23. *Analects* 1:2.

24. In translating this comment, it is challenge to find consistent renderings for *ch'iao* 巧 (Lau: cunning) and *ling* 令 (Lau: ingratiating) that allow for the different nuances that Hsieh is pointing out. "Artful" and "pleasing" are used here, respectively.

25. *Li-chi*, "Piao-chi" 32/26. Legge translates "*ch'iao*" in this passage as "susceptible of proof"; see *Li Ki*, vol. 2 (SBE, vol. 28), 349.

26. *Shih-ching* #260 "Ching min." Legge (*Chinese Classics*, vol. 4, 542) translates "*ling*" as "good."

27. *Analects* 15:18, Lau 134.

28. *Analects* 10:4, Lau 101.

29. See *Analects* 17:12, "A cowardly person who puts on a brave front."

30. *Analects* 8:4, paraphrased.

31. The last question, "*ch'uan pu hsi hu?*" 傳不習乎, can also be interpreted as asking whether one passed on to others things that one has not applied for oneself.

32. For the "nine streams" (*chiu liu* 九流), see the *Han-shu* "Yi-wen chih."

33. Literally, does not have two extremities (*wu erh chih* 無二至).

34. I have not been able to locate a source for this phrasing.

35. *Chung-yung* 13; see Chan, *Source Book*, 101 and Legge, *Chinese Classics*, vol. 1, 394.

36. That is, taking "*wu*" 物 and "*wo*" 我 as two; see discussion in chapter 3.

37. *Analects* 11:25; Lau 110, modified.

38. *Analects* 11:25 begins with "On the occasion Tzu-lu made Tzu-kao the prefect of Pi, the Master said, 'He is ruining another man's son.'"

39. *Analects* 19:25, Lau 157, modified.

40. Paraphrasing *Mencius* 2A2.

41. *Mencius* 3A3, Lau 97.

42. Literally, a "younger brother and son" (*ti-tzu* 弟子); the term has come to mean "disciple" or "pupil."

43. *I-ching*, Wen Yen commentary on "Ch'ien" hexagram (#1), second line. See Wilhelm/Baynes 380, Legge, *Yi King* (SBE, vol. 16), 410.

44. *Mencius* 7B31, Lau 200.

45. See *Analects* 6:30: "A person of humanity, wishing to establish his or her own character, also establishes the character of others." See Chan 31 (6:28, modified).

46. *Analects* 7:6, Lau 88. See also *Li-chi*, "Shao i" 17/15, Legge, *Li Ki*, vol. 2, 73.

47. The note attributed to K'ung An-kuo says it means "taking the heart-and-mind of loving beauty to love the worthy, then it is good." See Hsing Ping's edition, 1/3b. The word "*se*" 色 in both passages is generally taken to refer to beauty, especially to beautiful women. But this gender assumption is not necessary to the point about spontaneously appreciating worthy persons.

48. That is, it is a natural, unpremeditated response. See *Ta-hsüeh* 7, Chan 89.

49. *Analects* 9:18 and 15:13; see Lau 98 and 134.

50. *Mencius* 5A1; Lau 138.

51. The *Chu-tzu i-shu* edition has "not to dare to have a stopping point (*i* 已)."

52. *Mencius* 3A4; see Lau 102. In the *Mencius* text, "distinction between husband and wife" and "precedence of the old over the young" come before "faith between friends."

53. *Chung-yung* 6; Chan 99.

54. Paraphrasing *Mencius* 4B28; Lau 134.

55. See *Chung-yung* 20; Chan 105.

56. Hsing Ping (1/4a) notes that there are two traditional interpretations of this line. The interpretation followed by Hsieh and other Neo-Confucians reads *ku* 固 as *chien-ku* 堅固 (strong, firm). The gloss attributed to K'ung An-kuo interprets *ku* as a blockage, thus "obstinate" or "inflexible," so the phrase would be: "An exemplary person . . . who studies will not be inflexible."

57. See *Chung-yung* 20; Chan 105.

58. *Chung-yung* 20; Chan 106.

59. These descriptions are from *Li-chi* 13/16 "Yü tsao"; see Legge, *Li Ki*, vol. 2, 18. Hsieh has reversed the order of the latter two.

60. Continuing to cite *Li-chi* 13/16 "Yü tsao"; see Legge, *Li Ki*, vol. 2, 18.

61. See *Analects* 12:1.

62. *Analects* 20:2; see Lau 160.

63. *I-ching*, "Hsi-tz'u chuan, shang" 12; Legge, *Yi King,* 378, modified. Wilhelm/Baynes (324) has: "Silent fulfillment, confidence that needs no words, depend upon virtuous conduct."

64. "is cold when worn in the wind." *Shih-ching* #27 "Lü Yi"; Legge, *Chinese Classics*, vol. 4, 42.

65. *Chuang Tzu* 1/29; Graham 46. Note that Hsieh deliberately counters the logic of Chuang Tzu, by holding such claims up for ridicule.

66. See *Analects* 17:3.

67. *Analects* 15:10; see Lau 133.

68. *Analects* 19:16.

69. "*Kuo, kuo yeh*" 過過也. This may be a play on words, with the second "*kuo*" to be read as "passing," meaning either "something excessive" or "something past."

70. *Huai Nan Tzu,* "Yüan Tao" (as given by Yang in a note to *Analects* 14:25, 154). See a related passage in *Chuang Tzu* 25 translated by Graham (102): "Ch'ü Po-yü at the age of sixty had sixty times changed his mind . . . We do not yet know of anything which we now affirm that we shall not deny it fifty-nine times over."

71. Or: "content with old habits."

72. See *Mencius* 7B15; Lau 197: "The Sage is teacher to a hundred generations."

73. *Analects* 6:3.

74. *Mencius* 2A8; Lau 83.

75. *Hsün-tzu* 27/94 "Ta lüeh." See *Hsün-tzu tu-pen*, 387.

76. *Analects* 19:21.

77. "*Tzu-ch'i tzu-pao*" 自棄自暴. See *Mencius* 4A10; see Lau 122: "It is not worth the effort to talk to a person who has no self-respect [*tzu-pao che* 自暴者], and it is not worth the trouble to make common effort with a person who has no self-confidence [*tzu-ch'i che* 自棄者]."

78. See *Analects* 19:8.

79. *Mencius* 4B13; see Lau 130 and Legge, *Works of Mencius*, 322.
80. See my discussion of *Analects* 1:2 in chapter 3.
81. See *Mencius* 3A5, recounting that in ancient times, seeing that the bodies of their deceased parents were eaten by foxes, sons were moved to bury them.
82. See *Li chi* 21:1, Legge, *Li Ki*, vol. 2, 210—"When he treads on the dew which has descended as hoarfrost he cannot help a feeling of sadness, which arises in his mind and cannot be ascribed to the cold." Therefore, in the autumn, offspring sacrifice to their parents.
83. See *Mencius* 7B25 (Lau 199): "to shine forth with this full possession [is called 'great']."
84. *Chung-yung* 16; Chan (102) translates: "[Such is] the impossibility of hiding the real [*ch'eng* 誠]."
85. "*Hsing-hsing jan*" 悻悻然; see *Mencius* 2B12, Lau 94.
86. *Li-chi* 2/16 "Chü li, hsia"; Legge, *Li Ki*, vol. 1, 112.
87. *Analects* 10:2; Lau 101.
88. *Analects* 10:2; Lau 101.
89. See *Shih-ching* #107, "Ko chü," Legge, *Chinese Classics*, vol. 4, 163.
90. "*Tsung-tsung*" 總總; translation tentative.
91. These phrases are from *Analects* 8:4.
92. "*Wu-wo chih hsin* 物我之心," a key term in Hsieh's thought. The connection with being deferential may be that the perceived opposition between self and others puts one constantly on guard against others. See discussion in chapter 3.
93. *Mencius* 7B15; see Lau 197.
94. See *Mencius* 2B2, Lau 87: "Hence a prince who is to achieve great things must have subjects he does not summon. If he wants to consult them, he goes to them."
95. *Analects* 13:14; Lau 120, modified. See also Legge, *Chinese Classics*, vol. 1, 268.
96. *Analects* 11:22; Lau, 109, modified.
97. *Hsiao-ching* (The Classic of Filial Piety), chapter 1; cf. Legge, SBE vol. 3, 466, and Fung Yu-lan/Derk Bodde, vol. 1, 361.
98. I.e., a brief instant of fleeting time. Hsieh is alluding to *Li-chi* 38/8, "Questions on the Three Years Mourning"; see Legge, *Li Ki*, vol. 2, 393.
99. For this phrase, see *Shih-ching* Odes #35 and #197. Alternatively, Legge (*Chinese Classics*, vol. 4, 56, 340) translates, "What avails it to care?" The sentiment here seems to be that one is too caught up in the sense of loss for it to matter whether one's father's ways should be changed or kept unchanged.
100. Hsieh assumes the gloss of "harmony" as "music" found in Hsing Ping (1/4b) and Huang K'an (see Yang 8). His explanation thus draws heavily on the "Yüeh chi" chapter of the *Li-chi* and focuses on the necessary balance between ritual and music.
101. Following Wang Meng-o's gloss for "*fan*" in his commentary on "Yüeh chi" 19/26, 648.
102. On some of these dyadic relationships, see *Li-chi*, "Yüeh chi," 19/6; Legge, *Li Ki*, vol. 2, especially 102–103.
103. *Li-chi*, "P'in i," 48/10; see Legge, *Li Ki*, vol. 2, 462. The occasion was ceremonial archery among diplomatic missions.

104. *Li-chi*, "Yüeh chi" 19/10; see Legge, *Li Ki*, vol. 2, 107. The whole passage reads, "Where there is (but) one presentation of the cup (at one time), guest and host may bow to each other a hundred times, and drink together all the day without getting drunk." See also Yang K'uan, "Hsiang chiu yü hsiang li hsin t'an," in *Ku shih hsin t'an* (New Discussions of Ancient Matters), 281.

105. See *Li-chi*, "Yüeh chi" 19/1. Legge (*Li Ki*, vol. 2, 98) translates, "where ceremony [*li* 禮, ritual] prevails [over music, there is] a tendency to separation [*li* 離]." Wang Meng-o glosses *li* (separation) as "*ke-he* 隔閡," no meeting of minds, a barrier of heart-and-mind.

106. See *Analects* 3:1, 2, 6.

107. *Li-chi*, "Li chi," 10/37; see Legge, *Li Ki*, vol. 1, 415. The context is that since the Chi family were overzealous in their performing of rites from before dawn until after dark, those who performed were not able to be consistently reverent in their performance.

108. *Analects* 14:43; Lau translates, "Yüan Jang sat waiting with his legs spread wide." The idea is that even this complete lack of courtesy is better than excessive ritualism.

109. This term appears in the "Autumn Floods" section of the *Chuang-tzu* 17/6; see Graham (145): "You can't talk to hole-in-the-corner scholars [*ch'ü-shih* 曲士] about the Way, because they are constricted by their doctrines."

110. For example, Hsün Tzu; see especially chapter 23, on human nature as evil and ritual as the result of "conscious activity" (*wei* 偽).

111. *Lao-tzu* 38; Lau 99.

112. *Mencius* 7B37; see Lau's translation, 203.

113. Following Hsing Ping (1/4b) but different from Lau, this passage would mean that "[ritual] followed alike in matters great and small [without harmony] will not always work." Although this is in accord with Hsieh's overall interpretation (as in his concluding sentence), he uses the passage here to show that harmony requires ritual.

114. See for example *Li-chi*, "Hsiang yin chiu i" 45/8, Legge, *Li Ki*, vol. 2, 440–41.

115. *Analects* 10:2; see Lau 101.

116. See *Analects* 4:26.

117. See *Li-chi* "Yüeh chi" 19/26, repeated in "Chi i" 24/34; Legge, *Li Ki*, vol. 2, 126–27 and 225–26, respectively.

118. I have largely followed Lau's rendering here, taking "*yin*" 因 (relation, cause) as "*yin*" 姻 (marriage), as this accords with Hsieh's interpretation. For a different interpretation, having nothing to do with marriage, see Ames and Rosemont 74.

119. *Analects* 11:6; Lau 106.

120. *Analects* 18:8; Lau 151.

121. "Performing in measure" for "*chung-chieh*" 中節 draws on the image from music and ritualized archery of "hitting the beat" or striking the rhythm. I would like to thank Prof. Chiang I-pin of Chinese Culture University for suggesting this point on the importance of "the beat" in ritualized performance.

122. This phrase is found in *Chuang Tzu* 4/20, "Jen-chien shih." Graham (68) translates, "Lifting up the tablet in his hands and kneeling and bowing from the waist [are the etiquette of a minister]." However, the context in *Chuang Tzu* is rather ironic.

123. For Confucius's similar action in passing the court, see *Analects* 10:3.

124. *Li-chi* 1/11–12; see Legge, *Li Ki*, vol. 1, 68.

125. *Shu-ching* 17, "Yüeh ming"; Legge, *Chinese Classics*, vol. 3, 257. See also *Tso-chuan*, first year of Duke Ting.

126. "*I-shih t'ung-jen*" 一視同仁." The source of this saying is Han Yü's essay, "Yüan jen* lun" 原人論 (On Human Origins). Generally, it means being impartial and extending the same generous treatment to all.

127. *Analects* 12:5; Lau 113.

128. See *Analects* 8:3, on Tseng Tzu's showing his hands and feet.

129. See *Li-chi* 9/5, Legge, *Li Ki*, vol. 1, 369.

130. *Shih-ching*, Ode #237, "Mien"; Legge, *Chinese Classics*, vol. 4, 437.

131. *I-ching*, "Hsi-tz'u chuan" 2.2; Wilhelm/Baynes 331.

132. *Mencius* 7B24; Lau 198, slightly modified.

133. "joy can still be found," *Analects* 7:16; see Lau 88.

134. "is a hardship most people would find intolerable, but Yen Hui does not allow this to affect his joy," *Analects* 6:11, paraphrased. See also *Mencius* 4B29.

135. At the time his father died, Mencius had only the rank and means for a smaller offering. *Mencius* 1B16; Lau 72.

136. *Li-chi* 3/18, paraphrased; see Legge, *Li Ki*, vol. 1, 128. According to the text, Tseng Tzu was extremely ill, yet insisted that the mat on which he was lying be changed from one beyond his rank.

137. That is, they did not have the rank of counselors (*tai-fu* 大夫). See *Analects* 11:8, in which Confucius thus describes his official rank.

138. See *Analects* 13:17; Lau 121.

139. See *Mencius* 7B37, "the wild rush forward." See also *Analects* 5:22.

140. *Mencius* 7B37, following Legge's interpretation of "*pu wang ch'i ch'u*" 不忘其初 as "cannot forget their early ways." Hsieh's understanding of this passage takes "rushing forward" and "not forgetting their early ways" as a reciprocal pair of shortcomings: either being overly ambitious or clinging to old ways. See also *Analects* 13:21.

141. *Analects* 10:2, slightly paraphrased; Lau 101.

142. *Analects* 10:1, shortened; Lau 101.

143. See *Analects* 7:38, Lau 91: "The Master is cordial yet stern."

144. *Analects* 19:6.

145. *Chung-yung* 8; Legge, *Chinese Classics*, vol. 1, 389, modified.

146. See *Analects* 8:5, on that toward which Yen Hui directed his efforts.

147. *Mencius* 6A10; Lau 166.

148. The reference here is to *Li-chi* 4/62, "T'an kung, hsia"; see Legge, *Li Ki*, vol. 1, 195.

149. *Analects* 5:9; see Lau 77.

150. *Analects* 7:8; see Lau 86.

151. *Shih-ching*, "Odes of Wei" # 55.

152. The reference is to *Mencius* 6B3, in which Mencius criticizes Master Kao's interpretation as "rigid" (*ku* 固); see Lau 173. Hsieh is taking Kao as representing a pedantic approach to the *Odes*.

153. See *Ta-hsüeh* 7; Chan translates, "as if they see his very heart."

154. This phrasing seems to imply that "anxiousness about being known by others" is both what those engaged in learning are troubled about and what is troubling their learning.

Notes to Appendix 2

1. See *Analects* 6:11 on Yen Hui living in a narrow alley. The implied criticism of Yen Hui as a model is somewhat surprising, given Hsieh's general admiration for him.

2. On Yü and Chi, see *Shu-ching* 5, "I Chi," Legge, *Chinese Classics*, vol. 3, 76f.

3. *Mencius* 4A11, Lau 122–23: "If only everyone loved his parents and treated his elders with deference, the Empire would be at peace." Cf. the description of the Age of Great Unity in the "Li yün" chapter of the *Li-chi* (9/1, Legge, *Li Ki*, vol. 1, 365) as the time when people "did not love their parents only, nor treat as children only their own sons."

4. The passage is from *Li-chi*, "Ta-hsüeh" (The Great Learning), 42/10, see Wing-tsit Chan, *A Source Book*, 91 (#9). The skeptical sentiment in the commentary here is rather remarkable. But compare this with Hsieh's comment on *Analects* 2:21.

5. Chan (*Source Book*, 22) translates the phrase ("*ssu wu hsieh*" 思無邪) as "Have no depraved thoughts," citing *Ode* #297 and commenting, "The word *ssu* means 'Ah!' in the poem but Confucius used it in its sense of 'thought.'" However Confucius used the phrase, by the time of Chu Hsi it was definitely understood to refer to thoughts (as in CTYL 23/538f.). That seems to be Hsieh's understanding as well, although Chu Hsi complained that he did not address the issue (CTYL 23/546).

6. Lit., "sputtered out [*hsi* 熄]."

7. The quality of "stopping in propriety and righteousness" is attributed in the "Great Preface" of the *Odes* to "the beneficent influence of the former kings." See Legge's prolegomena, *Chinese Classics*, vol. 4, 36.

8. *I-ching* "Hsi-tz'u chuan, hsia," 4; Legge, *SBE*, vol. 16, 393: The Master said: "The superior man . . . makes his mind restful and easy before he speaks." Similarly, Wilhelm/ Baynes 343.

9. *Analects* 3:20, Lau 70. See also the "Little Preface" to Ode #1, Legge's prolegomena, *Chinese Classics*, vol. 4, 37.

10. *Odes* #27 "Lü yi"; Legge, *Chinese Classics*, vol. 4, 42. Hsieh condenses the title from the "Little Preface"; see Legge's prolegomena, Ibid., 41.

11. *Odes* #31 "Chi ku"; Legge, *Chinese Classics*, vol. 4, 48. The extended title is implied in the "Little Preface"; see Legge's prolegomena, Ibid., 42.

12. *Odes* #33 "Hsiung chih"; Legge, *Chinese Classics*, vol. 4, 51. The narrative title comes from the "Little Preface"; see Legge's prolegomena, Ibid., 42.

13. *Odes* #66 "Chün-tzu yü yi"; Legge, *Chinese Classics*, vol. 4, 113. The long narrative title is taken from the "Little Preface"; see Legge's prolegomena, Ibid., 48.

14. From the description of the *Ya* forms of the Odes in the "Great Preface"; see Legge's prolegomena, *Chinese Classics*, vol. 4, 36.

15. Part of the description of the *Sung* forms of the Odes from the "Great Preface"; see Legge's prolegomena, *Chinese Classics*, vol. 4, 36. Hsieh replaces "*sheng*" 盛 (complete) with "*sheng*" 聖 (sagely).

16. *Li-chi* 31/20, "Chung-yung"; see Chan's *Source Book*, 105.

17. See *Mencius* 2A2; Lau 79.

18. That is, when the experience of taste becomes so enjoyable that the distinction between taste and taster is forgotten.

19. *I-ching*, "Ch'ien" hexagram (#1), "Wen yen"; Wilhelm/Baynes 376: "Because he is persevering and firm, he is able to carry out all his actions."

20. This may be understood as coherence between heavenly Mandate and the principle in things, and also between heavenly Mandate and the nature of the person, and therefore as coherence between these two also. Chu Hsi remarked (CTYL 23/557) that Hsieh's interpretation of "knowing the heavenly Mandate" was "the best" among all those in the LYCI; he did not, however, include it in the LYCC.

21. For the term "*ch'ou-tsuo*" 酬酢 (give and take/social interaction), see *I-ching*, "Hsi-tz'u chuan, shang," 8; Wilhelm/Baynes (313) translate it as "meet[ing] everything in the right way."

22. The idea seems to be that an arbitrary, subjective intention can neither be added to, nor subtracted from, the flow of the Way to which one is attuned.

23. See *Mencius* 6A11.

24. Both "knowing innately" and "practicing naturally and easily" are the highest of three comparative levels described in "*Chung-yung*" 20; see *Source Book* 105.

25. *Analects* 14:35; Lau 129.

26. These phrases on the grades of learning come from *Li-chi*, "Hsüeh chi," 18/2; see Legge, *Li Ki*, vol. 2, 83.

27. *Li-chi*, "Hsüeh chi," 18/2, following the gloss of Wang Meng-o, 595; Legge (*Li Ki*, vol. 2, 83) renders "*pu fan*" 不反 as "would not fall back."

28. Echoing and reversing the logic of *Analects* 1:7, in which Tzu-hsia remarks that even though someone may say [of himself or of others] that he does not yet have learning, if the person has certain qualities in action, Tzu-hsia would definitely say the person has learning.

29. See *Li-chi*, 27/7 (Questions of Duke Ai); Legge, *Li Ki*, vol. 2, 269: "Therefore a [person of *jen*] serves his parents as he serves Heaven, and serves Heaven as he serves his parents."

30. The text has "in bed" (*ch'in* 寢), which may indicate a contrast with Tsai Wo (*Analects* 5:10). Chu Hsi has placed the small character "*i*" 疑 (doubtful) at this point, and so it is.

31. See *Analects* 16:3. Meng Yi Tzu and Meng Wu Po belonged to one of the Three Families.

32. In contrast with *Analects* 5:13, in which Tzu-kung said, "one cannot get to hear [the Master's] views on human nature and the Way of Heaven."

33. See *Li-chi* 24/35, "Chi i" (The meaning of sacrifice). Legge (*Li Ki*, vol. 2, 228) translates, "when they are dead, to ask (the help only of) the good to obtain grain with which to sacrifice to them." Wang Meng-ou (p. 765) suggests that it means, "one must use one's own rightful income to offer sacrifice to them." The translation here is more

literal, with the thought that "the grain of a person of *jen*" might be like the fruit of good seed.

34. "*Wu wei* 無違," that is, contrary to the rites. This is the phrase translated by Lau as "Never fail to comply." "*Wei*" also has the connotation of "disobedience."

35. "*Hao hao-se*" 好好色" *Li-chi*, "Ta hsüeh" 7; see *Source Book*, 89.

36. *Li-chi* 12/12, "Nei tse"; Legge, *Li Ki*, vol. 1, 456.

37. *Li-chi* 2/17, "Chü li, hsia"; Legge, *Li Ki*, vol. 1, 114 (modified).

38. *Li-chi* 24/35, "Chi i"; Legge, *Li Ki*, vol. 2, 226 (modified).

39. "*Che*" 折 is read as "*che-chuan*" 折饌 (removing sacrificial dishes).

40. *Mencius* 7B15; see Lau 197. The *Mencius* passage originally refers to Po Yi and Liu Hsia Hui, but Hsieh applies it to Confucius.

41. "*Pu-wei*," 不違, i.e., no internal opposition. Translated here as "disagreeing," the character "*wei*" is the same as "violation" in the previous section.

42. Followed by an editorial "*i*' 疑 (doubtful). Possible meanings might be: "it is the same as simply reading a book" or "reading books is just the same [one must reach to 'no internal opposition']."

43. *Analects* 6:3, 11:7.

44. See *Analects* 12:1, Confucius's answer to Yen Hui's question about *jen* as entailing not looking, listening, speaking, or acting in impropriety.

45. See "Chung-yung" 8; Legge, *Chinese Classics*, vol. 1, 389 and Chan 99.

46. As in Yü's saying, *Shu-ching* 5; Legge, *Chinese Classics*, vol. 3, 76.

47. *Analects* 6:17.

48. *Analects* 14:6.

49. See *Analects* 4:2.

50. "Ta-hsüeh" 7; Chan 90.

51. "Ta-hsüeh" 7; Chan (90) translates " as if they see his very heart." See Hsieh's commentary on 1:16.

52. That is, from the viewpoint of having obtained the one Way.

53. "Chung-yung" 27; Chan 110.

54. *Analects* 13:21, *Mencius* 7B37; in the *Analects*, Lau (122) translates "enterprising," but in *Mencius* (202), "rushing forward."

55. *Mencius* 7B37; Lau (202) translates "[rushing forward] while not forgetting their origins." However, Hsieh understands "*pu wang ch'i ch'u*" 不忘其初 as juxtaposed with "rushing forward," in the pattern of the wild and the squeamish. Therefore, Legge's (498) "cannot forget their early ways" is followed here. See Hsieh's comment on *Analects* 1:14.

56. *Li-chi* 18/10 "Hsüeh chi," Legge (*Li Ki*, vol. 2, 89–90) translates, "He who gives (only) the learning supplied by his memory in conversations is not fit to be a master."

57. "Chung-yung" 13. Chan (101) translates, "There are four things in the Way of the superior man, none of which I have been able to do."

58. See *Mencius* 2A2, "A sage is something even Confucius did not claim to be"; Lau 79.

59. *Analects* 14:6.

60. In this sentence, Hsieh is quoting from *Analects* 4:16, 4:11, 14:23, 35, and 15:34, respectively.

61. *Mencius* 7A21; Lau 186.

62. See *Mencius* 2A2; Lau 79.

63. But rather from Confucius, see *Mencius* 5B1; Lau 150.

64. See *Mencius* 7A21; Lau 186.

65. *Shu-ching* 1, "Yao tien"; Legge (*Chinese Classics*, vol. 3, 26) translates the description of Shun: "He is the son of a blind man. His father was obstinately unprincipled, his step-mother was insincere, his half brother Seang was arrogant. He has been able, however, by his filial piety to live in harmony with them."

66. *Mencius* 7B11; Lau 196: "A man who is out to make a name for himself will be able to give away a state of a thousand chariots, [but in a different context would show resentment in giving away soup and rice]." However, Hsieh seems to use the phrase as a simple description, so I have added "genuinely."

67. See *Analects* 17:19.

68. A comment attributed to K'ung An-kuo in the *Lun-yü chu-shu* glosses "*chou*" 周 as "doing one's best and being trustworthy [*chung-hsin* 忠信]." Later commentators extend this in the direction of "nonpartisan."

69. The passage is obscure and the translation tentative at best. Hsieh seems to be characterizing the attitude of the petty person in forming cliques, each looking out only for his cohorts, by using an image from *Chuang Tzu* 14: "When the spring dries up and the fish are stranded together on land, they spit moisture at each other and soak each other in the foam." See Graham 129.

70. For Confucius's description of "the exaltation of virtue," see *Analects* 12:10 and 12:21.

71. See *Analects* 14:35.

72. *Mencius* 7A:5. Lau (182) translates: "[The multitude can be said never] to notice what they repeatedly do."

73. *Analects* 8:9.

74. This phrase alludes to *Analects* 15:33.

75. *I-ching*, "Hsü kua" 2; see Legge, *SBE*, vol. 16, 438: "He whose greatness reaches the utmost possibility, is sure to lose his dwelling" and Wilhelm/Baynes 675: "Whatever greatness may exhaust itself upon, this much is certain: it loses its home."

76. Referring to *Analects* 17:8, in which the Master enumerates the faults involved in loving six moral qualities without "loving learning."

77. I have translated this controversial passage in accord with Hsieh's comment on it. Lau gives the rather literal rendering, "To attack a task from the wrong end can do nothing but harm." The more usual interpretation of this passage, given by Hsing Ping (2/3b) without specific attribution and then followed by him, is that "*kung*" 攻 (Lau: to attack) means "*chih*" 治 (order, to study). Hsing continues, "The good Way has unity, therefore it has multiple paths which have a common return [*kuei* 歸, paraphrasing "Hsi-tz'u chuan," 2.3; see Wilhelm/Baynes 338], *i-tuan* do not have a common return." The interpretation is thus (as in Legge, *Chinese Classics*, vol. 1, 150): "The study of strange doctrines is injurious indeed!" Hsing Ping interprets "*i-tuan*" as referring to "the writings of the hundred schools." The same basic interpretation is

followed in the LYCC, with an added twist by Chu Hsi to direct the passage against Buddhist teachings. On the other hand, Yang Bojun (18) follows a different line of interpretation, taking "*kung*" as "attack" and the final "*i*" 已 as "*chih*" 止 (to stop), so that his rendering might translate, "Critique the various incorrect theories and harm can be eliminated." Ames and Rosemont point out (233, n. 34) that the recently discovered Dingzhou *Analects* fragments, which have 功 instead of 攻, support the more usual rendering. Hsieh has something in common with these other interpretations, yet differs intriguingly.

78. Duke Ting of Lu (r. 509–495 BCE) and his son Duke Ai (r. 494–466).

79. "Chung yung" 29; Chan 111. The original context concerns "the regulations of former times."

80. See also Chu Hsi's essay "Chih tao" (The Way of Governing). The meaning seems to be "adding fuel to the fire."

81. *Analects* 7:21; Lau 88: "The topics the Master did not speak of were prodigies, force, disorder, and gods."

82. That is, "the structure and implications of my teaching." See *Analects* 19:23 on Tzu-kung's description of Confucius's walls and gate.

83. See *Mencius* 3B9; Lau 115.

84. Again, following Hsieh's interpretation. A more common rendering would be "to recognize that you know when you know, and that you do not know when you do not."

85. "*Chih-chih wei chih-chih*" 知之爲知之; Lau and other interpreters: "To say you know when you know." The other Ch'eng disciples also seem to take the phrase in this way, but Hsieh interprets it in a remarkably different and innovative way.

86. *I-ching*, "Hsi-tz'u chuan" 3–4; Wilhelm/Baynes (294) translate the latter as "the conditions of outgoing and returning spirits."

87. *Chuang Tzu* 2/56; lit., "beyond the six combinations [*liu-he* 六合]": Heaven and Earth (or up and down), and the four directions. A. C. Graham (57) translates, "What is outside the cosmos [the sage locates as there but does not sort out]."

88. See *Mencius* 4B28, 7A1.

89. "*Shih-fei chih hsin*" 是非之心; see *Mencius* 2A6, 6A6.

90. "*Wen*" 聞 could be taken as "listen" or "using the ears," as in Lau's translation, or in light of Hsieh's examples, as "reputation."

91. The reference "alone" (*tu* 獨) recalls the image of vigilant solitariness (*shen-tu* 慎獨) from both "Ta-hsüeh" 7 and "Chung-yung" 1.

92. Interpreted by Lau as "mistakes," but here in accord with Hsieh's usage.

93. Hsieh is using the term "*chin-ssu*" 近思 in a different way than in *Analects* 19:6.

94. *Hsiao-ching* 4. See Legge's translation in SBE.

95. I.e., without a true standard, people will subjectively decide what is upright and what is crooked—the implication is that this leads to chaos.

96. *Analects* 8:9.

97. On "completing oneself" and "completing things," see Hsieh's comment on *Analects* 2:1: "Learning is to complete oneself; governing is to complete things." See also "Chung-yung" 25; Chan (108) translates: "Sincerity is not only the completion of

one's own self; it is that by which all things are completed. The completion of self means humanity. The completion of all things means wisdom."

98. *I-ching*, Judgement on hexagram #37, "Chia jen"; Legge's translation (*SBE*, vol. 16, 242) continues "let the husband be indeed husband and the wife wife;—then will the family be in its normal state. Bring the family to that state, and all under heaven will be established."

99. See *Mencius* 7A9: "In solitariness, one makes one's personal conduct good [*tu shan ch'i shen* 獨善其身]."

100. See *Analects* 8:7.

101. Compare Hsieh's comment on *Analects* 2:1, that such is not yet the full extent of governing.

102. *Mencius* 7B25.

103. See also *Analects* 19:2.

104. In *Mencius* 7A38 (Lau 191), Mencius said, "Our body and complexion are given to us by Heaven. Only a sage can give his body complete fulfilment [chien-hsing 踐形]."

105. Compare "Ta-hsüeh" 8 (Chan 90): "When the mind is not present, we look but do not see, listen but do not hear, and eat but do not know the taste of food."

106. In contrast to *Mencius* 7B:31: "If a person can fully extend the natural aversion to harming others, there will be an abundance of jen."

107. "Tz'e-yin" 惻隱; see *Mencius* 2A6, 6A6.

108. Continuation of the contrast with *Mencius* 7B31 (Lau 200): "If a man can extend his dislike for boring holes and climbing over walls, then there will be an overabundance of rightness." Compare *Mencius* 3B3, "those who bore holes in the wall to peep at one another, and climb over it to meet illicitly."

109. See *Mencius* 2A6, 6A6.

110. *I-ching*, "Hsi-tz'u chuan," 1.4; Wilhelm/Baynes 294.

111. "Wang-liang" 魍魎; see Chuang-tzu 2/92. A note in the Chuang-tzu tu-pen describes "wang-liang" as "in general, something which is neither this nor that . . . like a human but not human, like a ghost but not a ghost." Graham (60) translates it as "Penumbra," following Kuo Hsiang (see Chuang-tzu chi-shih 1b/110).

112. "Chung-yung" 29; Chan 111.

113. "Chung-yung" 29; Chan 111.

114. "Yin ko" 因革; another possibility is "building on and changing," following Lau's translation of "yin" as "built on."

115. See, for reference, the "Sun" 損 (decrease) and "I" 益 (increase) hexagrams of the *I-ching*, numbers 41 and 42, respectively.

116. Following D. C. Lau's convention of using "Tchou" 紂 for the evil last ruler of the Yin.

117. A possible reference to Chuang Tzu 28; Graham 232: "to exchange tyranny for a misrule pushed farther still."

118. "Chung-yung" 29; Chan 111.

119. See "Chung-yung" 29; Chan 111.

120. See *I-ching*, "Hsi-tz'u chuan," 1.5: "When Yin and Yang cannot be fathomed, it is called spirit [shen 神]."

121. A more philosophical interpretation would gloss "shen" 神 (spirit) as "shen" 伸 (extension) and "kuei" 鬼 (ghost) as "kuei" 歸 (returning), thus the extending and returning of the Yin and Yang. See *Li-chi*, "Chi-i" 24/24; Legge, *Li Ki*, vol. 2, 220: "All the living must die, and dying, return [kuei] to the ground; this is called 'kuei [ghost].'" Chan glosses "kuei-shen" as "positive and negative spiritual forces"; see Source Book 789.

122. Or: "cause them to approach." This reading of "ko" 格 recalls "Chung-yung" 16, quoting Ode #256 (Legge, *Chinese Classics*, vol. 4, 398): "The approaches of the spirits, you cannot surmise;—and can you treat them with indifference?" Chu Hsi glosses this as "the response of the spirits"; see his discussion of this comment at CTYL 101/2565.

123. This and the following sentence draw on Li-chi, "T'an kung, shang" 3/69. Legge (*Li Ki*, vol. 1, 148) translates: "Confucius said, 'In dealing with the dead, if we treat them as if they were entirely dead, that would show a want of [jen], and should not be done; or if we treat them as if they were entirely alive, that would show a want of wisdom, and should not be done.'" Hsieh apportions this advice according to whether or not the particular sacrifice is "permissible"(k'o 可).

124. See *Analects* 6:22: "Show reverence to ghosts and spirits, and keep them at a distance."

125. The phrase "ghosts will not be spiritual," with "shen" 神 (spiritual, cf. ling 靈) modifying "kuei" 鬼, recalls Lao Tzu 60 (see Chan's Source Book, 168). Hsieh's meaning here seems to be that for those for whom it is permissible (according to the rites), one should allow their ghost to become spiritual—that is, communicable and spiritually relevant—through the sacrifice, whereas one should not do so for those for whom it is not permissible.

126. The phrasing recalls *I-ching*, "Hsi Tz'u chuan" 1.4; see Wilhelm/ Baynes 294.

127. That is to say, able to be courageous in not sacrificing inappropriately.

128. On "knowing reaching to it," see *Analects* 15:33.

129. "Hsün-hsün" 恂恂, a description of Confucius in *Analects* 10:1.

130. Wu Yu, son of Wu Hui, was a regional governor during the Latter Han dynasty, who ran afoul of the wealthy and powerful minister and imperial relative Liang Chi (fl. 136–160) yet held his ground. See *Hou Han shu* 94/1a–3b (SPPY; cf. SPTK 64).

131. *Mencius* 2A2; see Lau 77: "if one finds oneself in the right, one goes forward even against men in the thousands."

Note to Appendix 3

1. The Chinese text has been digitally reproduced and formatted for inclusion in this book, hence the slight variation in the size of the characters in these selections. For *Analects* 1.7, the *Chu-tzu i-shu* edition has been substituted. The borders surrounding each selection have been added; open-ended borders indicate continuation of the text.

Glossary

ai chih li 愛之理

ch'ao-yüeh 超越

cheng-i 正義

Ch'eng Hao, Po-ch'un, Ming-tao 程顥，伯醇，明道

Ch'eng I, Cheng-shu, I-ch'uan 程頤，正叔，伊川

chiang-yu 講友

Chien-yen i-lai hsi-nien yao-lu 建炎以來繫年要錄

chih 知

chih-chüeh 知覺

chih-hsien 知縣

chih-che yao shui 知者樂水

chih-yen 知言

chin-shih 進士

Chin-ssu lu 近思錄

Ching-i k'ao 經義考

ching-tso 靜坐

ch'i 氣

ch'iao 巧

ch'in-jen 親仁

ch'in-jen i ch'eng-chi 親仁以成己

ch'ing 清

ch'iu-jen 求仁

Chou-li 周禮

Chu Chen, Han-shang 朱震，漢上

Chu Hsi 朱熹

Chu Nei-han lun K'ung-Meng chih hsüeh ch'uan yü Erh-Ch'eng 朱內翰論孔孟之學傳於二程

Chu Ron Guey 朱榮貴

chu-tzu 諸子

Chu-tzu hsin hsüeh-an 朱子新學案

Chu-tzu i-shu 朱子遺書

Chu-tzu nien-p'u 朱子年譜

Chu-tzu yü-lei 朱子語類

Chuang Tzu 莊子

chün-tzu 君子

chung 忠

chung-kuo li-shih ti-t'u chi 中國歷史地圖集

Chung-yung 中庸

ch'u tse ch'i 出辭氣

chü chih mo neng sheng 舉之莫能勝

chüeh 覺

Erh-Ch'eng chi 二程集

Erh-Ch'eng i-shu 二程遺書

Erh-Ch'eng wai-shu 二程外書

Fu-kou hsien-chih 扶溝縣志

fu tzu yu ch'in 父子有親

Han Fei Tzu 韓非子

Hsiao-ching 孝經

hsien-ju 先儒

Hsieh Liang-tso, Hsien-tao, Shang-ts'ai 謝良佐，顯道，上蔡

Hsieh Shang-ts'ai yü-lu hou-chi 謝上蔡語錄後記

hsin 心

hsin chih te 心之德

hsin-hsüeh 心學

hsin-te 心得

hsin yu suo chüeh 心有所覺

hsing 性

hsing-wu 醒悟

hsiu-ts'ai 秀才

Hsün Tzu 荀子

Hu An-kuo 胡安國

Hu-hsiang hsüeh (-p'ai) 湖湘學 (派)

Hu-shih ch'uan chia lu 胡氏傳家錄

hua-t'ou 話頭

Huai Nan Tzu 淮南子

Huang Kan 黃榦

Huang K'an 皇侃

Huang-ch'ao wen-chien 皇朝文鑑

hun-jan 渾然

Hung-shih T'ang shih ching kuan tsung-shu 洪氏唐石經館叢書

I-ching 易經

i-tuan 異端

i wan-wu wei i-t'i 以萬物爲一體

i wu wei wo 以物爲我

I-Lo yüan-yüan lu 伊洛淵源錄

jen 仁

jen* 人

jen i ch'eng chi, chih i ch'eng wu 仁以成己，知以成物

jen wu wei chi 認物爲己

jen* yü chi wei-i 人與己爲一

jen yü wei li 認欲爲理

jen-che jen* yeh 仁者人也

jen-che yao shan 仁者樂山

jen-hsüeh 仁學

Jen-shuo 仁說

ju 儒

ju-chiao 儒教

ju-chia ssu-hsiang 儒家思想

kan 感

ko-wu 格物

Kuei-shan yü-lu 龜山語錄

kung-fu 功夫

K'ung-tzu jen-hsüeh chung ti Tao, hsüeh, cheng 孔子仁學的道，學，政

Kuo-ch'ao chu lao hsien-sheng Lun-Meng ching-i 國朝諸老先生論孟精義

Lao Tzu 老子

li (principle, pattern) 理

li (ritual) 禮

Li-chi 禮記

Li Hsin-ch'uan 李心傳

li-hsüeh 理學

Lieh Tzu 列子

ling 靈

Lun-yü cheng-i 論語正義

Lun-yü chi-chieh 論語集解

Lun-yü chi-chu (LYCC) 論語集註
Lun-yü chi-i 論語集義
Lun-yü chieh 論語解
Lun-yü chieh hsü 論語解序
Lun-yü ching-i (LYCI) 論語精義
Lun-yü chu-shu 論語注疏
Lun-yü i-shu 論語義疏
Lü Ta-lin 呂大臨
Lü Tsu-ch'ien 呂祖謙

ma-mu pu-jen 麻木不仁
men-jen* 門人
Mien-ch'ih hsien-chih 澠池縣志
mu-chih ming 墓誌銘

nien 念

Pai-hu t'ung 白虎通
Pien-Tao lu 辨道錄
pu-ch'uan chih hsüeh 不傳之學
pu-jen 不仁

san-chiao 三教
Shang-ti 上帝
Shang-ts'ai Lun-yü chieh (STLYC) 上蔡論語解
Shang-ts'ai Lun-yü chieh hou-hsü 上蔡論語解後序
Shang-ts'ai yü-lu (STYL) 上蔡語錄
Shang-ts'ai yü-lu hou-chi 上蔡語錄後記
sheng-sheng 生生
Shih-chi 史記
shih-min ju-shang 視民如傷

Shih-ching 詩經
Shih-jen p'ien 識仁篇
shu 恕
Shu-ching 書經
Ssu-ma Kuang 司馬光
Ssu-shu huo-wen 四書或問
Su Shih 蘇軾
Sung 宋
Sung-hsüeh kai-yao 宋學概要
Sung wen-chien 宋文鑑
Sung-Yüan hsüeh-an (SYHA) 宋元學案

Ta-hsüeh 大學
Tao 道
Tao-hsüeh 道學
Tao-ming lu 道命錄
Tao-t'ung 道統
T'ai-chi 太極
T'ien 天
T'ien-chu 天主
T'ien-chu shih-i 天主實義
T'ien-li 天理
T'ien-ti chih hsin 天地之心
tsai-ch'uan 再傳
ts'e-yin chih hsin 惻隱之心
Tso-chuan 左傳
tsung-chiao 宗教
ts'ung 從
Ts'ung-shu chi-ch'eng 叢書集成
t'ung-t'i 同體
tzu-jan-erh-jan 自然而然
Tzu-ssu 子思
tzu-te 自得

wan-wei 玩味

wan-wu 萬物

wan-wu sang-chih 玩物喪志

Wang An-shih, Chieh-fu 王安石，介甫

Wang Fang, Yüan-tse 王雨方，元澤

Wang Pi 王弼

wen-chi 文集

wen-hsüeh 文學

Wu-ching cheng-i 五經正義

wu-wo chih fen 物我之分

wu-wo chih hsin 物我之心

wu-wo hsiang-tui 物我相對

Yang Hsiung 揚雄

Yang Shih, Kuei-shan 楊時，龜山

Yin T'un, Ho-ching 尹焞，和靖

Yu Tso, Ting-fu, Chai-shan 游酢，定夫，齋山

Yüan Tao lun 原道論

yung-hsin 用心

Selected Bibliography

Abbreviations

CITCS   Cheng-i t'ang chüan-shu 正誼堂全書
CTIS   Chu-tzu i-shu 朱子遺書
KHCPTS   Kuo-hsüeh chi-pen ts'ung-shu 國學基本叢書
KKS   Kinsei kanseki sōkan 近世漢籍叢刊
SKCS   Ying-yin Wen-yüan ko Ssu-k'u chüan-shu 景印文淵閣四庫全書
SPPY   Ssu-pu pei-yao 四部備要
SPTK   Ssu-pu ts'ung-k'an 四部叢刊

Ames, Roger T., and Henry Rosemont, Jr. *The Analects of Confucius: A Philosophical Translation*. New York: Ballantine Books, 1998.

Bäcker, Jorg. "'Prinzip der Natur' und 'Sein Selbest Vergessen,' Theorie und Praxis des Neokonfuzianismus Anhand der 'Aufgezeichneten ausspruche des Hsieh Liang-tso (1050–1121).'" Ph.D. diss., Rheinischen Friedrich-Wilhelms-Universität, Bonn, 1982.

Berthrong, John Hugh. "Chu Hsi's Ethics: *Jen* and *Ch'eng*." *Journal of Chinese Philosophy* 14 (June 1987): 161–78.

———. "Glosses on Reality: Chu Hsi as Interpreted by Ch'en Ch'un." Ph.D. diss., University of Chicago, 1979.

Bloom, Irene, trans. *Knowledge Painfully Acquired: The K'un-chih chi by Lo Ch'in-shun*. New York: Columbia University Press, 1987.

Bol, Peter K. "Ch'eng Yi as a Literatus." *The Power of Culture: Studies in Chinese Cultural History*, edited by Willard J. Petersen, Andrew Plaks, and Ying-shih Yü. Hong Kong: Hong Kong University Press, 1994, 172–94.

———. "Culture and the Way in Eleventh Century China." Ph.D. diss., Princeton University, 1982.

———. *"This Culture of Ours": Intellectual Transitions in T'ang and Sung China*. Stanford: Stanford University Press, 1992.

Booth, Wayne C. *Modern Dogma and the Rhetoric of Assent*. Notre Dame: University of Notre Dame Press, 1974.

Cai Fanglu (Ts'ai Fang-lu) 蔡方鹿. *Ch'eng Hao Ch'eng I yü Chung-kuo Wen-hua* 程顥程頤與中國文化 (Ch'eng Hao, Ch'eng I, and Chinese culture). Guiyang: Kuei-chou jen-min, 1996.

Carman, John, and Mark Juergensmeyer, eds. *A Bibliographic Guide to the Comparative Study of Ethics*. Cambridge: Cambridge University Press, 1991.

Chan Sin-wai, trans. *An Exposition of Benevolence: The Jen-hsüeh of T'an Ssu-t'ung*. Hong Kong: Chinese University Press, 1984.

Chan, Wing-tsit. *Chu Hsi: New Studies*. Honolulu: University of Hawaii Press, 1989.

_____. "Chu Hsi's Completion of Neo-Confucianism." *Etudes Song: In Memoriam Etienne Balazs*, 2nd ser., 1 (1972): 59–90.

_____ 陳榮捷. *Chu-tzu men-jen* 朱子門人 (Chu Hsi's Disciples). Taipei: Student Book Co., 1982.

_____. "The Evolution of the Confucian Concept *Jen*." *Philosophy East and West* 4.4 (January 1955): 295–315.

_____. "Patterns for Neo-Confucianism: Why Chu Hsi Differed from Ch'eng I." *Journal of Chinese Philosophy* 5 (1978): 101–26.

_____, ed. *Chu Hsi and Neo-Confucianism*. Honolulu: University of Hawaii Press, 1986.

_____, trans. *Neo-Confucian Terms Explained (The Pei-hsi tzu-i) by Ch'en Ch'un, 1159–1223*. New York: Columbia University Press, 1986.

_____, trans. *Reflections on Things at Hand: The Neo-Confucian Anthology Compiled by Chu Hsi and Lü Tsu-ch'ien*. New York: Columbia University Press, 1967.

_____, trans. and comp. *A Source Book in Chinese Philosophy*. Princeton, Princeton University Press, 1963.

Chang, Carsun. *The Development of Neo-Confucian Thought*, vol. 1. New York: Bookman Associates, 1957.

Chang Shih 張栻. *Chang Nan-hsien hsien-sheng wen chi* 張南軒先生文集. KHCPTS edition. Shanghai: Shang-wu yin-shu-kuan, 1937.

Chang Tsai 張載. *Chang Tsai chi* 張載集. Peking: Chung-hua shu-chü, 1985 [1978].

Chang Yung-chün 張永俊. *Erh-Ch'eng hsüeh kuan-chien* 二程學管見 (Humble Views on the Learning of the Two Ch'engs). Taipei: Tung-ta t'u-shu, 1988.

_____. "Tu 'Shang-ts'ai yü-lu' suo chien" 讀「上蔡語錄」所見 (Thoughts on Reading "The Sayings of [Hsieh] Shang-tsai"). *National Taiwan University Philosophical Review* (*Che-hsüeh Lun-p'ing*) 8 (January 1985): 145–73.

_____. "Yang Kuei-shan che-hsüeh ssu-hsiang shu-p'ing" 楊龜山哲學思想述評 (A Critical Account of Yang Kuei-shan's Philosophical Thought). *National Taiwan University Philosophical Review* (*Che-hsüeh Lun-p'ing*) 7 (January 1984): 163–97.

Ch'ao Pu-chih 晁補之. "Pa Hsieh Liang-tso suo shou Li T'ang ch'ing-chuan ch'ien-tzu wen" 跋謝良佐所收李唐千字文 (Colophon to a Thousand-word Precious Seal Character Writing of the T'ang Dynasty Collected by Hsieh Liang-tso) in *Chi-le chi* 雞肋集 33/23b. SKCS edition. Taipei: Shang-wu yin-shu-kuan, 1983.

Chen Lai (Ch'en Lai) 陳 來. *Sung Ming Li-hsüeh* 宋明理學 (Neo-Confucianism of the Sung and Ming Periods). Reprint, Taipei: Hung-ye wen-hua, 1993.

Chen Te-hsiu 真德秀. *Hsi-shan tu-shu chi* 西山讀書集 ([Chen] Hsi-shan's Reading Journal). Ch'in-ting Ssu-k'o chüan shu edition. Taipei: Shang-wu yin-shu-kuan, 1976.

Ch'eng Hao 程 顥 and Ch'eng I 程 頤. *Erh Ch'eng chi* 二程集 (Collected Writings of the Two Ch'engs). Ed. Wang Hsiao-yü, from SPPY. 2 vols. Reprint Taipei: Han-ching wen-hua, 1983.

_____. *Honan Ch'eng-shih i-shu* 河南程氏遺書 (Surviving Works of the Ch'engs of Honan). KHCPTS edition. Shanghai: Shang-wu yin-shu-kuan, 1935.

Ch'eng I 程 頤. "Ming-tao hsien-sheng mu-piao" 明道先生墓表 (Epitaph for Master [Ch'eng] Ming-tao). *Honan Ch'eng-shih wen-chi* 河南程氏文集 11, in *Erh Ch'eng chi* 二程集. Taipei: Han-ching wen-hua, 1983.

Chiang I-pin 蔣義斌. *Sung-ju yü Fo-chiao* 宋儒與佛教 (Sung Dynasty Confucians and Buddhism). Hong Kong: Hai-hsiao 海嘯 ch'u-pan shih-ye, 1997.

_____. *Sung-tai ju shih t'iao-ho-lun chi p'ai-fo-lun chih yen-chin* 宋代儒釋調和論及排佛論之演進 (The Evolution of the Confucian-Buddhist Synthesis and Anti-Buddhism in the Sung Period). Taipei: Shang-wu yin-shu-kuan, 1988.

Chiang Yung 江 永. *Chin-ssu lu chi-chu* 近思錄集註 (Collected Annotations on Reflections on Things at Hand). Shanghai: Shang-wu yin-shu-kuan, 1933, reprinted by Shang-hai shu-tien, 1987.

Ch'ien Mu 錢 穆. *Chu-tzu hsin hsüeh-an* 朱子新學案 (A New Scholarly Record on Chu Hsi). 5 vols. Taipei: San-min Book Co., 1982 [1971].

_____. *Sung Ming Li-hsüeh Kai-shu* 宋明理學概述 (A General Account of Sung and Ming Neo-Confucian Thought). Taipei: Student Book Co., 1984 [1975].

_____. *Sung-tai Li-hsüeh San-shu Sui-cha* 宋代理學三書隨劄 (Notes to Three Texts of Sung Dynasty Neo-Confucian Thought). Taipei: Tung-ta, 1983.

Ching-shu 經書 (Korean edition, Kyong so) Songgyun'gwan Taehakkyo, Seoul, 1965. (Facsimile reproduction of 1777 edition).

Ching, Julia. *Confucianism and Christianity: A Comparative Study.* New York: Kodansha International, 1977.

Ching, Julia, et al., trans. *The Records of the Ming Scholars*. Honolulu: University of Hawaii Press, 1987.

Chu Chen 朱 震. "Chu Nei-han lun K'ung-Meng chih hsüeh ch'uan yü Erh-Ch'eng" 朱內翰論孔孟之學傳於二程 (Secretary Chu Discusses the Transmission of the Learning of Confucius and Mencius to the Ch'eng Brothers). Collected in Li Hsin-ch'uan 李心傳, comp., *Tao-ming lu* 道命錄 (Record of the Destiny of the Tao) Ming Hung-chih edition 3/2a–b, and *Chien-yen i-lai hsi-nien yao-lu* 建炎以來繫年要錄 (Important Records Chronologically Interrelated from the Chien-yen Period [1127–1130] Onward) 101/12b–13b, *Ts'ung-shu chi-ch'eng* ed. Kyoto: Chūbun shuppansha indexed edition, 1983: 837-38.

Chu Hsi 朱 熹. *Chu-tzu i-shu* 朱子遺書 (Surviving Works of Master Chu). Taipei: I-wen shu-kuan, 1969. (Facsimile reproduction of Pai lu tung edition).

_____. *Chu-tzu yü-lei* 朱子語類 (Classified Conversations of Master Chu). Ed. Li Ching-te, punctuated edition, Beijing: Chung-hua shu-chü, 1986. Reprint of 1473 ed., 8 vols., Taipei: Cheng-chung, 1962. Indexed edition by Sato Hitoshi, Kyoto: Chūbun shuppansha, 1984 [1970].

_____. *Hui-an hsien-sheng Chu Wen-kung wen-chi* 晦庵先生朱文公文集 (Chu Hsi's Collected Writings). SPTK edition, Shanghai: Shang-wu yin-shu-kuan, 1929. Edition with name index by Satō Hitoshi, Taipei: Ta-hua shu-chü, 1985.

_____, comp. *Ssu-shu chang-chü chi-chu* 四書章句集註 (Collected Commentaries on the Four Books). Punctuated edition. Taipei: E-hu, 1984.

_____, comp. *I-Lo yüan-yüan lu* 伊洛淵源錄 and *I-Lo yüan-yüan lu hsin-tseng* 伊洛淵源錄新增 (Records of the Origin of the Loyang School [of Ch'eng Hao and Ch'eng I], with Supplement). TSCC edition, Shanghai: Shang-wu yin-shu-kuan, 1936. KKS annotated edition, Taipei: Kobun Shokyoku, 1972.

_____, comp. *Kuo-ch'ao chu lao-hsien-sheng Lun-Meng ching-i* 國朝諸老先生論孟精義 (Essential Meanings of the *Analects* and *Mencius* by the Old Masters of Our Dynasty). Hung-shih T'ang shih-ching kuan tsung-shu 洪氏唐石經館叢書 edition, Kuang-hsü period, 1875-1908. CTIS edition, Taipei: I-wen shu-kuan, 1969. SKCS edition, Taipei: Shang-wu yin-shu-kuan, 1983.

_____, comp. *Yen-p'ing ta-wen* 延平答問 (Li T'ung's Answers to [His Student Chu Hsi's] Questions). CTIS edition, Taipei: I-wen shu-kuan, 1969. KKS edition, Taipei: Kobun Shokyoku, 1972.

Chu I-tsun 朱彝尊. *Ching-i k'ao* 經義考 (Research on the Meaning of the Classics). SPPY edition. Shanghai: Chung-hua shu-chü, 1936.

Chu Ron-Guey 朱榮貴. "*Recorded Sayings of Hsieh Liang-tso (Shang-ts'ai hsien-sheng yü-lu)*: An Annotated Translation with an Introduction." M.A. thesis, Columbia University, 1982.

Chung Tsai-chun. *The Development of the Concepts of Heaven and of Man in the Philosophy of Chu Hsi.* Nankang, Taiwan: Academia Sinica, 1993.

Chung-kuo li-shih ti-t'u chi 中國歷史地圖集 (The Historical Atlas of China), ed. Tan Qixiang (T'an Ch'i-hsiang) 譚其驤, vol. 6, *Sung, Liao, Chin.* Shanghai: Cartographic Publishing House, 1982.

de Bary, Wm. Theodore. *Learning For One's Self.* New York: Columbia University Press, 1992.

_____. *The Message of the Mind in Neo-Confucianism.* New York: Columbia University Press, 1989.

_____. *Neo-Confucian Orthodoxy and the Learning of the Mind-and-Heart.* New York: Columbia University Press, 1981.

Dunne, George H., S.J. *Generation of Giants.* Notre Dame: University of Notre Dame Press, 1962.

Eno, Robert. *The Confucian Creation of Heaven: Philosophy and the Defense of Ritual Mastery.* Albany: State University of New York Press, 1990.

Fingarette, Herbert. *Confucius: The Secular as Sacred.* New York: Harper & Row, 1972.

_____. *Self-Deception.* New York: Humanities Press, 1969.

Franke, Herbert, ed. *Sung Biographies.* Weisbaden: Franz Steiner Verlag, 1976.

Fu-kou hsieh-chih 扶溝縣志 (Gazette of Fu-kou County). Kuang-hsü period edition. Ta-ch'eng shu-yüan, 1893.

Fung Yu-lan. *A History of Chinese Philosophy.* Trans. Derk Bodde, vol. 2. Princeton: Princeton University Press, 1983 [1953].

Gardner, Daniel K. *Chu Hsi and the Ta-hsüeh: Neo-Confucian Reflection on the Confucian Canon.* Cambridge: Harvard University Press, 1986.

_____. "Transmitting the Way: Chu Hsi and His Program of Learning." *Harvard Journal of Asiatic Studies* 49 (June 1989): 141–72.

_____, trans. *Learning to be a Sage, Selections from the Conversations of Master Chu, Arranged Topically.* Berkeley: University of California Press, 1990.

Gernet, Jacques. *China and the Christian Impact: A Conflict of Cultures.* Trans. Janet Lloyd. New York: Cambridge University Press, 1985.

Girardot, N. J. "Chinese Religion: History of Study." *The Encyclopedia of Religion,* edited by Mircea Eliade. New York: Macmillan, 1987.

Graham, A[ngus] C[harles]. *Disputers of the Tao: Philosophical Argument in Ancient China.* LaSalle, IL: Open Court, 1989.

_____. *Two Chinese Philosophers: Ch'eng Ming-tao and Ch'eng Yi-ch'uan.* London: Lund Humphries, 1978 [1958]. Reprinted as *Two Chinese Philosophers: The Metaphysics of the Brothers Ch'eng* by Open Court, 1992.

_____, trans. *Chuang Tzu: The Inner Chapters*. London: George Allen & Unwin, 1981.

Graham, William A. *Beyond the Written Word: Oral Aspects of Scripture in the History of Religion*. Cambridge: Cambridge University Press, 1987.

Hall, David L., and Roger T. Ames. *Thinking Through Confucius*. Albany, NY: State University of New York Press, 1987.

Hao Wanzhang (Hao Wan-chang) 郝萬章. *Ch'eng Hao yü Ta-Ch'eng shu-yüan* 程顥與大程書院 (Ch'eng Hao and the Elder Ch'eng Academy). Zhengzhou 鄭州: Chung-chou ku-chi 中州古籍 ch'u-pan-she, 1993.

Hartman, Charles. "Han Yü as Philosopher: The Evidence from the *Lun Yü Pi-chieh*." *Tsing-hua Journal of Chinese Studies*, ns. 16 (December 1984): 57–94.

Henderson, John B. *Scripture, Canon, and Commentary: A Comparison of Confucian and Western Exegesis*. Princeton: Princeton University Press, 1991.

Hervouet, Yves, ed. *A Sung Bibliography/Bibliographie des Sung*. Hong Kong: Chinese University of Hong Kong, 1978.

Hsia Chün-yü 夏君虞. *Sung-hsüeh Kai-yao* 宋學概要 (Essentials of Sung Learning). Shanghai: Shang-wu yin shu kuan, 1937.

Hsieh Liang-tso 謝良佐. "Lun-yü chieh hsü" 論語解序 (Preface to Explanations of the *Analects*). Lun-Meng ching-i edition, see Chu Hsi, *Kuo-chao chu lao hsien-sheng Lun-Meng ching-i*. Sung wen-chien edition, see Lü Tsu-ch'ien, *Sung wen chien*. Ching-i k'ao edition, see Chu I-tsun, *Ching-i k'ao*.

_____. *(Shang-ts'ai) Lun-yü chieh* (上蔡) 論語解. See Chu Hsi, *Kuo-chao chu lao hsien-sheng Lun-Meng ching-i*.

_____. *Shang-ts'ai yü-lu* 上蔡語錄 or *Shang-ts'ai hsien-sheng yü-lu* 上蔡先生語錄 (Recorded Conversations of Hsieh Liang-tso). Ed. Chu Hsi. CITCS edition, Fuzhou: Cheng-i yin-shu-yüan, 1868. CTIS edition, Taipei: I-wen shu-kuan, 1969. KKS edition, Taipei: Kobun Shokyoku, 1972. SKCS edition, Taipei: Shang-wu yin-shu-kuan, 1983.

Hsing Ping 邢昺. *Lun-yü chu-shu* 論語注疏. SPPY edition. Shanghai: Chung-hua shu-chü, 1934.

Hsiung Wan 熊琬. *Sung-tai li-hsüeh yü fo-hsüeh chih t'an-t'ao* 宋代理學與佛學之探討 (A Discussion of Sung Period Neo-Confucian and Buddhist Learning). Taipei: Wen-chin ch'u-pan-she, 1985.

Hsü Fu-kuan 徐復觀. *Chung-kuo ssu-hsiang shih lun chi hsü-p'ien* 中國思想史論集序篇 (Supplemental Edition of Discourses on the History of Chinese Thought). Taipei: Shih-pao wen-hua ch'u-pan-she, 1982.

Hu Hung 胡宏. *Hu Hung chi* 胡宏集. Beijing: Chung-hua, 1987.

Hu Yin 胡 寅. "Shang-ts'ai Lun-yü Chieh hou-hsü 上蔡論語解後序 (Postface to Hsieh Liang-tso's *Analects* Commentary)." *Fei-jan chi* 斐然集 19/7b–9a. SKCS edition. Taipei: Shang-wu yin-shu-kuan, 1983.

Huang, Chichung. *The Analects of Confucius: A Literal Translation with an Introduction and Notes.* New York: Oxford University Press, 1997.

Huang Kan 黃 乾. *Huang Mien-chai chi* 黃勉齋集. CITCS edition. Fuzhou: Cheng-i yin-shu-yüan, 1868.

Huang K'an 皇 侃. *Lun-yü i-shu* 論語義疏 (Elaboration of the Meanings of the *Analects*). Tsung-shu chi-ch'eng edition. Shanghai: Shang-wu yin-shu-kuan, 1937.

Huang Tsung-hsi 黃宗羲. *Ming-ju hsueh-an* 明儒學案. Trans. Julia Ching as *The Records of Ming Scholars.* Honolulu: University of Hawaii Press, 1987.

Huang Tsung-hsi 黃宗羲 and Ch'üan Tsu-wang 全祖望, et al. *Sung-Yüan hsüeh-an* 宋元學案 (Records of Sung-Yüan Period Scholars). 3 vols. Shanghai: Shang-wu, 1934. Punctuated edition, Beijing: Chung-hua, 1986.

Hucker, Charles. *A Dictionary of Official Titles in Imperial China.* Stanford: Stanford University Press, 1985.

Hung Ju-k'uei 洪汝奎, comp. *Hung-shih T'ang shih ching kuan ts'ung-shu* 洪氏唐石經館叢書 (Mr. Hung's Collection from the Office of T'ang Stone Classics) in *Kuang-hsü chung jing Hung-shih kung shan-t'ang ji-ch'eng* 光緒中涇洪氏公善堂集成. Library Collection of the Institute for Research in Humanities, Kyoto University. Kuang-hsü period, 1875-1908.

Jameson, Melanie Alison. "South-returning Wings: Yang Shih and the New Sung Metaphysics." Ph.D. diss., University of Arizona, 1990.

Kalton, Michael. *To Become a Sage: The Ten Diagrams on Sage Learning by Yi T'oegye.* New York: Columbia University Press, 1988.

Kusumoto Bun'yū 久須本文雄. *Sōdai jugaku no zen shisō kenkyū* 宋代儒学の禅思想研究 (An Investigation of Zen Thought in Sung Dynasty Confucian Learning). Nagoya: Nisseido, 1980.

Lau, D. C., trans. *Confucius: The Analects.* Harmondsworth: Penguin Books, 1979.

————, trans. *Lao Tzu: Tao-te Ching.* New York: Penguin Books, 1963.

————, trans. *Mencius.* Harmondsworth: Penguin Books, 1970.

Leder, Drew. *The Absent Body.* Chicago: University of Chicago Press, 1990.

Lee, Thomas H. C. *Government Education and Examinations in Sung China.* Hong Kong: Chinese University Press, 1985.

Legge, James. *The Chinese Classics.* Vol. 1, Confucian Analects, the Great Learning, the Doctrine of the Mean; vol. 2, The Work of Mencius; vol. 3, The Shoo King [*Shu-ching*]; vol. 4, The She King [*Shih-ching*]; vol. 5, The Ch'un ts'ew [*Ch'un-ch'iu*], with the Tso chuen [*Tso-chuan*]. Oxford: Clarendon Press, 1893–95. Reprint, 5 vol. in 4, Taipei: Southern Materials Center, 1985.

_____. *Confucius: Confucian Analects, The Great Learning, and The Doctrine of the Mean*. New York: Dover Publications, 1971. Reprint of vol. 1 in The Chinese Classics Series published by Clarendon Press, Oxford, 1893.

_____. *The Notions of the Chinese Concerning Gods and Spirits: With an Examination of the Defense of an Essay on the Proper Rendering of the Words* Elohim *and* Theos *into the Chinese Language by William J. Boone, D. D.* Hong Kong: Hong Kong Register, 1852.

_____. *The Sacred Books of China: The Texts of Confucianism*. Pt. 1, The Shu King [*Shu-ching*], the Religious Portions of the Shih King [*Shih-ching*], [and] the Hsiao King [*Hsiao-ching*]; pt. 2, The Yi King [*I-ching*]; pt. 3–4, The Li Ki [*Li-chi*] vols. 1–2. Published as vols. 3, 16, 27–28 of *Sacred Books of the East* [SBE]. Oxford: Clarendon, 1879–85. Reprint Delhi: Motilal Banarsidass, 1977.

_____. *The Works of Mencius*. New York: Dover Publications, 1970. Reprint of vol. 2 in The Chinese Classics Series published by Clarendon Press, Oxford, 1895.

Levering, Miriam. "Ch'an Enlightenment for Laymen: Ta-hui and the New Religious Culture of the Sung." Ph.D. diss., Harvard University, 1978.

_____, ed. *Rethinking Scripture: Essays from a Comparative Perspective*. Albany: State University of New York Press, 1989.

Levey, Matthew A. "Chu Hsi as a 'Neo-Confucian': Chu Hsi's Critique of Heterodoxy, Heresy, and the 'Confucian' Tradition." vols. 1–2. Ph.D. diss., University of Chicago, 1991.

Li Hsin-ch'uan 李心傳, comp. *Chien-yen i-lai hsi-nien yao-lu* 建炎以來繫年要錄 (Important Records Chronologically Interrelated from the Chien-yen Period [1127–1130] Onward). Kuang-hsü edition, with index. Kyoto: Chūbun shuppansha, 1983. *Ts'ung-shu chi-ch'eng* edition.

_____, comp. *Tao-ming lu* 道命錄. Ming Hung-chih edition (1488–1504). New York: Columbia University Microfilm collection.

Li Zehou (Li Tse-hou) 李澤厚. *Lun-yü chin tu* 論語今讀(Reading the Analects Today). Hefei: An-hui wen-yi chu-pan-she, 1998. Reprinted, Taipei: Yün-ch'en wen-hua, 2000.

Lindbeck, George. *The Nature of Doctrine: Religion and Theology in a Postliberal Age*. Philadelphia: Westminster Press, 1984.

Liu, James T. C. *China Turning Inward: Intellectual-Political Changes in the Early Twelfth Century*. Cambridge, MA: Council on East Asian Studies, Harvard University, 1988.

_____. "How Did a Neo-Confucian School Become the State Orthodoxy?" *Philosophy East and West* 23/4 (October 1973): 483–506.

_____. *Reform in Sung China: Wang An-shih and the New Policies*. Cambridge: Harvard University Press, 1959.

Liu Ts'un-yan. "The Syncretism of the Three Teachings in Sung-Yüan China." *New Excursions from the Hall of Harmonious Wind.* Leiden: E. J. Brill, 1984.

Liu Xiangbin (Liu Hsiang-pin) 劉象彬. *Er-Ch'eng Li-hsüeh Chi-pen Fan-ch'ou Yen-chiu* 二程理學基本範疇研究 (Researches on the Fundamental Categories of the Two Ch'engs' Neo-Confucianism). N.p.: Henan Daxue chu-pan-she, 1987.

Lo Kuang 羅 光, "Ch'eng Hao te Che-hsüeh Ssu-hsiang" 程顥的哲學思想 (Ch'eng Hao's Philosophical Thought). *Jen-wen hsüeh-pao* (*Journal of Human Culture*) 5 (May 1976): 1–36.

Lo, Winston Wan. *The Life and Thought of Yeh Shih.* Gainesville: University Presses of Florida; Hong Kong: Chinese University of Hong Kong, 1974.

Lü Tsu-ch'ien 呂祖謙, comp. *Sung wen chien* 宋文鑑 (Literary Mirror of the Sung Dynasty). KHCPTS edition. Shanghai: Shang-wu yin-shu-kuan, 1937.

Lundbaek, Knud. "The Image of Neo-Confucianism in *Confucius Sinarum Philosophus.*" *Journal of the History of Ideas* 44.1 (January–March 1983): 19–30.

Mao Huaixin (Huai-hsin). "The Establishment of the School of Chu Hsi and Its Propagation in Fukien." *Chu Hsi and Neo-Confucianism*, edited by Wing-tsit Chan, 503–20.

McRae, John R. *The Northern School and the Formation of Early Ch'an Buddhism.* Honolulu: University of Hawaii Press, 1986.

Mien-ch'ih hsien-chih 澠池縣志 (Gazateer of Mien-chih County). Reprinted, Shanghai: Han-yü ta-tzu-tien chu-pan-she, 1991.

Mou Tsung-san 牟宗三. *Hsin-t'i yü Hsing-t'i* 心體與性體 (The Substance of the Heart-and-Mind and the Substance of Human Nature). 3 vols. Taipei: Cheng Chung Book Company, 1985 [1963].

Mungello, David E. "The Seventeenth-Century Jesuit Translation Project of the Confucian *Four Books.*" *East Meets West: The Jesuits in China, 1582–1773*, edited by Charles E. Ronan and Bonnie B. C. Oh. Chicago: Loyola University Press, 1988, 252–68.

Neville, Robert Cummings. *Behind the Masks of God: An Essay Toward Comparative Theology.* Albany: State University of New York Press, 1991.

_____. "Religious Studies and Theological Studies." AAR 1992 Presidential Address in *JAAR* 59.2 (Summer 1993): 185–200.

_____. *The Tao and the Daimon.* Albany: State University of New York Press, 1982.

Niebuhr, H. Richard. *Faith on Earth.* Ed. Richard R. Niebuhr. New Haven: Yale University Press, 1992.

Niebuhr, Richard R. *Experiential Religion.* New York, Harper & Row, 1972.

Oxford English Dictionary. Ed. J. A. H. Murray. Compact edition. Oxford: Oxford University Press, 1971.

Perls, Fritz. *The Gestalt Approach and Eye Witness to Therapy*. N.p.: Science & Behavior Books, 1973.

Petersen, Willard. "Another Look at Li." *The Bulletin of Sung-Yüan Studies* 18 (1976): 13–31.

Pfister, Lauren. "The 'Failures' of James Legge's Fruitful Life for China." *Ching Feng* 31:4 (December 1988): 246–271.

Pye, Michael, and Robert Morgan, eds. *The Cardinal Meaning: Essays in Comparative Hermeneutics: Buddhism and Christianity*. The Hague: Mouton, 1973.

Ricci, Matteo, S.J. *The True Meaning of the Lord of Heaven (T'ien-chu-shih-i)*. Translated with introduction and notes by Douglas Lancashire and Peter Hu Kuo-chen, S.J., and edited by Edward J. Malatesta, S.J. St. Louis, MO: The Institute of Jesuit Sources, in cooperation with The Ricci Institute, Taipei, Taiwan, 1985. Original text found in *Fonti Ricciane*, ed. Pasquale M. d' Elia, S.J. Rome: Libreria dello Stato, 1942–1949.

Satō Hitoshi. "Chu Hsi's 'Treatise on *Jen*.'" Trans. Richard Shek in *Chu Hsi and Neo-Confucianism*, edited by Wing-tsit Chan, 212–227.

———— 佐藤仁. "Sha Ryō-sa 'Rongo kai jo' ni yosete" 謝良佐 '論語解序' によせて (Concerning Hsieh Liang-tso's "Lun-yü chieh hsü"). *Kokugo no kenkyū* 10 (Showa 52 [1977]): 77–86.

Schirokauer, Conrad. "Chu Hsi and Hu Hung." *Chu Hsi and Neo-Confucianism*, edited by Wing-tsit Chan, 480–502.

————. "Neo-Confucians Under Attack: The Condemnation of Wei-hsüeh." *Crisis and Prosperity in Sung China*, edited by John W. Haeger. Tucson: University of Arizona Press, 1975, 163–198.

Schwartz, Benjamin. *The World of Thought in Ancient China*. Cambridge: Belknap Press of Harvard University Press, 1985.

Selover, Thomas W. "*San-chiao*: Religious Dimensions of Pacific Culture." *Religion in the Pacific Era*, edited by Frank K. Flinn and Tyler Hendricks. New York: Paragon House, 1985, 95–110.

Shang-ts'ai hsien-chih 上蔡縣志 (Gazateer of Shang-ts'ai County). 8 vols. Preface dated 1690.

Shih-san ching chu shu 十三經注疏 (The Thirteen Classics with Commentaries and Subcommentaries). Ed. Juan Yüan 阮元. 16 vols. Kuang-hsü edition. Mo wang hsien kuan, 1887.

Shushi no senku 朱子の先駆 (Chu Hsi's Forerunners). In Morohashi Tetsuji 諸橋轍次, et al., *Shushigaku taikei* 朱子学大系. Tokyo: Meitoku Shuppansha, 1976–1978.

Smith, G. E. Kidder, Jr. "Ch'eng Yi's (1033–1107) Commentary on the 'Yijing.'" Ph.D. diss., University of California at Berkeley, 1979.

Smith, Kidder Jr., Peter K. Bol, Joseph A. Adler, and Don J. Wyatt. *Sung Dynasty Uses of the I Ching*. Princeton: Princeton University Press, 1990.

Smith, Wilfred Cantwell. *The Meaning and End of Religion.* San Francisco: Harper & Row, 1978.

———. *Towards a World Theology: Faith and the Comparative History of Religion.* Philadelphia: Westminster Press, 1981.

Streng, Frederick. *Understanding Religious Life.* 3rd ed. Belmont, CA: Wadsworth, 1985.

T'ang Chün-i 唐君毅. *Chung-kuo Che-hsüeh Yüan-lun* 中國哲學原論 (A Basic Exposition of Chinese Philosophy). Taipei: Student Book Co., 1984.

T'o T'o 脫 脫, et al. *Sung shih* 宋史. 20 vols. Beijing: Chung-hua shu-chü, 1977.

Takeuchi Teruo 竹內照夫. *Jin no kogi no kenkyū* 仁 の 古 儀 の 研 究 (Investigation of the Early Meanings of *Jen*). Tokyo: Meiji Shoin, 1964.

Taylor, Rodney. *The Confucian Way of Contemplation: Okada Takehiko and the Tradition of Quiet Sitting.* Columbia, SC: University of South Carolina Press, 1988.

———. *The Religious Dimensions of Confucianism.* Albany: State University of New York Press, 1990.

Tillman, Hoyt. *Confucian Discourse and Chu Hsi's Ascendancy.* Honolulu: University of Hawaii Press, 1992.

———. "A New Direction in Confucian Scholarship: Approaches to Examining the Differences between Neo-Confucianism and *Tao-hsüeh.*" *Philosophy East and West* 42.3 (July 1992): 455–74.

———. *Utilitarian Confucianism: Ch'en Liang's Challenge to Chu Hsi.* Cambridge: Harvard University Press, 1982.

Tracy, David. *The Analogical Imagination: Christian Theology and the Culture of Pluralism.* New York: Crossroad, 1981.

———. "Comparative Theology." *Encyclopedia of Religion,* edited by Mircea Eliade. New York: Macmillan, 1987.

Ts'ai Jen-hou. "A Reappraisal of Chu Hsi's Philosophy." Trans. Lee Shui-chuen. *Chu Hsi and Neo-Confucianism,* edited by Wing-tsit Chan, 461–79.

——— 蔡仁厚. *Sung Ming li-hsüeh* 宋明理學 (Sung and Ming Neo-Confucian Thought). Vols. 1–2, new edition. Taipei: Student Book Co., 1983.

Ts'ai Yen-zen. "*Ching* and *Chuan*: Towards Defining the Confucian Scriptures in Han China (206 BCE–220 CE)." Th.D. diss., Harvard, 1992.

Ts'ai Yung-ch'un. "The Philosophy of Ch'eng I: A Selection of Texts from the Complete Works, Edited and Translated with Introduction and Notes." Ph.D. diss., Columbia University, 1950.

Tu Wei-ming. *Centrality and Commonality: An Essay on Confucian Religiousness.* Albany: State University of New York Press, 1989.

_____. *Confucian Thought: Selfhood as Creative Transformation.* Albany: State University of New York Press, 1985.

_____. "The Creative Tension between *Jen* and *Li.*" *Philosophy East and West* 18:1-2 (January–April 1968): 29–39. Reprinted in *Humanity and Self-Cultivation: Essays in Confucian Thought,* 5–16.

_____. *Humanity and Self-Cultivation: Essays in Confucian Thought.* Berkeley: Asian Humanities Press, 1979.

_____. "*Jen* as a Living Metaphor in the Confucian *Analects.*" *Philosophy East and West* 31.1 (January 1981): 45–54. Reprinted in *Confucian Thought: Selfhood as Creative Transformation,* 81–92.

_____ 杜維明. "K'ung-tzu Jen-hsüeh ti Tao, Hsüeh, Cheng" 孔子仁學的 道、學、政 (The Way, Learning and Politics in Confucius's Humane Learning). *Chung-kuo che-hsüeh,* no. 5, 17–32, and *Chung-kuo wen-hua ti wei-chi yü chan-wang: Tang-tai yen-chiu yü chu-hsiang.* Taipei: Shih-pao wen-hua chu-pan-she, 1981,19–36.

_____. "Pain and Suffering in Confucian Self-cultivation." *Way, Learning, and Politics: Essays on the Confucian Intellectual.* Singapore: Institute of East Asia Philosophies, 1989. Reprint Albany: State University of New York Press, 1993.

_____. *Way, Learning, and Politics: Essays on the Confucian Intellectual.* Singapore: Institute of East Asia Philosophies, 1989. Reprint Albany: State University of New York Press, 1993.

Veith, Ilza. *Huang Ti Nei Ching Su Wen: The Yellow Emperor's Classic of Internal Medicine.* Berkeley: University of California Press, 1972.

Van Zoeren, Steven. *Poetry and Personality: Reading, Exegesis, and Hermeneutics in Traditional China.* Stanford: Stanford University Press, 1991.

Waley, Arthur, trans. *The Analects of Confucius.* New York: George Allen & Unwin, 1938.

Walker, James Lynwood. *Body and Soul: Gestalt Therapy and Religious Experience.* Nashville: Abingdon Press, 1971.

Wang An-shih 王安石. *Lin-ch'uan chi* 臨川集 (Wang An-shih's Literary Collection). Beijing: Chung-hua shu-chü. Reprint Taipei: Shih-chieh shu-chu, 1988.

Wang K'ai-fu 王開府. *Hu Wu-feng te hsin-hsueh* 胡五峰的心學 (Hu Hung's Learning of the Heart-and-Mind). Taipei: Student Book Co., 1978.

Wang Mao-hung 王懋竑, comp. *Chu-tzu nien-p'u* 朱子年譜 (Yearly Record of Chu Hsi). Reprint of KHCT edition. Taipei: World Book Co., 1973.

Watson, Burton, trans. *Writings of Mo Tzu, Hsün Tzu, and Han Fei Tzu.* New York: Columbia University Press, 1963.

Watts, Fraser, and Mark Williams. *The Psychology of Religious Knowing.* Cambridge: Cambridge University Press, 1988.

Weber, Max. *The Religion of China: Confucianism and Taoism.* Trans. Hans H. Gerth. New York: Free Press, 1951.

Wile, Douglas David. "T'an Ssu-t'ung: His Life and Major Work, the '*Jen Hsüeh.*'" Ph.D. diss., University of Wisconsin, 1972.

Wilhelm, Richard. *The I Ching or Book of Changes.* Trans. Cary F. Baynes. Princeton: Princeton University Press, 1967.

Wilson, Thomas A. "Genealogy of the Way: Representing the Confucian Tradition in Neo-Confucian Philosophical Anthologies." Ph.D. diss., University of Chicago, 1988.

Yamaguchi Satsujō 山口察常. *Jin no kenkyū* 仁の研究 (Investigation of *Jen*). Tokyo: Iwanami Shoten, 1936.

Yanagida Seizan. "The 'Recorded Sayings' Texts of Chinese Ch'an Buddhism.'" Trans. John R. McRae. *Early Ch'an in China and Tibet,* edited by Whalen Lai and Lewis R. Lancaster. Berkeley: Berkeley Buddhist Studies Series, 1983, 185–205.

Yang Po-chün 楊伯峻. *Lun-yü i-chu* 論語譯注 (Modern Translation and Notes on the *Analects*). Hong Kong: Chung-hua shu-chü, 1980.

———. *Meng-tzu i-chu* 孟子譯注 (Modern Translation and Notes on the *Mencius*). Hong Kong: Chung-hua shu-chü, 1984.

Yang Shih 楊 時. *Yang Kuei-shan chi* 楊龜山集 (Complete Works of Yang Shih). KHCPTS edition. Shanghai: Shang-wu, 1937.

Ying-ch'eng chih 應城志 (Gazateer of Ying-ch'eng County). Kuang-hsü edition. Pu-yang shu-yüan, 1882.

Young, John D. *Confucianism and Christianity: The First Encounter.* Hong Kong: Hong Kong University Press, 1983.

Yuasa Yasuo. *The Body: Toward an Eastern Mind-Body Theory.* Ed. Thomas P. Kasulis. Albany: State University of New York Press, 1987.

Zhang Delin (Chang Te-lin) 張德麟. *Ch'eng Ming-tao Ssu-hsiang Yen-chiu* 程明道思想研究 (Researches on Ch'eng Hao's Thought). Taipei: Student Book Co., 1986.

Zhou Fengwu (Chou Feng-wu) 周鳳梧 and Zhang Canjia (Chang Ts'an-chia) 張燦玾, *Huang-ti nei-ching su wen yü-shih* 黃帝內經素問語釋 (An Explanation of the Language of the *Simple Questions on the Yellow Emperor's Internal [Medicine] Classic*). Jinan: Shan-tung k'o-hsüeh chi-shu chu-pan-she, 1985.

Zhu Hanmin (Chu Han-min) 朱漢民 and Chen Gujia (Ch'en Ku-chia) 陳谷嘉. *Hu-Hsiang hsüeh-p'ai yüan-liu* 湖湘學派源流 (The Story of the Hunan School). N.p.: Hunan chiao-yü chu-pan-she, 1992.

Index